The Safeguard of Liberty and Property

The Safeguard of Liberty and Property

The Supreme Court, Kelo v. New London, *and the Takings Clause*

Guy F. Burnett

LEXINGTON BOOKS
Lanham • Boulder • New York • London

Published by Lexington Books
An imprint of The Rowman & Littlefield Publishing Group, Inc.
4501 Forbes Boulevard, Suite 200, Lanham, Maryland 20706
www.rowman.com

Unit A, Whitacre Mews, 26-34 Stannary Street, London SE11 4AB

British Library Cataloguing in Publication Information Available

Library of Congress Cataloging-in-Publication Data

Burnett, Guy F., 1979– author.
The safeguard of liberty and property : the Supreme Court, Kelo v. New London, and the takings clause / Guy F. Burnett.
p. cm.
Based on author's dissertation (doctoral—Claremont Graduate University), 2013.
Includes bibliographical references and index.
ISBN 978-0-7391-9783-7 (cloth : alk. paper) – ISBN 978-0-7391-9784-4 (ebook)
1. Kelo, Susette–Trials, litigation, etc. 2. New London (Conn.)–Trials, litigation, etc. 3. Eminent domain–United States–Cases. I. Title.
KF229.K45B87 2015
343.73'0252–dc23
2014036681

™ The paper used in this publication meets the minimum requirements of American National Standard for Information Sciences Permanence of Paper for Printed Library Materials, ANSI/NISO Z39.48-1992.

Printed in the United States of America

Contents

Acknowledgments

This book grew out of a lengthy discussion on property rights and eminent domain one sunny afternoon at Claremont Graduate University in the office of Michael M. Uhlmann. What began as a discussion over the nature of property and law quickly took on a life of its own thanks to the help, guidance, and constructive criticism of so many friends and colleagues. I would be remiss if I did not thank those who helped along the way as well as those who tirelessly and selflessly donated their time to continually discussing *Kelo* with me.

I would especially like to thank Michael M. Uhlmann for helping me understand the law and the Constitution and for being such a good mentor and close friend. Ralph A. Rossum for his tireless and continual friendship, advice, and help, and whose guidance was crucial throughout the entire process. Tony A. Peacock as well for all of his suggestions and whose continued friendship I value greatly.

I would also like to thank Kenneth P. Miller, Zack Kronberg, Esq., Charles Johnson, Peter and Carol McNamara, Jean Schroedel, Jennifer L. Merolla, William Baude, James W. Muller, Landry Signé, Kimberly Pace, Forrest Nabors, Bradley A. Jensen, Ryan P. Williams, Christopher Chrappa, Jordan Bradley, Daniel and Katy O'Toole, Brandon P. Dabling, Mike and Petria Hoffpauir, Robert Garrow, Rebecca Papanicolas, Lindsay Eberhardt, Benjamin Judge, Murray S. Y. Bessette, Randy Huth, and Ian A. Sundwall-Byers.

I must also thank the students in my classes at the University of Alaska Anchorage, especially those in my two sections of Constitutional Law. Their feedback and discussions were always lively and insightful.

Lastly, I'd like to thank my mom and pop for all of their love, patience, and help through it all.

Chapter One

Introduction

The small city of New London is a tiny and picturesque seaport town along the Thames River in Connecticut. A true harbor town, New London borders the Long Island Sound between Niantic Bay and Fishers Island Sound, separated from both New York and Rhode Island by large white lines drawn by cartographers over large swaths of the Atlantic Ocean on official maps.[1] The city itself is geographically small, and varies between five and ten square miles, depending on which map you're using.[2] In 2006, the city's small population of approximately 27,000 residents celebrated the city's 360th birthday, its heritage reaching back to its founder John Winthrop, Jr. and the Pilgrims.[3] It boasts a rich history including a visit by the twenty-four-year-old Virginia Militia officer and future father of his country George Washington. The city is also where patriot and spy Nathan Hale enjoyed his living as a schoolteacher before he volunteered for the Revolutionary War and the fateful espionage mission against the British.

New London is home to a thriving little community of tightly knit locals, and is a true slice of Americana. Glancing over the city's events calendar, one runs across such public activities as: "Community Knit at New London Public Library," "New London History," "Field of Greens Farmers Market," and "Ribbon Cutting: Holiday Inn."[4] The median age for the city in 2010 was exactly 30.3, and it's ethnic makeup included Whites (60%), Hispanics (28%), Blacks (17%), Asians (3%), and other groups including Native Americans (1%) as well as a small number of Native Hawaiian/Pacific Islanders (<1%).[5] New London is not a wealthy city. In fact, according to the rhetoric, New London is still a depressed city, one with a median income almost $20,000 less than Connecticut's median income.[6] Its economy slowly began to decrease after the U.S. Naval Undersea Warfare Center, which was located in New London, closed in 1996. Two years after the base closed, the unemployment rate nearly doubled that of the state.[7] It is against the backdrop of this little depressed and historic waterfront town that one of the most unpopular Supreme Court decisions ever produced was handed down.

In February 2005, the Supreme Court heard the case of *Susette Kelo, et al., Petitioners v. City of New London, Connecticut, et al.* In June 2005, it issued a highly controversial and damaging decision on the nature of property rights. The decision, made by a slim majority of justices, held that private property could be taken for economic redevelopment. The press and public heralded the decision as one of the worst decisions the Supreme Court ever made, and the outcry was loud and vicious. It made Levy and Mellor's list of the twelve worst Supreme Court decisions of all time in their book *The Dirty Dozen: How Twelve Supreme Court Cases Radically Expanded Government and Eroded Freedom*. *The Economist* called it Justice John Paul Stevens' worst decision. In a speech at the University of Chicago Law School, Justice Antonin Scalia placed the case in the same category as *Dred Scott*. Even the humor website Cracked.com featured it as one of the "5 Most Terrifying Supreme Court Decisions."[8] Both the right and the left roundly condemned the decision. Immediately after the decision, over forty states began, to varying degrees, to implement their own legislation in response. Ilya Somin noted, "[t]he *Kelo* backlash probably resulted in more new state legislation than any other Supreme Court decision in history."[9] Such a universal and coordinated repulsion is almost without parallel in Supreme Court history.

The case involved the homes of several citizens in the Fort Trumbull area of the southern part of New London. In order to make way for a revitalization project aimed at boosting the economy, the city approved redevelopment efforts by the newly created non-profit New London Development Corporation (NLDC). When several citizens refused to leave their waterfront homes that were blocking redevelopment plans, the city allowed the NLDC to condemn and seize the homes. The citizens sued the city and the case eventually ended up in the Supreme Court of Connecticut and the United States Supreme Court. The case raised several important constitutional issues. Perhaps the most important of these was the nature of property in the American regime. In the corpus of American law, the Fifth Amendment's Takings Clause has evolved and been redefined over time by the Court and legislatures. *Kelo* represents the most recent development in the evolving conception of private property.

At the center of the case, a tension was apparent regarding interpretations of property rights in America. Early conceptions of property held it to be "sacred and inviolable," and the Founding Fathers viewed it as a natural right which could only be taken away in very limited circumstances.[10] These traditional views of private property held firm throughout the eighteenth and nineteenth centuries. In the latter half of the nineteenth century, changes to the political and legal conceptions of property began to occur. State legislators began to see property as a tool to be used by urban and city planners, agencies, and other public officials for the public good, and this began to supersede any traditional notion of natural rights. One of the themes highlighted by the decision in *Kelo* was the tension between competing conceptions of property rights that were held by the American public and the Supreme Court.

Another reason *Kelo* became so infamous was the tension it presented between understandings of state and Federal power. The Tenth Amendment very briefly laid the foundation for the police powers of the states, but how far those extended over property became unclear. Polls showed that citizens wanted the states to continue to have power to benefit the local population, but the line was drawn at the taking of private property for anything but a strict public use. The decision in *Kelo* showed that the Court believed the states should ultimately decide where the line should be drawn regarding public use. Conceptions of police power played a major role in the case, and the opinions spent ample time discussing the proper role of states.

In order to find out how the Court arrived at its opinion in *Kelo* requires a look back at the last century of American legal history. In the majority opinion, the takings doctrine revolved around the meaning and application of the phrase "public use" in the Fifth Amendment. As it is stated there, "[no person shall] be deprived of life, liberty, or property, without due process of law; nor shall private property be taken for public use, without just compensation." The Court decision in *Kelo* began with a consideration of the evolution of the Public Use Clause that began largely during the Progressive Era (notably with Justice Oliver Wendell Holmes). The Court then continued to follow the evolution over the course of the next hundred years of jurisprudence, most notably in the cases of *Berman v. Parker* (1954) and *Hawaii Housing Authority v. Midkiff* (1984). Justice Stevens, who wrote the majority opinion, utilized a "living constitution" method of interpretation, and it is apparent in *Kelo*. Consequently, the dissenting opinions by both Justice Sandra Day O'Connor and Justice Clarence Thomas, questioned Stevens' interpretive approach to the case. As the dissents forcefully noted, Stevens' interpretation had no place in an original or correct understanding of the Fifth Amendment, and it created a dangerous precedent that would affect decisions at national, state, and local levels.

The Court's plethora of divergent opinions has caused many observers to remark on the problem of interpretation concerning the Takings Clause. That the Court was so split in *Kelo,* and that the public continues to strongly disagree with the decision, is evidence that takings is far from being a well understood, applied, or interpreted body of law. Written a little over a decade before the decision was handed down, Supreme Court commentator Jed Rubenfeld noted: "Throughout constitutional jurisprudence, only the right to privacy can compete seriously with takings law for the doctrine-in-most-desperate-need-of-a-principle prize."[11] His words are still relevant. Several states have taken steps to marginalize the takings principles found in *Kelo* by additions to their own state constitutions, and five state high courts have already cast doubt on the ruling.[12] Even Justice Antonin Scalia said he believes the decision will soon be overturned.[13]

The reason the decision remains so influential and sparks so much debate a decade later is that it speaks to fundamental questions of governance, democracy, and natural rights. Humans have long acknowledged the fundamental role that property plays in their lives, articulated throughout history by such philosophers as Aristotle, St. Thomas Aquinas, John Locke, and Karl Marx, to name a few. Modern academics and commentators such as Charles Beard, Richard A. Epstein, Bruce J. Ackerman, Ilya Somin, and many others, continue to debate and discuss the importance and role of property. While all of these scholars have not agreed on the legal limits, protection, or ownership of property in human affairs, they have all agreed that property plays a major role in human affairs, and that it is an indispensable part of governance. The *Kelo* case speaks deeply to this fundamental human attribute, and the decision helps shed light on where the modern U.S. government has delineated the question of private property.

It is important that a book be written examining the *Kelo* case in detail. For the reasons mentioned above, the case shows the different interpretations of ownership of property, of rights, and of governmental power. In order to better understand these essential themes in the modern American regime, this book will deeply focus on the case itself, including its reasoning, logic, and validity. It will also look at the reaction in the public, legal, legislative, and academic spheres. Overall, this will provide valuable insight into the Court's modern interpretation of the Takings Clause and the natural right to private property.

OUTLINE

The book will be broken into several chapters examining the case and related material. Where several studies stop at the law itself, this book will spend considerable time on the path to, and the fallout from, the decision, noting the most important developments in American politics and law since the case was decided in 2005. *Kelo* is an important case for legal scholars as well as political scientists, and is one of the best cases to better understand how the Supreme Court, the public, and legislative politics interact with each another.

Chapter 2 will look more closely at the facts surrounding the case. In *Kelo*, the case began with the city of New London's plan to revitalize a sagging economy. The plans of the NLDC will be looked at, including the rationale for specific development. The plight and arguments of the petitioners, including the case's namesake, Susette Kelo, will be examined here as well. After the case was argued before the Superior Court of Connecticut, Judge Thomas Corradino issued the longest opinion from any of the courts the case was heard in. Corradino considered every conceivable argument in the case, including the more salient constitutional questions, and it is worth examining in detail because it raises questions answered in the Supreme Court. After the Superior Court decided the case, the Supreme Court of Connecticut further streamlined the arguments that would eventually end up in the U.S. Supreme Court, and both the majority and dissenting opinions are examined.

In chapter 3, the approach and argument at the federal level will be examined. Once the case was decided in Connecticut, those friendly and those opposed to the decision offered advice in droves. Thirty-seven amicus curiae briefs were submitted to the Court (twenty-five siding with the petitioners), and taken altogether their sundry reasoning was as diverse and introspective as any the Supreme Court has ever seen.[14] The briefs are broken down into two categories and several subcategories based on their prescriptions. As important, but often ignored is the oral argument before the Court which took place several months before the decision was handed down. A study of the oral argument is vital because it contains fragments and streams of thought which ultimately end up coloring each of the opinions. In each of the opinions, the justices are answering questions from the oral argument, and it became clear during the argument that the Court had already begun to draw up sides This becomes even clearer when the questions and answers from both the justices and the attorneys are considered.

Chapter 4 will look at the majority opinion as Justice Stevens wrote it. The majority opinion only represented the slimmest majority of five members on the Court, but Stevens's interpretation of the Public Use Clause presents the modern interpretation of Fifth Amendment. He noted that the clause had changed long ago to mean "public purpose," and that the Court had established guidelines in pervious cases, and he argued that the city's takings were not unconstitutional. Most of his opinion was based on the precedent of two other takings cases, *Berman v. Parker* (1954) and *Hawaii Housing Authority v. Midkiff* (1984). He referenced several other cases, but none were as important as these two.

Following Stevens's majority opinion, chapter 5 will focus on Justice Anthony Kennedy's concurring opinion, which stood in stark relief against the majority. Kennedy believed the majority voted the correct way, but erred by not following the rational basis test as laid forth in the Due Process cases of the first half of the twentieth century. For him, the majority opinion did not go far enough in establishing and outlining a principle for future public use takings.

Chapter 6 will consider Justice O'Connor's dissenting opinion, where Chief Justice William Rehnquist and Justice Scalia joined her. Based on a strong textual analysis, O'Connor, the author of the majority opinion in one of Stevens's linchpin cases (*Midkiff*), offered a full-throated rejection of the majority in *Kelo*.

Chapter 7 will look at Justice Clarence Thomas's dissenting opinion which focused heavily on an originalist interpretation. The Framers of the Constitution, Thomas argued, would never have supported such an intrusion into the private property of the citizens of the republic. For him, the majority opinion was the exact opposite of what the Framers believed in. This dissent is perhaps the most far-reaching and introspective of all of the opinions because he brought up larger questions about natural rights and constitutional democracy. As with the decisions before, each of these questions will be considered. Where the Court has gone with the takings doctrine is much more evident after seeing the broad strokes of the four opinions.

Public opinion polls and the media reaction surrounding the case showed that an overwhelming majority of Americans vehemently disagreed with the Supreme Court's interpretation of the Takings Clause. Americans were stirred into a frenzy, and put pressure on their legislators to change the laws regarding eminent domain. Legislatures in many of the states, as well as the United States Congress, became involved in trying to fix the perceived problems of the decision. Interestingly, almost all of the reactive reforms came to nothing.[15] After a short time, the public shifted its focus away from the case, and considerations of the Takings Clause lay largely dormant once again. Although recent polls show that Americans still feel the same about property and takings, the battle is being waged on a much smaller scale. Why the public became quiet again after such a large and disgusted outcry speaks to a larger set of questions and reflections on the nature of democratic governance itself. Chapter 8 will look at the backlash against the decision, and is broken down into the following categories: personal, public, legal, academic, and legislative.

The legal backlash has been significant because of the number of major cases which relied almost completely on *Kelo*, including *Goldstein v. Pataki* (2008), *Fideicomiso de la Tierra del Cano Martin Pena v. Fortuno* (2010), and *Whittaker v. County of Lawrence* (2011) to name a few. Each of these represents a direct application of *Kelo* to a different and unique set of circumstances.

When anything is done in American government, there is almost always academic speculation and response, and chapter 8 will also contain a survey of academic scholarship surrounding the decision. *Kelo* produced a large number of academics both criticizing and supporting the decision, but more have found reason to respond negatively to it. The literature grew quickly after the case and scholars have devoted numerous articles and even a few books to it. Several authors, including Carla T. Main, Bruce L. Benson, and Robert A. Levy and William Mellor, among others, have devoted entire books or significant portions of books to the case and these will be considered here. Important authors such as Richard A. Epstein, and others who had already written extensively on takings also had much to say regarding the case. The academic literature on *Kelo* is important because it represents innovative and well-researched viewpoints in the fields of political science and legal studies.

The final part of the chapter will act as an epilogue to the parties involved in the case. The personal stories are some of the most fascinating, strangest, and ironic in American legal history. While the city was triumphant and the petitioners had their homes seized for redevelopment, New London did not ultimately redevelop the area. The plan was permanently tarnished after the decision, and because of the negative publicity surrounding the case the plan was eventually neutralized. New London is still trying to revitalize to this day, and has even changed the name of the NLDC to avoid any reminders of the *Kelo* drama.

The Court meant the *Kelo* decision to be another step in the direction of a more perfect delineation of liberty and property under the Constitution. While many saw the decision as the erosion of both liberty and property rights, the Court had a very specific reason for deciding the case the way it did. This book discovers how and why the Court arrived at the decision and the repercussions of that decision within the regime. It is important to take these repercussions seriously because of their impact on American law and constitutional interpretation. The case also brought people together from all over the nation in strong opposition against the Supreme Court. The opposition contained members on both the right and the left of the political spectrum, although they were united in their opposition for completely different reasons. The sheer amount of reaction to the case and the negative connotation it still holds is a testament to the lasting impression it made. Since property is such an important part of any government, especially in the United States, this case will no doubt be one of the most important cases ever decided by the Supreme Court.

NOTES

1. A local historian wrote in the city's historical journal that the lines were drawn incorrectly over the ocean maps. The historian noted, "It is obvious to anyone looking at a map that Long Island and especially Fishers Island should be part of Connecticut and not New York. . . . If there were justice or logic in the world, and the Pequots, the island's first occupants, would probably be among the first to suggest that their existence is an iffy thing, Fishers Island today would be part of Connecticut and part of New London. Actually, despite the artificial political designation, Fishers Island is historically and spiritually part of New London." "The Richest

Gem of the Sound," The New London Gazette, accessed May 13, 2013, http://newlondongazette.com/fisherisland.html.

2. According to the New London Gazette, the city is "six square miles" ("Surprises, Features, and Facts of New London, Connecticut, USA," The New London Gazette, accessed May 13, 2013, http://newlondongazette.com/surprise.html). According to Google Maps, the city is 10.76 square miles ("New London, CT," Google Maps, accessed May 31, 2013, https://www.google.com/maps/place/New+London,+CT/@41.3458062,-72.1057119,12z/data=!3m1!4b1!4m2!3m1!1s0x89e60e6eb612cdbd:0xd01603e69c2b939d). The 2010 U.S. Census says the city is only 5.62 square miles ("New London (city) Connecticut," U.S. Census Bureau, accessed May 31, 2013, http://quickfacts.census.gov/qfd/states/09/0952280.html).

3. The city's actual residents for 2010 was listed as 27,569 by the U.S. Census. "New London (city) Connecticut," U.S. Census Bureau, accessed May 31, 2013, http://quickfacts.census.gov/qfd/states/09/0952280.html.

4. "Upcoming Fun Events," New London Historic Waterfront website, accessed October 10, 2012, http://www.newlondonmainstreet.org/pub/gen/eventspage.

5. 2010 U.S. Census, accessed May 1, 2014 (http://ci.new-london.ct.us).

6. According to the 2010 U.S. Census, the median income was $43,551, with 17.3 percent living below the poverty line (http://quickfacts.census.gov).

7. Justice John Paul Stevens notes this in the opinion of *Susette Kelo et al., Petitioners v. City of New London, Connecticut, et al.* (2005) (hereafter *Kelo v. New London*).

8. Robert A. Levy and William Mellor, *The Dirty Dozen: How Twelve Supreme Court Cases Radically Expanded Government and Eroded Freedom*. (New York: Sentinel, 2008); Lexington, "The Worst Decision of Justice Stevens," *The Economist*, April 14, 2010, accessed October 10, 2013, http://www.economist.com/blogs/lexington/2010/04/kelo_john_paul_stevenss_worst_decision; Debra Cassens Weiss, "Scalia Lumps Kelo Decision with Dred Scott and Roe v. Wade." *ABA Journal*. October 19, 2011, accessed May 12, 2013, http://www.abajournal.com/news/article/scalia_lumps_kelo_decision_with_dred_scott_and_roe_v._wade/; J.F. Sargent and Ricardo R. Read, "The 5 Most Terrifying Supreme Court Decisions," Cracked.com, September 6, 2012, accessed October 31, 2013, http://www.cracked.com/article_19991_the-5-most-terrifying-supreme-court-decisions.html.

9. Ilya Somin, "The Limits of Backlash: Assessing the Political Response to *Kelo*," in *Property Rights: Eminent Domain and Regulatory Takings Re-Examined*, ed. Bruce L. Benson, (New York: Palgrave Macmillan, 2010), 101–48.

10. *Kelo v. New London*, 545 U.S. 469 (2005) (Thomas, J., dissenting).

11. Abraham Bell and Gideon Parchomovsky, "Takings Reassessed," *Virginia Law Review* 87 (2001): 278.

12. Scott G. Bullock, "The Inadequacy of the Planning Process for Protecting Property Owners from the Abuse of Eminent Domain for Private Development," in *Property Rights: Eminent Domain and Regulatory Takings Re-Examined*, ed. Bruce L. Benson, (New York: Palgrave Macmillan, 2010), 89–100.

13. Justice Scalia said to a crowd at the University of Chicago Law School in 2011, "I do not think that the *Kelo* opinion is long for this world." Debra Cassens Weiss, "Scalia Lumps Kelo Decision with Dred Scott and Roe v. Wade." *ABA Journal*, October 19, 2011, accessed May 12, 2013, http://www.abajournal.com/news/article/scalia_lumps_kelo_decision_with_dred_scott_and_roe_v._wade/.

14. Patricia E. Salkin, Lora A. Lucero, and Allyson Phillips, "Friends of the Court: The Role of Amicus Curiae in *Kelo v. City of New London*," in *Eminent Domain Use and Abuse: Kelo in Context*, eds. Dwight H. Merriam and Mary Massaron Ross, (Chicago: American Bar Association, 2006), 165–66. A diverse array of political groups and ideologies were represented amidst the thirty-seven amicus curiae briefs. Thinktanks and associations filed briefs, including those from the more conservative-leaning groups such as the Claremont Institute and the CATO Institute, as well as more liberal-leaning groups such as the NAACP. There were also regional interests who filed, including the Tidewater Libertarian Party, The New London Railroad Co., Inc., Brooklyn United for Innovative Local Development, and Develop Don't Destroy [Brooklyn] Inc. et al. Academics and activists also filed briefs, including such names as law professor David L. Callies (et al.), Robert H. Freilich (et al.), and author and activist Jane Jacobs. Other

special interests also weighed in, including city planners, planning commissions, historic preservation societies, and legal institutes. Perhaps in no other Supreme Court case has such a response been so varied and diverse. The full list can be found on the Supreme Court's Website: "Susette Kelo, et al., Petitioners v. City of New London, Connecticut, et al.," Supreme Court of the United States Website, Accessed May 23, 2014, http://www.supremecourt.gov/Search.aspx?FileName=/docketfiles/04-108.htm.

15. Ilya Somin, "The Limits of Backlash: Assessing the Political Response to *Kelo*," in *Property Rights: Eminent Domain and Regulatory Takings Re-Examined*, ed. Bruce L. Benson's (New York: Palgrave Macmillan, 2010).

Chapter Two

The Facts of the Case and the Original Decisions

The Fort Trumbull area of New London had a grand history even before the case made it famous. Fort Trumbull is just that—a fort. During the Revolutionary War, the city itself, as well as the future site of the fort, was captured and burned under the command of the American traitor Benedict Arnold.[1] The strategic importance of New London was well known to both sides, and the United States had always retained a heavy military presence in the area. The present fort, which stands today overlooking the harbor at New London, was erected between 1839 and 1852. Its impressive masonry and stonework are in the Egyptian Revival style, and harken back to an era when the fledgling United States Navy was beginning to build more and larger fortresses to protect against coastal attacks. Over the years, residents who populated the small seaport town found it necessary to always retain a working relationship with the military. In 1911, Connecticut College was erected on a hilltop overlooking the small and bustling little city. The city continued to grow until the 1970s.[2]

During the 1970s, the small city fell on hard times. It suddenly was in major stagnation and financial trouble. Even though it boasted one of the largest nuclear submarine facilities in the United States (the Naval Underwater Systems Center which later changed its name to the Naval Undersea Warfare Center) and employed over 1,500 people, the city itself had taken a turn for the worse.[3] The city council became increasingly worried as businesses were vacated and empty lots continued to pile up in and around the Fort Trumbull area of the city. Scores of city council officials attempted to turn the problem around through different plans and redevelopment ideas. Between 1985 and 1997, four different consultants were hired to research the economic problems of the city. Each of them concluded that the city needed to do something—fast.[4]

Republican John G. Rowland was elected governor of Connecticut in 1994, but he had not won with a decisive victory. In order to further his political career on the national stage, he sought out Democratic strongholds in the state that he might persuade to support him. New London, the city with major financial worries, was just that place for him. New London had always been a heavily Democratic district and had always had heavily Democratic city councils. Rowland knew that he would not be able to work with the council itself, and instead offered the job of creating a redevelopment plan to former Democratic state legislator Jay B. Levin. Levin searched for a way to redevelop New London without publicizing the assistance of Governor Rowland, and he found it in the dormant New London Development Corporation (NLDC). Created in 1978, the NLDC was a non-profit organization complete with its own by-laws, board of directors, and a president, and was tasked with helping revitalize the city. The NLDC began well but as author Jeff Benedict notes, it "had faded into dormancy."[5] Levin talked Connecticut College President and rising star, Dr. Claire Gaudani, into becoming the president of the NLDC. Once she agreed in 1997, the NLDC went to work recruiting high-powered individuals to construct a redevelopment plan unlike anything the city had ever imagined. The NLDC also wanted the Pfizer Corporation, one of *Fortune 500*'s largest companies and creator of the increasingly popular Viagra, to select the site for their headquarters. As the two sides courted one another, a plan evolved which would drastically alter the city's financial landscape.[6]

Things went well enough at first. Pfizer signed on after seeing the initial redevelopment plans that were tailored to them. The NLDC's website boasted that the acquisition of Pfizer created a unique private-public partnership interested in working with the community. It read, "With a corporate culture that emphasizes participation and contribution in the community, Pfizer management participates on the NLDC Board of Directors and NLDC committees. Employees also take on active roles in the corporation's planning and community development services."[7] The newly developed redevelopment project called for the ninety-acre area of Fort Trumbull (excluding the Fort itself) to be cleared, including an old Amtrak station and two wastewater treatment sites, as well as the homes, which dotted the area in parcels 3 and 4a.[8] The namesake of the case, Susette Kelo, lived on parcel 4a in a little 107-year old house that she had purchased in August 1997 and had remodeled herself. A recently divorced, single parent of five grown sons who worked as a paramedic and nurse, Kelo had never owned a house before. She bought the house specifically for the waterfront view and worked for years to restore the old house.[9]

With Pfizer on board and under the skilled leadership of Gaudani, the state began to support the NLDC plans, which were rapidly being solidified. In July 1998, a state consultation team was appointed to approve the environmental portions of the plan, as well as to come up with a working schedule. The eventual final plan, known as the Municipal Development Plan (MDP), was presented to and accepted by the NLDC Board in early 2000. The MDP was also reviewed and accepted by several state departments including the Department of Economic and Community Development, the Department of Environmental Protection, the State Office of Policy and Management, and the non-state Southeastern Connecticut Council of Governments. Each of these departments had the power to veto the plan with the takings aspect fully disclosed, but none of them did.[10] The New London City Council was not excited about the new powerful behemoth the NLDC had turned into, but recognized that the state was ready to pour millions of dollars into New London if the plan was accepted. They accepted the NLDC plans, which included the delegation of eminent domain power to the corporation. By the year 2000, the state, under the watchful eye of Governor Rowland, had promised the NLDC $23 million in grants and a $50 million bond in order to push the redevelopment plans through.[11]

In November of 2000, Kelo came home from work to a notice of condemnation of her house by the City of New London acting through the NLDC. Her property had been officially taken and she was to evacuate to make way for the razing of her house. She called her newfound attorney and friend, Scott G. Bullock from the Institute of Justice in Washington, D.C., and informed him of the news. The following month, amidst a throng of interested and irate citizens, Kelo and her neighbors from the inhabited parcels 3 and 4a held a rally and told the city and the press that they were going to fight the action. In December of 2000, the case was officially filed.[12]

THE SUPERIOR COURT OF CONNECTICUT

The first trial was held in July 2001 in the New London District Court, and was decided in March 2002, in a lengthy decision handed down by Superior Court Judge Thomas Corradino.[13] The decision focused on a myriad of aspects the plaintiffs had chosen, and in all but one of the arguments, the City of New London was successful in its justification of its eminent domain. The Corradino decision deserves attention, because it set up both the Supreme Court of Connecticut's and the U.S. Supreme Court's decisions.

In his opening remarks, the loquacious Corradino wrote that "life, after all, is short, unlike this decision and the excellent briefs filed by the parties."[14] He is not lying. The decision is over 65,000 words, and is far longer than the U.S. Supreme Court's decision three years later. Part of this is due to the myriad of different questions. The Kelo team focused on a variety of issues at first, including the constitutionality of delegation, the specific disposition of the parcels, and city favoritism. However, the Kelo case's fame ultimately came from the new understanding of the Public Use Clause.

One of the main objections the plaintiffs had against the city was the questionable authority to delegate eminent domain. As noted previously, the NLDC was given the power of eminent domain for the redevelopment project by the City of New London. The plaintiffs argued that if a taking was to occur, it could only be done by a public or political body, and that since the NLDC was neither, nor subject to the political process, it could not have the power. The NLDC, according to the plaintiffs, was a purely private, non-stock entity, completely apart from public responsibility.

This objection over the authority to delegate became one of the most important in the early cases, and it should be for Americans in general, especially in a natural-rights-based republic. If owning and holding property is a natural right, and if the taking of one's property by the government is allowed in certain circumstances, should it be possible to delegate this power to a body unconnected to democratic responsibility? In other words, can a democracy simply delegate its authority for convenience and efficiency? This question ultimately became a large one for each of the three courts and part of the larger question in the Supreme Court case. More discussion on the issue of natural rights occurred in both Thomas's and O'Connor's dissents than the majority opinion, and more attention will be given to them in a future chapter.

Corradino noted that according to the Connecticut General Statutes, a city may delegate such power to an organization like the NLDC because it was not a "private" organization in the way the plaintiffs had claimed. The NLDC was instead a non-profit corporation and "in many ways the NLDC is subject to the political process and the control of its activities by city and state."[15] Connecticut law expressly stated that such a corporation was properly enmeshed in the public process in the Connecticut General Statutes, chapter 132, Section 8-188:

> Any municipality which has a planning commission is authorized, by vote of its legislative body, to designate the economic development commission or the redevelopment agency of such municipality or a nonprofit development corporation as its development agency and exercise through such agency the powers granted under this chapter.[16]

He further noted that during the process of designing and implementing the plan, the redevelopment agency was required to get approval from numerous publicly-elected and publicly-appointed officials (such as the city council, the city's chief executive, the State Commission of Economic Development, and its commissioner), thus making it part of the political process.[17] According to the law, at any given point in the process, the elected officials might stop the process or demand a change, which, according to Corradino, denoted the public nature of the NLDC. Be not deceived, he warned, by arguments over the constitutionality of such delegation, and instead recognize what the plaintiffs were doing: "the plaintiffs had . . . set up an analytical strawman then, because they were very able lawyers, proceeded to demolish it."[18] Delegation was constitutional as long as public officials could still influence the process in some way.

Corradino's argument about the legality of the takings according to the Connecticut General Statutes was correct and undeniable according to state law. That the state had given the power of delegation to city councils was clearly expressed. However, what he did not address was the constitutionality of such legislation when compared to the Fifth Amendment of the Constitution of the United States as well as the Constitution of the State of Connecticut.[19] The redevelopment takings legislation Corradino cited was written during the 1960s on the heels of the Supreme Court case *Berman v. Parker* (1954). When it was being written, a new wave of urban planning and economic redevelopment studies was on the rise in the nation. In the Connecticut case *Graham v. Houlihan* (1960), the opinion called the era "these days of advanced city planning and urban improvement."[20]

Stemming from a political tradition stretching back to the Progressive Era, expertise and public policy became enmeshed and began to replace the more mundane political processes at all levels of government.[21] This tradition of delegating city and urban planning to experts free from public pressures and inconsistencies paved the way for the delegation of takings to the City of New London. Progressive reforms in both the early twentieth century and the 1960s–1970s sought to bypass the messiness of the political procedure and provide a guided evolution found in planning bodies separate from direct politics. The Connecticut legislation followed the urban planning trend which was later adopted by the Supreme Court. As the Court noted, the notion where the proper line between experts and the democratic process in takings is somewhat of an evolving concept over time—one that permeated the *Kelo* case. In a future article, Bullock remarked that this deference to elites outside of the political process had produced an area that operated as "a constitution-free zone."[22]

Building off of the delegation argument, the plaintiffs struck at the constitutional heart of the matter. They claimed that under both federal and state constitutions the taking in the case was not made for a legitimate public use. While they didn't argue the merits of economic takings per se, they focused on the problem of taking private property and transferring it to another private owner for an incidental or perceived public benefit. In other words, it was not a "public" use if the public was not allowed to use the property once taken. The plaintiffs were interpreting the Takings Clause of the Fifth Amendment very strictly: "No person shall . . . be deprived of life, liberty, or property, without due process of law; nor shall private property be taken for public use, without just compensation."[23]

Corradino explained that there existed a distinction between narrow and broad interpretations of public use, and that the legal system had settled on the broad interpretation. In his discussion of public use, Corradino relied heavily on eminent domain scholar Philip Nichols and his work *The Law of Eminent Domain: a Treatise on the Principles Which Affect the Taking of Property for the Public Use.*[24] Nichols noted that public use was a difficult term to define and there were many who still held to the narrow interpretation that meant "use by the public" or "employment" by the public. However, there were many who espoused the broad interpretation that public use meant "public advantage."[25] It was of some notice that Corradino focused on the Nichols text that was written in 1917 and enjoyed wide publication during the Progressive Era. The principles were consistent with the era. However, even Nichols would not go so far as to allow a taking purely for an economic redevelopment plan. He noted in chapter VI:

> It is well settled, as a general principle of law, that the power of eminent domain cannot be constitutionally employed to enable private individuals to cultivate their land or to carry on their business to better advantage, even if the prosperity of the community will be enhanced by their success.[26]

Corradino was most likely nudged away from this specific scholastic limitation by later cases such as *Berman*.

After demarcating the narrow and broad interpretations, Corradino wrote, "trying to determine if a particular use is a public use, however, cannot depend on a linguistic analysis."[27] In reasoning that can best be described as the needs of the many outweighing the needs of the few, he wrote that the broad view had prevailed out of necessity.[28] Redevelopment takings had been seen as a public use in Connecticut since the 1954 Supreme Court of Connecticut case *Gohld Realty Co. v. Hartford.*[29] The primary body, which ultimately defined the term according to the Supreme Court of Connecticut, was the state legislature. Referring back to Nichols, Corradino noted, "The presumption is that a use is public when the legislature has declared it to be."[30] Following this logic, the taking agent was now able to define what its limitations for takings are. Of course, argued Corradino, the legislature's takings power was not absolute. The courts were in place to determine whether or not the takings went too far on a case-by-case basis. The legislature was allowed to determine the takings, but not without immunity from judicial review. The job of the judge in redevelopment takings cases was to "discover whether it [the legislature] has acted unreasonably or in bad faith, or has exceeded its powers."[31] Where that scope of proper powers exists became more of a judgment than a distinctly demarcated line.

One can sympathize with the problem Corradino faced when trying to define the proper judicial role in cases of an undefined concept of public use. Where might one draw the limits on the takings power? How was a judge to know where these lines are? Corradino implies a mild solution to the problem by claiming that there was "One such limit adopted in the case law . . . the so-called 'heightened scrutiny' test."[32] In order to determine the proper limits, a judge must "determine the validity of a taking where eminent domain power benefits specific private interests."[33] In a two-part qualification of the test, Corradino wrote that the judge must determine if a) the taking was in line with the redevelopment plan itself, and b) if the purpose of the taking was "primarily to benefit the public."[34] The proper role of a judge in the takings case, according to Corradino, would be to understand the facts of the case and determine whether or not the taking was a real public use. In this case, Pfizer was specifically courted for the sites by the NLDC, but the seizure was not to boost Pfizer's profits as much as benefit the public through a revitalization of revenue and a remodeling of blighted areas along the waterfront.

The public use question was largely dealt with using Nichols and Connecticut case law, as well as an appeal to several other states' precedents.[35] However, he noted "one gets the feeling that in the eminent domain area each state court seems to operate in its own little universe."[36] This presents a major problem with the universal applicability of law, and a more comprehensive discussion of it was found in both the Supreme Court of Connecticut and the U.S. Supreme Court, which will be discussed in future chapters.

Aside from the more lofty legal arguments, the plaintiffs argued a practical issue, namely, that the specific parcels their homes were situated on (parcels 3 and 4a) were not needed for the redevelopment plan because the "MDP and its goals can be accomplished as to this parcel without tearing down their houses."[37] They argued that the takings were in excess. Parcel 3 contained only a small cluster of homes, which were to be torn down to make office buildings and parking lots. Parcel 4a was designated as something termed "park support" and a "marina training facility." Corradino decided to split the judgment on the parcels, finding that parcel 3 was a legitimate part of the plan, but parcel 4a was not.

Beginning with parcel 3, Corradino relied on the testimony of University of Massachusetts Amherst urban development professor, John R. Mullin. Mullin noted that "it is uncommon for land to be entirely cleared for new development and it is not reasonably necessary to take the four homes in parcel 3 to accomplish the goals of the MDP." However, on cross-examination, Mullin "brought out that his alternative would place a projected office building overlooking a sewer treatment plant" thus making the plan not desirable to incoming companies.[38] After professor Mullin's testimony, Jimmy Hicks, Executive Vice President and one of the principals in RKG Associates (an economic development firm), testified as to why to incorporate the parcel in the plan. It was all about attractiveness, which plays a vital role in any redevelopment plan. Hicks explained that developers wanted the most certainty they could get from a redevelopment plan they were investing in. He called the decision by the NLDC to clear the parcels the "spotted leopard defense." When asked to further elaborate, he replied:

> It's where a leopard has spots, spots are things that stay the same and you've got to work around them. Spotted leopard is just a way to refer at the configuration of land uses. If you're gonna attract developers, if you're gonna put out what you call requests for proposals and get them interested in the site, and after they overcome all the inherent problems with redevelopment, say to them also, well, you've got to work around this contingency, you greatly diminish your ability to finding competent capable people to come in. You take things that would possibly risk and turn them into uncertainty. Developers operate with very short time frame financial conditions, and it was our recommendation that because the housing wasn't adaptable and a long-term use to the office related things, and that three, four kinds of the hodgepodge of certain things that we recommended, that most of those facilities be demolished.[39]

As this explanation made clear, the NLDC needed to create an area attractive to developers, free from the restraints of working around pre-existing houses and the limitations they might bring.

In a more lengthy exposition, Corradino wrote that redevelopment plans could not be subjected to the whim of every owner within a tract of land. He said, "If each property owner were allowed to contest…that his property was being taken for a public use, redevelopment plans for blighted areas would be hopelessly bogged down" and would become "useless."[40] It is legislature, or in this case the city council (through the NLDC), that must be trusted. Examining the case, Corradino found no bad faith or unreasonableness and because of that, deferred to the decision of the NLDC.

The plaintiffs had yet another question surrounding the disposition of parcel 3 when they found that the plans were speculative and not definite. To take property for a speculative benefit was something that could invite all kinds of problems. This became a much larger issue at the United States Supreme Court, but Corradino explained that such a worry dismissed the intentions of the plan. As he noted previously, there was no bad faith in the designation of parcel 3 for seizure. In order to understand whether or not the taking was in bad or good faith, one must look to the "larger context of the public use this court had already found to be the goal of chapter 132."[41] He then proceeded to point out that the municipality was severely distressed and that the influx of revenue would be vital to spur job growth and create a larger tax base. According to this logic, the good faith requirement was met by the intent of the planning agency because it had laid out its goals in the originally accepted plans by the legislature or city council. The judges' only role was to scrutinize the intent, and the intent was good in the NLDC plans.

Parcel 4a was another matter. After his lengthy exposition on parcel 3 and the necessity of deferring to the originally accepted plans, Corradino took the opposite conclusion on the neighboring parcel. The intended uses of parcel 4a were markedly different in the MDP than those of parcel 3. Parcel 4b, adjacent to 4a, was designated as a possible "marina training facility" with parcel 4a possibly used as "marina support." In order to keep the plan flexible for investors, parcel 4a was also designated as a possible site of "park support."[42] This was a bridge too far for Corradino who emphatically wrote, "What on earth is a 'marina training facility'?" Each of the expert witnesses, including Mullin and Hicks, had no idea what either of these terms meant. Since the terms and the ultimate disposition of the parcel were unclear, the plan for parcel 4a was not deemed necessary, but far too speculative to justify any takings.[43]

For Corradino, the law was silent when the terms were unclear or the plan remained so inflexible that no reasonable or concrete good could issue from it. This seems at odds with his former discussion of legislative and agency deferment. If the "spotted leopard defense" was to be taken seriously, as Corradino did, it was difficult to strike down a part of the overall plan that remained open for other opportunities and investors. If a comprehensive plan were approved by the legislature, where would the difference lie between the possibility of having office buildings or parking lots and the possibility of having another related business being part of the plan? If the overall faith of the plan was good, and the intent was to economically build the distressed area, why was this as-yet-undetermined parcel of the plan so problematic? The overall intent of the plan as presented to numerous political bodies was good, as noted in parcel 3, and yet in 4a the overall intent was not good—or at least it was not good enough. This imaginary line Corradino drew was immediately reversed in the Supreme Court of Connecticut's decision after brief consideration. It was clear that the "heightened scrutiny" test Corradino tried to apply was not developed well enough to pass muster at the higher level.

The Superior Court opinion was, by all accounts, an understandable one. Chapter 132 of the Connecticut General Statutes made it clear that an economic redevelopment plan was a valid taking under Connecticut law. The NLDC was also vindicated as a legitimate instrument since it could be given authority under Section 8-188 to exercise the powers of eminent domain. Corradino's interpretation of public use also seemed to be consistent based on the case law up to that point. Using the same cases as the U.S. Supreme Court eventually would in its majority opinion, as well as Connecticut case law and statutory law, the opinion demonstrated what the current legal interpretation of the term was. This was not to say that there weren't constitutional problems with how the term was being understood, but strictly according to precedent, Corradino seemed to be very much in line.

THE SUPREME COURT OF CONNECTICUT

Immediately after the decision in favor of the City of New London was released, the plaintiffs appealed the decision to the Supreme Court of Connecticut. Interestingly enough, Susette Kelo's house was among those spared by the emancipation of parcel 4a from the plan. However, she did not want to give up the fight for her neighbors. As Jeff Benedict noted, she said "all for one and one for all," and appealed the case with her neighbors.[44] The initial hearing was conducted in December 2002 but the decision was not officially released until March of 2004. The state Supreme Court trial was originally argued in front of a panel of five justices and two were added later.[45]

The split on the court was 4-3 with Justice Flemming L. Norcott, Jr. writing the opinion for the majority. Concurring with the opinion were Justices David M. Borden, Richard N. Palmer, and Christine S. Vertefeuille; the dissent being written by Justice Peter T. Zarella, who was joined by William J. Sullivan and Joette Katz. The split numbers in both of the *Kelo* cases remained close up through the final decision made by the U.S. Supreme Court, being decided in each case by one vote. Norcott's opinion contained nothing new or remarkably novel that would set it apart from Corradino's opinion with perhaps the major exception of reversing the judgment regarding parcel 4a. Zarella's dissent was far more indecisive and one can get the feeling that he was hedged in by precedent, but was ultimately uncomfortable with the broader ramifications of the majority opinion.

By the time the case reached the Supreme Court of Connecticut, the plaintiffs had honed their argument over public use problem down to three major points. First, a taking specifically for redevelopment was not valid under chapter 132. Second, even if it were permitted, this particular instance would not pass state constitutional muster since the takings "don't promote significant public benefit" to be legitimized which the constitution required.[46] Third, parcels 3 and 4a (where Kelo and her neighbors lived) would be taken but would not be for a public use or benefit because they would remain in private hands for private purposes.

It was noteworthy that Norcott had foreseen the importance of the definition of public use from the very beginning of the case. He began the opinion by saying, "The principal issue in this appeal is whether the *public use clauses of the federal* and *state constitutions* authorize the exercise of the eminent domain power in furtherance of a significant economic development plan."[47] The public use question became the linchpin of the *Kelo* case.

The opinion addressed the points in turn. Regarding the absence of redevelopment takings in chapter 132, Norcott pointed to the same reasoning as the superior court, and noted that while Corradino had focused mainly on the statute, this was an even bigger question surrounding the constitutionality of the statute itself. Without going into any scholastic inquiry, Norcott stated "This court has long taken a flexible approach to construction of the *Connecticut public use clause*."[48] Using Connecticut precedent stretching back to 1866, he proceeded to demonstrate just how broadly the term had been interpreted. He noted that the court had construed public use as being synonymous with "public purpose" since 1953.[49] With such a broad definition being used by both the legislatures and the courts, Norcott argued that that public use included such redevelopment schemes as the NLDC had enacted. Norcott also cited the U.S. Supreme Court cases of *Berman* and *Midkiff* as proof that the federal government thought along the same lines.[50] Norcott also demonstrated the trend of academic disdain of the definition. He noted:

> Moreover, beyond the case law, we observe that many commentators within the academic community also have addressed the issue of whether economic development satisfies the constitutional public use requirement. Support for both sides of the issue, of course, may be found within this array of law review articles. We note that most, however, tend to express alarm at what they consider to be a situation rife with the potential for abuse of the eminent domain power.[51]

While scholarly debate had led most scholars to fear the evolution of public use, Norcott made it clear: "We, however, conclude that responsible judicial oversight over the ultimate public use question does much to quell the opportunity for abuse of the eminent domain power."[52] In other words, while academics might find an avenue for potential abuse, the judges' oversight would ultimately provide the safeguard against such abuses.

Considering the public benefit objection as well as the disposition of parcels 3 and 4a, Norcott held, as did Corradino, that the public benefit from the plan was enough to justify such a taking. Not only did chapter 132 expressly state that it was legitimate, but when "successful achievement of the public purpose of economic development necessarily requires private sector involvement," the takings are entirely justified.[53] This harkened back to Corradino's arguments over the intent and good faith of the taking itself. If the public would ultimately benefit according to the redevelopment plan, the taking fell under the protection of chapter 132. If the potential for public benefit was shown and agreed to by the city legislature, the public use requirement had been met.

When the plaintiffs brought up the problem of the delegation of authority, the majority sided with the City of New London by using Corradino's reasoning. Norcott noted that the process had not gone from a public one to a private one, but that by virtue of the process, the NLDC was still to be considered publicly accountable to the city and the legislature. In much the same terms of the superior court, he noted, "as the city resolved in January, 2000, after approving the development plan, the development corporation acquired the properties *in the name of the city*, pursuant to § 8-193."[54] According to chapter 132, the delegation was allowed. The constitutionality of the delegation was never fully addressed by the majority, and instead was only lightly touched upon and implicitly relied heavily on Corradino's reasoning.

The plaintiffs also appealed the disposition of parcel 3. Norcott reiterated Corradino's reasoning that the plan for parcel 3 did not need to comport with each inhabitant's desires. He wrote, "We conclude that the trial court did not commit clear error in upholding as a factual matter the development corporation's determination that the parcel 3 takings were reasonably necessary to effectuate the goals of the development plan."[55] As for parcel 4a, Norcott took the opportunity to effectively annul Corradino's idea for a new heightened scrutiny test: "we conclude that the trial court's review of the parcel 4A taking utilized a legal standard that permitted review far in excess of that provided for by our well established case law."[56]

The new test Corradino created was far too intrusive to legislative functions, which, as both Corradino and Norcott pointed out, were to be deferred to in the disposition of parcel 3. Norcott believed the test was not in keeping with the principle of limited judicial review in the case of eminent domain. That the courts may get involved was not in question for the majority. Instead, as Justice Anthony Kennedy worried about, the question became: what was the criterion for getting involved? For Norcott, it was somewhere between natural right and legislative prerogative. However, this line was not as clearly defined as it was in the superior court's treatment of parcel 4a. The question of intent, used on parcel 3, was reestablished for parcel 4a, and the majority reversed that part of the superior court decision.

The Supreme Court of Connecticut did not spend time with the more minute details, but it did a thorough job explaining the preexisting state and federal takings law and focused on the major issue of public use. While the majority found for the defendants on every question, the dissent, lead by Justice Zarella, took issue with the constitutional interpretation of the Public Use Clause and the disposition of parcels 3 and 4a.

Zarella sensed that the case was going to have more far-reaching effects than simply Connecticut case law. He wrote, "There is a gathering storm of public debate as to whether the use of eminent domain to acquire property for private economic development in non-blighted areas is justified."[57] Zarella sensed the uneasy tension between the public and the redevelopment laws which had been quietly put into place for the last several decades. In his objection to the public use interpretation, he stuck a spear directly into the heart of the matter by astutely noting, "This court has not considered…whether chapter 132 of the General Statutes is constitutional."[58] He continued, "In addition, for nearly a century, this court has not examined the authority of the state—or a subdivision thereof—to exercise its power of eminent domain for the public benefit when that public benefit is accompanied by a corresponding private benefit."[59]

The dissent laid out the historical foundations of takings and the evolution of the Public Use Clause that began with cases in the Progressive Era (with the exception of *Olmstead v. Camp* [1866]). During these times, the Public Use Clause was given the more expansive reading it would continue to adopt over the next century, whether the case was explicitly decided in favor of the defendant or not.[60] Zarella explained that by employing the broad interpretation of public use, "it is well established that judicial deference to determinations of public use by state legislatures is appropriate."[61] Citing only *Berman* and *Midkiff*, Zarella made it clear that this had been in practice in the recent past. However, it was not beyond the reach of the judicial responsibility to examine the trend. Taking a page from Corradino's opinion, Zarella called for a heightened scrutiny test in takings of this sort. He went further than Corradino and briefly set forth a four-step process that would shift the burden of proof to each side (condemner and condemned) during the process.[62]

Jumping to the parcel 3 and 4a takings, Zarella believed the takings were unjustified in the case. He did not deny that chapter 132 was constitutional, especially looking at the aforementioned cases, however, he did argue that in redevelopment takings, there must be a stronger burden of proof on the entity using eminent domain than simply vague speculation about increasing revenue for the city. He said, "The record, as it stands, contains scant evidence to suggest that the predicted public benefit will be realized with any reasonable certainty."[63] The NLDC did not do a thorough job in proving that parcels 3 and 4a were elemental to the plan as a whole. Where the majority found the general intent of the MDP was sufficient, Zarella believed that when a taking occurred of places with homes and where people are already living, the burden of proof was much higher and required specifics. He disagreed with the majority and wished for both parcels to be returned to their former owners.

CONCLUSION

Both of the original majority opinions hinted at a multifaceted and expansive discussion on the nature of takings in general. Citing precedent going back fifty years, both courts recognized that takings had evolved from the narrow definition present in the first 100 years of the republic. This evolution had occurred quietly, although not expressly hidden to the public, and only a few court cases as well as a small number of legislative provisions in each state bore any record of it. When the *Kelo* case was noticed by the public, thanks to the help of the young attorney Scott G. Bullock and his friends at the Institute for Justice, it became a national interest. The public had finally been made aware of the broad understanding of public use that had been used by courts and legislatures for decades. Suddenly there was an outpouring of interest in the eminent domain, and the case was painted as a David and Goliath story. While much of the media surrounding the case was sensationalized and oversimplified, it offered the public the rudimentary legal arguments that allowed them to begin questioning the interpretation and laws that had been made over the past fifty years. The case continued to gather steam when it was called for by the Supreme Court in 2004. It would be the Supreme Court that would bring the case to its position of prominence in America, and, as both in the superior and state supreme courts, the fight in that court would not be an easy one for either side.

In both of these opinions, the law found that Kelo and her neighbors could lose their property as a consequence of an economically distressed area. In this way, the individual was being more directly punished for the problem of the many. In the American republic, the Bill of Rights was written to delimit the intrusion of the many on the individual, including Amendment V, and the new understanding of eminent domain, namely redevelopment, stood in stark opposition to the original intent. Many people were shocked by the new definition of takings that they believed was strictly limited. The Declaration of Independence stated that the government was instituted on the principles of people's "Safety and Happiness." In the *Kelo* case, people found that neither happiness in the enjoyment and use of one's own property, nor safety from government seizure was being upheld, and the case became a sensation. People began to question the evolution of takings and began to make their voices known.

NOTES

1. "The Battle of Groton Heights and The Burning of New London," Department of Energy and Environmental Protection, accessed May 12, 2013, http://www.ct.gov/deep/lib/deep/stateparks/general_info/the_battle_of_groton_heights_and_the_burning_of_new_london.pdf.
2. Ibid.
3. *Kelo v. New London*, 545 U.S. 469 (2005); see also Carla T. Main, *Bulldozed: "Kelo," Eminent Domain, and the American Lust for Land*. (New York: Encounter Books, 2007), 154.
4. Claire Guadani, "New London Development Corporation Case Study," ClaireGuadani.com, accessed March 21, 2013, http://www.clairegaudiani.com/default.aspx.
5. Jeff Benedict, *Little Pink House: A True Story of Defiance and Courage*. (New York: Grand Central Publishing, 2009), 18. One cannot say enough about Benedict's work on the

people and timeline of events presented in his study. An investigative journalist by trade, Benedict uses scores of interviews with the actors on all sides of the controversy, official documents, media snippets; and nothing has been written to compare with his narrative of the events. For those interested in the human element in the case, Benedict's book cannot be recommended enough.

6. "Putting the New back in New London," *The Economist*, June 13, 1998, accessed February 11, 2013, http://www.economist.com/node/134291.

7. Main, *Bulldozed*, 156.

8. Ibid., 156–57. See Figure 2.1 at the end of this chapter for a map of the proposed area.

9. Benedict, *Little Pink House*, 3–42.

10. *Susette Kelo et al. v. City of New London et al.*, 2002 Conn. Super. LEXIS 789.

11. Main, *Bulldozed*, 156.

12. Benedict, *Little Pink House*, 204–14; see also *Susette Kelo et al. v. City of New London et al.*, 2002 Conn. Super. LEXIS 789.

13. Benedict, *Little Pink House*, 252.

14. *Susette Kelo et al. v. City of New London et al.*, 2002 Conn. Super. LEXIS 789.

15. Ibid.

16. *Connecticut General Statutes*, 132 C. § 8 §§ 188.

17. *Susette Kelo et al. v. City of New London et al.*, 2002 Conn. Super. LEXIS 789; see also Connecticut General Statutes, 132 C. § 8 §§ 191, §§ 195.

18. Ibid.

19. *Constitution of the State of Connecticut*, Art. I, §11 reads: "The property of no person shall be taken for public use . . ." This emphasizes that the taking will be for a public use, which is precisely the interpretational debate in the case.

20. *Graham v. Houlihan*, 147 Conn. 321, 160 A.2d 745 (1960) (quotation cited in *Susette Kelo et al. v. City of New London et al.*, 2002 Conn. Super. LEXIS 789.).

21. For a further discussion of Progressive reforms including views of expertise in government, see Bradley C.S. Watson, *Living Constitution, Dying Faith: Progressivism and the New Science of Jurisprudence*. Wilmington: ISI Books, 2009, 94–109.

22. Scott G. Bullock, "The Inadequacy of the Planning Process for Protecting Property Owners from the Abuse of Eminent Domain for Private Development," in *Property Rights: Eminent Domain and Regulatory Takings Re-Examined*, ed. Bruce L. Benson's (New York: Palgrave Macmillan, 2010).

23. U.S. Const. amend. V.

24. Philip Nichols, *The Law of Eminent Domain: A Treatise on the Principles Which Affect the Taking of Property for the Public Use*. Albany: Matthew Bender & Company Incorporated, 1917. There are several reprintings of this text, and it is unclear which Corradino uses based on the brief reference given on page 17.

25. *Susette Kelo et al. v. City of New London et al.*, 2002 Conn. Super. LEXIS 789; also Nichols, *The Law of Eminent Domain*, 128-33.

26. Nichols, *The Law of Eminent Domain*, 217.

27. *Susette Kelo et al. v. City of New London et al.*, 2002 Conn. Super. LEXIS 789.

28. Ibid. He asserted that "If this narrow view had prevailed in our history, it could be said that we might still be huddled along the eastern seaboard or presently our central cities would be severely handicapped in trying to recover from the mailing of our state." He did not explain further.

29. *Gohld Realty Co. v. Hartford*, 141 Conn. 135, A. 2d 365 (1954).

30. *Susette Kelo et al. v. City of New London et al.*, 2002 Conn. Super. LEXIS 789.

31. Ibid., (quoting *Graham v. Houlihan* (1960)).

32. Ibid.

33. Ibid.

34. Ibid.

35. There is a myriad of cases outside of Connecticut that Corradino mentions but does not delve into including *Poletown Neighborhood Council v. City of Detroit*, 410 Mich. 616, 304 N.W.2d 455 (Mich. 1981); *City of Jamestown v. Leevers Supermarkets, Inc.*, 552 N.W.2d 365, 369 (N.D. 1996); *City of Duluth v. State*, 390 N.W.2d 757, 763 (Minn. 1986); *In the Matter of*

Northeast Parent & Child Society, Inc. v. Schenectady, 114 A.D.2d 741, 494 N.Y.S.2d 503 (N.Y. 1985); *Hogue v. Port of Seattle,* 54 Wash. 2d 799, 341 P.2d 171, 187 (Wash. 1959); *Sweetwater Valley Civic Assoc., Inc. v. City of National City,* 18 Cal. 3d 270, 555 P.2d 1099, 133 Cal. Rptr. 859, 863 (Cal. 1976); and *Williamington Parking Auth. v. Land with Improvements,* 521 A.2d 227 (Del. 1987).

36. *Susette Kelo et al. v. City of New London et al.*, 2002 Conn. Super. LEXIS 789.

37. Ibid.

38. Ibid.

39. Ibid.

40. Ibid.

41. Ibid.

42. Ibid.

43. He gives several more descriptions of times when the legislature can go, or has gone, too far in its speculations: "Even if the court were prepared to give the legislative agency all the deference in the world under these circumstances, it cannot perform what is a constitutionally mandated function. In other words, this is not a case where if we are going to have an airport, it has been decided we need plaintiffs' land (*Carlor Co.*); or if we are going to build a convention center, the condemners' land must be taken (*Broida*); or if GM is going to build its assembly line, its width and length required the seizure of a whole neighborhood (*Poletown*); or the pipeline has to go through Mrs. Jones' house if we are going to access reservoir water; or the highway expansion means we need to take the nice house in the valley—this is a case where the court just cannot make the requisite constitutionally required necessity determination based on the information before it" (Ibid.).

44. Benedict, *Little Pink House*, 20.

45. Those on the original panel were Justices Borden, Norcott, Palmer, Vertefeuille, and Zarella. Added after were Justices Sullivan and Katz. *Susette Kelo et al. v. City of New London et al.*, 2004 Conn. LEXIS 54.

46. Ibid.

47. Ibid. (italics in original).

48. Ibid. (italics in original).

49. Ibid.

50. More on these two cases will be found in a further chapter.

51. Ibid.

52. Ibid.

53. *Susette Kelo et al. v. City of New London et al.*, 2004 Conn. LEXIS 54.

54. Ibid. (italics added).

55. Ibid.

56. Ibid. (italics added).

57. Ibid.

58. Ibid.

59. Ibid.

60. Cases including *Olmstead* (1866), but also *Gohld Realty Co. v. Hartford,* 141 Conn. 135 (1954), *Hawaii Housing Authority v. Midkiff,* 467 U.S. 229 (1984), *Poletown Neighborhood Council v. Detroit,* 410 Mich. 616 (1981), and *Pequonnock Yacht Club, Inc. v. Bridgeport,* 259 Conn. 601 (2002).

61. *Susette Kelo et al. v. City of New London et al.*, 2004 Conn. LEXIS 54.

62. His four-step process was as follows: (1) "Judicial review should begin with consideration of whether the statutory scheme is facially constitutional. In light of well established judicial deference to determinations of public use by state legislative bodies, the party opposing the taking should bear the initial burden of proving that the contemplated public use of private economic development is unconstitutional." (2) "If the court concludes, however, that the proposed economic development is a valid public use, the party opposing the taking should bear the additional burden of proving, in accordance with the deferential standard of review afforded to legislative determinations of public use, that the primary intent of the particular economic development plan is to benefit private, rather than public, interests." (3) "In the event that the court concludes that the plan is constitutional, the burden should shift to the taking

party to prove that the specific economic development contemplated by the plan will, in fact, result in a public benefit. . . . Accordingly, shifting the burden of proof is appropriate at this point in the inquiry because the taking party has greater access than the opposing party to information regarding developer interest in the properties and the progress of negotiations relating to the disposition of the properties." And finally (4) "Finally, if the trial court concludes that the condemned property will be used for a public purpose, it should be incumbent upon the party opposing the taking, on the basis of the deferential standard of review that we accord to legislative determinations of public use, to prove that the specific condemnation at issue is not reasonably necessary to implement the plan." (Ibid.)

63. Ibid.

Chapter Three

The Object of Society

The Amicus Briefs and Oral Argument

During the summer of 1787, the delegates to the Constitutional Convention covered a vast array of topics affecting the fledgling American experiment. One of those delegates was thirty-five-year-old Gouverneur Morris from Pennsylvania. Complete with a wooden peg leg and a bombastic style of oratory, Morris was a vociferous federalist during the convention's proceedings. Remarking upon the principle of representation, Morris spoke of the necessity of property in all societies and governments. James Madison wrote:

> He thought property ought to be taken into the estimate as well as the number of inhabitants. Life and liberty were generally said to be of more value, then property. An accurate view of the matter would nevertheless prove that property was the main object of Society. The savage State was more favorable to liberty than the Civilized; and sufficiently so to life. It was preferred by all men who had not acquired a taste for property; it was only renounced for the sake of property which could only be secured by the restraints of regular Government.[1]

Madison's notes showed that John Rutledge of South Carolina immediately followed by agreeing with Morris, concluding, "Property was certainly the principal object of Society."[2] The convention then continued to discuss apportionment and representation further, and the issue of property as the "object of society" was never objected to.

While the Morris quote was a good insight into the views and feelings of a popular delegate, it was of perhaps even greater importance to note the lack of reaction to the sentiment. Rutledge quickly agreed with Morris, and no one else said a word refuting the idea. It was safe to say that most, if not all, of the Framers viewed owning property as one of the chief ends of civil society. Morris noted that both liberty and life were more valuable than property, but could be easily had outside of civil society—in fact it was much easier outside of government to have them both. However, a government came into necessity when one "acquired a taste for property." Only then would a person renounce the freedoms of the state of nature (or the "savage state") and agree to live in a less-than-totally free society.

Americans have always held their property in the highest regard. Owning, holding, and disposing of property, was seen as one of the earliest recognized rights in America. Tocqueville said, "Each one [American], having a particular good to defend, recognizes the right of property in principle."[3] It was little wonder that Americans have always been interested in their own property in relation to the government. Some scholars have gone so far as to propose that the Constitution was a purely economic document, drafted by rich propertied men who sought to consolidate their own property and power by creating laws favorable only to themselves. The idea of private property had always been inseparable from constitutional considerations, and, until recently, was an area into which the government dared not tread except under the most important circumstances.

Thirty-seven amicus briefs were filed between November 2004 and January 2005. Twenty-five of the briefs supported the petitioners, which was more than twice as many than for the respondents.[4] The briefs filed with the Supreme Court pointed to the idea that Americans took their property very seriously. In the amici, the range and scope of property in the American regime was explored. From farmers to churches, from minority groups to the elderly, from scholars to realtors, each of those supporting the petitioners represented a strain of thought on the proper sphere of takings. The supporters of the respondents were also indicative of trends in the modern regime, and consisted almost wholly of cities and redevelopment corporations. Taken altogether, it was a good exploration of how property is seen through different lenses in America. In the pages that follow, relevant arguments found in the amici will be examined.

IN SUPPORT OF THE PETITIONERS

The twenty-five amici supporting Kelo and her neighbors attacked the modern interpretation of takings and public use in a variety of ways.[5] Many of the arguments overlapped, as would be expected with such a large number on the same side. It would be far too lengthy and superfluous to simply summarize each of the briefs one-by-one here. Instead, it is much easier to consider the briefs and find the patterns that emerged. Running throughout the briefs are three broad categories: (1) original interpretation of the Public Use Clause,

(2) a need for heightened scrutiny, and (3) discrimination. Admittedly many of these overlap, but the patterns remain strong enough for differentiation.

In the first category, the originalist interpretation amici appealed to the Framers, philosophers, and early common law practices surrounding the drafting of the Constitution. Groups such as the American Farm Bureau Federation, the Becket Fund for Religious Liberty, the CATO Institute, and the Claremont Institute all fell under this category. The category itself can be further broken into two subcategories: (a) those fearing an attack on their property that was their livelihood and (b) those relying on scholarship and philosophic inquiry.

In the first category, farmers, churches, realtors, and small business owners (among others), had recognized that a ruling updating and legitimizing the Public Use Clause past its original interpretation would establish a precedent which could jeopardize the very future of their careers and lives. Looking exclusively at both the superior court and Supreme Court of Connecticut's opinions, these amici forecasted the problem of a redevelopment taking as a public use. The general argument was that if a city wanted to increase the tax base (and what city does not desire more money?), property being used as farms, churches, or homes would be the first to go, since they did not produce as much tax revenue as a more profitable private enterprise might.[6] The Becket Fund for Religious Liberty brief asserted,

> Religious institutions will always be targets for eminent domain actions under a scheme that disfavors non-profit, tax-exempt property owners and replaces them with for-profit, tax-generating businesses. Such a result is particularly ironic, because religious institutions are generally exempted from taxes *precisely because* they are deemed to be "beneficial and stabilizing influences in community life."[7]

Churches were seen to be non-profit and tax-exempt entities, which did not produce as much revenue as possible, but instead acted as "beneficial and stabilizing" parts of society. For a city to increase the tax base, the property a church sat on would not realize its potential. Spirituality, which churches seek to influence and increase, cannot be measured by the same profit standards, therefore the Becket Fund believed that they would eventually be unwisely discriminated against.

The American Farm Bureau Federation also feared for their interests. Farms were not sources of high revenue, and fewer and fewer have been found each year in America. While the tax profits were not there, another tangible benefit was produced: "the . . . feeding of the American populace."[8] Farmers often had large tracts of land that could be more profitable in the hands of a private developer, which made the argument over increasing the tax base a valid concern. A shopping mall or a Costco could generate far more tax revenue than a cornfield or alfalfa field. The Farm Bureau noted that if the Public Use Clause were interpreted in such a way, Americans would be in far more severe trouble later as they became unable to grow enough food for their populace.

The National Association of Home Builders and the National Association of Realtors voiced concern over the tax generating power of individual homes against commercial establishments. They wrote, "housing will almost never afford a community with the economic development benefits that a commercial application will."[9] Houses can always be torn down for more profitable commercial projects, just as farms and churches may.

Businesses are not all alike, as the Develop Don't Destroy (Brooklyn) Inc. and the West Harlem Business Group stated in their brief. At the outset, the West Harlem Business Group described the bullying of their members and small businesses by Columbia University, which sought nearby land to expand its campus. The Group noted the alarming trend that occurred all over New York, "Most disturbingly, such takings had been affected at the behest of private corporations and developers, who selected the property to be taken and derive the principle benefits from the taken land."[10] In other words, it was not the city planners who were seeking such takings, but private entities that stood to profit from them. Manhattan, the brief also noted, had little commercial land available, and developers were beginning to look to smaller businesses outside the area to condemn and develop, using the excuse of increasing tax revenue for the city. However, the Group argued that even though fair compensation for the property could be awarded, "Many of the businesses . . . have a long-term local customer base, so that relocation would cause enormous economic hardships for such businesses far beyond the fair value of the real estate."[11] The main conclusion being that if a business was not performing better than a larger one that would like to take the property, the city would side with the larger business for the increase in tax revenue.

Altogether, these groups represented a large swath of the American populace, a swath which does not have the financial or political power of larger and more successful developers. A ruling in favor of the petitioners would have, for them, alleviated their fears that economic redevelopment takings occurred willy-nilly at the behest of those promising higher taxes and more employment.

The second subcategory in the originalist interpretation group was the scholars and philosophers who sought a more principled repudiation of the modern public use jurisprudence. The CATO Institute, long known for its libertarian stance on politics, issued a lengthy brief authored (in part) by the eminent legal scholar Richard A. Epstein from the New York University School of Law. Professor Epstein has written many articles on takings, including a book on the subject, and his views were consistent with his previous scholarship. CATO's brief contained numerous appeals to the problem of economics in takings jurisprudence. The brief asserted that the new interpretation of the "public use test was so broad that no major government initiative failed to meet it, for every large-scale project could be justified in the name of economic development even if the plan was a dead loser from the moment of its conception."[12] Indeed, subjecting the rule of law in this case to purely economic rationale subverted the very principles of private property that the nation was founded on. It further implied that often such "redevelopment" was hardly ever in the best interest of the citizens, and more in the interest of the city council or city planners themselves: "The romantic assumption that legislatures act only for the common good leads to travesties like this New London project." For CATO, even the blight rulings in *Berman* led to an over expansive and unnecessary takings doctrine. If an area was "blighted," then it was a "nuisance-like" place that could be "eliminated under the traditional police power (through condemnation of dilapidated structures)."[13] As it stood in this case, however, Kelo's home was not blighted, and therefore did not fall under the power to be taken for a private developer. Public use meant just that: use by the public. This was the "strict definition" which Corradino noted had changed in the superior court opinion.[14] The CATO brief distinctly argued: "On its face, the Constitution blocks such a taking."[15] In a four-part process, the CATO brief laid out why the Court's current interpretation, from *Berman* to *Midkiff*, was incorrect and dangerous to the principles of the Constitution.

Along the same lines as CATO was the brief from the Claremont Institute. Claremont is known for its appeal to history and the original principles of the Founders, and the brief focused heavily on both. Beginning with questioning the very statute the NLDC justified its actions with, the brief found that the whole developing interpretation was flawed: "Chapter 132 of Connecticut's statutory code presumes that city officials may and should redistribute land in whatever way is most advantageous for their cities."[16] From the beginning of American history, property was seen as untouchable and, as Sir William Blackstone called it, "The third absolute right."[17] The departure from this idea was disturbing, and had placed too much power in the hands of the state legislature, when in reality the lines of distinction were drawn to keep the power out of the hands of that body. This was evident in Judge Patterson's opinion in *Van Horne's Lessee v. Dorrance* (1795): "The preservation of property . . . is a primary object of the social compact. . . . No man would become a member of a community, in which he could not enjoy the fruits of his honest labour and industry."[18] The Claremont Institute pointed out that the shift occurred gradually beginning in the Progressive Era because of the new theories of government popular at that time. The brief pointed out that Progressive historian Charles Merriam, wrote that by 1924 the "question is now one of expediency rather than of principle."[19]

By following such legal realism, legislatures and courts had gradually come to reinterpret the Public Use Clause far beyond its original idea. The

Claremont brief offered a simple solution to the problem: return to the original understanding of the clause in cases and commentaries. It concluded, "Government takes property for a public use if it retains ownership of the property, or if it assigns the property to a private party subject to common carrier duties of public access."[20] As far as the Claremont evidence was presented, this simple test produced the understanding of original intent, and the court would do well to put an end to the confusion of public use by reverting back to the ideas of the Founding.

Each of these briefs called for a return to the original intent of the Takings Clause, and produced slightly different ways of advocating their position. These would be categorized as those seeking the narrow interpretation that Corradino brought up in his opinion. In the originalist briefs, the old legal maxim "a man's home is his castle" was completely undermined by the modern interpretation of public use. However, not every supporter of the petitioners believed that a return to original intent would be the solution to the problem. Too much time had passed, and the legal doctrine had changed so much, that a return would be untenable. Instead, the advocates of the second category, heightened scrutiny, called for retaining the status quo in the public use interpretation, but added a stricter (or heightened) scrutiny test to redevelopment takings. The dissenting justice on the Supreme Court of Connecticut, Zarella, saw the need for such a test to be created, as did Supreme Court Justice Anthony Kennedy in his concurring opinion in *Kelo*. This trend had other advocates during the oral argument in the Supreme Court in the form of Justices Stephen Breyer and Sandra Day O'Connor.[21]

The amici dealing with the heightened scrutiny test all shared the same basic reasoning that in cases of redevelopment takings, the courts or legislatures should be involved to a higher degree because such a taking was prone to corruption or suspect by its very nature. The brief of professors David L. Callies, James T. Ely, et al., spoke to the very idea by saying, "Whatever the precise formulation adopted by the Court, the government should be required to make some sort of individualized determination of the need for the particular parcel in question before condemning private property."[22] The test would require the legislature to provide more than simply a "rational basis" test to show that the public use was a rational use. The briefs of the Cascade Policy Institute, et al., and the New London Railroad Company, Inc., agreed that a scrutiny test was the only way to put a lid on corruption and favoritism.[23] Other amici mentioned the same type of heightened scrutiny, but most placed the onus on the legislatures taking the property—not the court. O'Connor picked this up in the oral argument who did not want to establish a new and improved test that courts would be using on every new eminent domain case. This would have proven far too burdensome.

The last set of pro-petitioner amici dealt with a facet of the case that was heavily taken up by both the media and scholarly journals, but hardly saw any consideration by the courts. Many believed that an element of discrimination was apparent in redevelopment cases. Where the petitioners sought relief from a violation of the Fourteenth Amendment in the Superior and Connecticut Supreme Court decisions, the elements of race, class, and age were picked up by several of the amici. One of the most powerful interest groups in America, the NAACP joined together with another interest group behemoth, the AARP, as well as others, and together wrote a brief, pointing out the problems such takings had for minority groups. The brief stated, "Elimination of the requirement that any taking be for a true public use will disproportionately harm racial and ethnic minorities, the elderly, and the economically underprivileged . . . they are affected differently and more profoundly."[24]

For example, the NAACP brief focused on several cases, but especially salient to the *Kelo* case was the Michigan case *Poletown Neighborhood Council v. City of Detroit* (Mich. 1981).[25] In *Poletown*, the Michigan Supreme Court ruled that public use was synonymous with a public purpose, and even though no blight was being specifically cleared, the economic benefits were enough to condemn the houses.[26] However sound the ruling was in 1981, the brief noted that in another case, *County of Wayne v. Hathcock* (Mich. 2004), the Michigan Supreme Court overruled the *Poletown* decision.[27] The *Hathcock* decision became the rallying cry for those who saw redevelopment takings as specifically aimed at minority and less affluent groups. In the same way *Poletown* was overturned based on these considerations, so must the *Kelo* decision be decided, the brief reasoned.

The brief pointed out that redevelopment condemnations often targeted minority groups because "these groups were less likely, or often unable, to contest the action."[28] Being in such a destitute state, these minority groups were unable to pay to contest the action, much in the same way Susette Kelo and her fellow petitioners were. The brief did not contend that the blight rulings in *Berman* were wrong since they sought to alleviate the "decay of the area." However, the ruling in the Connecticut Supreme Court was beyond the Public Use Clause because it sought goals which were to "create jobs, increase tax and other revenues, encourage public access to and use of the city's waterfront, and eventually 'build momentum'" for the city.[29] By using such vague terms, the city can and would seek minority groups to discriminate against as others had in the past. The brief concluded that any such broad ruling on public use (in favor of New London) would render "the eminent domain power open to abuse" and prevent future cases from "rein[ing] in potential abuses."[30]

IN SUPPORT OF THE RESPONDENTS

The twelve briefs filed for the City of New London are useful in helping explore the modern arguments surrounding the takings doctrine. The amici in this section will be broken into three general categories that serve to encompass what they are proposing. The categories are (1) broad public use interpretation, (2) police powers, and (3) discrimination.

The first category stood in direct opposition to the narrow public use reading that the originalists espoused. Beginning with the amici for the Connecticut Conference of Cities et al., and largely joined by the National League of Cities et al., the argument was one that mirrored that of the superior court. It began, "The rise and decline of Connecticut cities was [sic] a familiar story," and continued to outline the problems faced by such small communities packed into tiny waterfront areas.[31] If cities were not allowed to employ takings for redevelopment purposes, the cities in areas like Connecticut would be doomed to fail forever since they could never attract any new businesses or projects to such a depressed area. Reading public use broadly included the welfare of the cities and state which was something that had to be done if anything was to be done to save the state. In their briefs, they wrote that the Court dismissed all of the arguments against a narrow interpretation long ago, and that broad interpretations were "well-established principles" which had been in place for the past half century.[32] In the respondents' briefs, the categories and new tests introduced by the petitioners were nothing but a veiled reversal of the modern public use doctrine.[33] The Court had never required proof that a redevelopment plan would succeed, and trying to push one now was to refute the rulings of the past fifty years.

The second category used scholarship and philosophic inquiry to refute the amici for the petitioners and focused on the proper role of the police powers. In the brief of Law Professors Robert H. Freilich, Richard Briffault, et al., the authors argued that "This Court held that the definition of the police power [of the scope of public use] 'is essentially the product of legislative determination addressed to the purposes of government. . . .'"[34] Here, the professors assumed that part of the police powers given to a state included defining how the legislature would interpret the Public Use Clause in eminent domain cases. This fact, they claimed, was well established in *Berman,* and to challenge such a finding would be to challenge the doctrine of police powers itself.[35] The Court had never in its history used a heightened scrutiny test, they argued, and to subject takings cases to a new kind of test would dangerously erode the police powers of a state. Instead, the "judicial restraint by this [Supreme] Court had worked well," and those who sought to impose a new test were trying to tamper with something that had worked fine.[36]

The third category was in direct opposition to the last category of the pro-petitioner group; namely the category of discrimination. The amicus brief for BUILD et al., focused on the impact that such takings had on blighted areas where disproportionately large numbers of minorities resided.[37] They directly confronted the NAACP's findings by saying,

> [T]he Court should not decide the case on the jarring premise . . . that government promoted economic development projects should be viewed as transferring wealth *from* individuals of modest means *to* the wealthy or that such efforts are opposed by poor and working people and people of color. The purpose of projects like the one at issue is to make a material difference in the lives of residents of economically distressed cities, the vast majority of whom are themselves of extremely modest means; our experience with similar projects teaches that these purposes can in fact be accomplished.[38]

The brief continued that in many of the strictly public use takings (i.e., a highway) used in the 1950s and 1960s often used a "racial animus" that targeted black neighborhoods.[39] They continued to say that because of demographic and voting rights shifts elected officials "are far more accountable to poor and minority elected constituents" and therefore would not be devising plans to target minorities as many did in the 1950s and 1960s.[40] The implication here was that by taking away the elected officials' power of redevelopment takings, those supporting the petitioner were being insensitive to minority groups who benefit most from such takings. While the NAACP brief found that racial problems pervaded redevelopment takings, the BUILD brief argued that the opposite was true: redevelopment takings helped destroy racism and its attendant problems.

All of these amici pointed to the diverse views on the Takings Clause and the nature of property rights in modern America. Arguments about social justice and redistribution, absolute natural rights, police powers, race, class, and others mentioned, were all part of the national dialogue on takings. Looking over these amici, it is clear that Americans have differing views on the place of property under the Constitution. This became problematic for many reasons, and the Court was forced to consider these views while attempting to figure out the proper interpretation of the Fifth Amendment. Although no specific consensus was reached, the amici did a good job of presenting the regnant themes in America, and the justices undoubtedly drew from them in the oral argument as well as their opinions.

ORAL ARGUMENT

On February 22, 2005, Susette Kelo and her legal team (headed by attorneys Scott Bullock, Dana Berliner, and Chip Mellor) were to report for oral argument at the Supreme Court. Not all of the nine justices were present that day—Chief Justice William Rehnquist was at home sick from the cancer that was spreading throughout his body, and Justice John Paul Stevens, who would later write the majority opinion, was "stranded at an airport."[41] As per usual, the gallery to hear the argument was full. According to the rule of seniority, Justice O'Connor presided. She announced that the Court would hear the case of *Kelo v. New London*, with the petitioners, represented by Bullock, speaking first.[42]

The oral argument in *Kelo* contained a number of questions and explanations of eminent domain, the limits of the Public Use Clause, and the issue of redevelopment takings. Much in the same way the amici were struggling to come to a clear and concise determination of takings, the Court seemed to be divided between several different viewpoints. One of the largest and most pervasive questions coming from the oral argument was the notion of natural rights vs. distributive justice.

In an article entitled "Takings and Distributive Justice" (1999) by Hanoch Dagan, the author set out a view that was consistent with a Progressive notion of takings. Dagan derived his thesis in his article from a quote by Justice Hugo Black: "[the] Fifth Amendment guarantee . . . [is] designed to bar Government from forcing people alone to bear public burdens which, in all fairness and justice, should be borne by the public as a whole." Dagan wrote, "It [the idea of distributive justice] requires that we consider what distributive criteria should guide the distribution of the burden of the public project, activity, or regulation between the landowner and the community that benefits from this public use (i.e., the taxpayers of that jurisdiction)."[43] Dagan's article sought to show that distributive justice must weigh the benefits of the "public burdens" with the right of property, and find a way to balance the two so that the public unequal distribution of wealth was "borne by the public as a whole." This encapsulated the major argument of those seeking the more Progressive notion (he uses the term in his article) of takings. Takings should be able to be carried out by experts and elites who understand and may redistribute the property so that all may benefit from it. This was in direct confrontation with the view that property was a natural right and should be retained at all costs except for something that would specifically be used by the public, not taken and redistributed to other private owners for the public's benefit. This became the major underlying theme that both sides brought up implicitly, but never directly.

BULLOCK

Attorney Bullock began his remarks by bringing up the precarious situation he believed every "home, church, or corner store" was in if the Connecticut ruling in the case were allowed to stand.[44] Immediately into his description of the case, Justice Ruth Bader Ginsburg interjected and pointed out that this case was not about a private-to-private taking by New London, but that the city had been severely depressed and wanted to create more jobs.[45] Bullock immediately countered by saying that chapter 132 of the Connecticut General Statutes was not circumscribed to depressed cities only, and that this sort of taking was without limits. This, according to Bullock, was why the case was so important because, as he noted, "Every city has problems."[46]

Justices O'Connor and Ginsburg then began to discuss with Bullock the limitations that the Court had put in place by referring to the blight case of *Berman*. This case was like *Berman*, they argued, and the only thing the petitioners seem to be doing was coming up with a newer, stricter test for the Court to enforce. O'Connor bluntly asked Bullock, "What kind of standard were you proposing we should get into here to second guess the public use aspect?"[47] She brought this question up later, asking Bullock to propose a new standard or test, since he seemed to be walking the line between not overturning *Berman* and heightening the scrutiny in *Kelo*. Bullock, after not having an answer the first time said, "The test should be that the government cannot take property simply so that the new owners can put it to ordinary private uses of land."[48] He referred to his test as the "reasonable foreseeability test."[49] In other words, there must be an immediate foreseeable benefit in the condemnation or else it was not truly public use. Instead, it became a private-to-private taking with an incidental public benefit. He noted that in *Berman*, the benefit was immediate. O'Connor was not satisfied with this test, and said, "that was not what was asserted here [in *Kelo*] . . . the city says, we were doing this for the purposes of enhancing economic development of a very poor city. . . . What was your test?" Several minutes later, Breyer picked up on the idea of a new test and asked what the minimal standards for such a test should be. Bullock's answer and the subsequent exchanges are worth noting as they point out the major problems of such a test:

> **Justice Breyer:** . . . it comes to me now you're getting to what I think is a possible realm of reason here. But the second part now you said has minimum standards. What minimum standards?
> **Mr. Bullock:** Well, the dissent in the Connecticut Supreme Court talked a lot about minimum standards that should be in place in order to ensure that public benefits actually come about. Those could be such things as a commencement date for the project, a construction schedule, financial eligibility for the developers, there's a number of different things.
> **Justice Breyer:** No, I mean, are you advocating particular ones?
> **Mr. Bullock:** Not particular ones, just the standard actually be in place and we think that the dissent provides some good guide posts for establishing—
> **Justice Scalia:** Isn't that in effect changing the test from public use to efficient public use? I mean, what's . . . you know, if I condemn land for a public utility

> and the public utility turns out to be very inefficient, has the condemnation been valid?
> **Mr. Bullock:** No. Your Honor.
> **Justice Scalia:** Do you want us to sit here and evaluate the prospects of each condemnation one by one?
> **Mr. Bullock:** No, Your Honor, what we are advocating for, and utilities of course are justified, have long been justified under a separate line of cases, common carrier regulations. But what we are talking about are certain minimum standards in place at the time of condemnation to try to have some type of reasonable certainty that the public benefits are to come about so we are not talking about ongoing oversight. We are simply talking about minimum standards at the time of the, at the time of the condemnation.[50]

This badgering of Bullock was instructive. O'Connor, Breyer, and Scalia were all pushing for clarification because they were confused by Bullock's reasoning. Throughout his argument, several of the justices peppered him with questions about whether or not to overturn *Berman*.[51] He answered first that *Berman* was a fundamentally different case, and it did not need to be overturned. However, he also answered that the public uses in *Berman* were direct and immediate, but in *Kelo* they were at a time far too distant.[52]

The lawyer for the respondents, Wesley W. Horton, picked up on this confusion and during his argument said that the petitioners were presenting two tests, "One for *Berman* and *Midkiff* and *National Railroad*, and another test for *Kelo*."[53] Many of the amici brought up the same language, including National League of Cities and the several law professors. If the Court were to adopt a new bright line rule governing takings, the respondents argued that the Court would be so weighed down with cases that the evolution of the public use doctrine would be reversed. Horton proclaimed that if such a test was adopted, or the Court demarcates the line between public use and purpose the way the petitioners wanted, then "you're going to overrule Holmes' decisions from 1905 and 1906."[54] Scalia, in typical humorous fashion, immediately replied to Horton, "It wouldn't be the first of Holmes' decisions to be overruled." The Court and the chambers erupted into audible laughter. It is unclear which of Holmes's decisions Horton is referring to, although they are most likely *Clark v. Nash* (1905) and *Strickley v. Highland Boy Gold Mining Co.* (1906).[55] Both cases dealt with conveyances over land in the arid desert of Utah. In *Clark* the issue was over irrigation water conveyed through another's land, and in *Strickley* it was the use of an aerial to transport coal across someone's land. Holmes only wrote the opinion in *Strickley*, but in it he agreed with Justice Peckham's opinion in *Clark* that emphasized the deference of defining public use to the state legislatures who knew the local circumstances better.[56] One year later in *Strickley*, Holmes wrote, "In discussing what constitutes a public use, it [*Clark*] recognized the inadequacy of use by the general public as a universal test."[57] He continued further, "If the state Constitution restricts the legislature within narrower bounds, that is a local affair, and must be left where the state court leaves it in a case like the one at bar. . . . The Constitution of the United States does not require us to say that they are wrong."[58] Peckham and Holmes both agreed that there are extenuating circumstances for a private taking, and that the "use by the general public" test was an insufficient one for general applicability.

After Scalia's response, Horton reiterated his previous argument over Holmes's precedent, "Plus I thought Holmes was right when he said that to say that the public actually had to use the property was not an appropriate meaning of the phrase, so I would not think you'd want to revisit that case, even if you wanted to revisit some other of Holmes' decisions."[59]

The justices themselves were wary of the idea of a heightened scrutiny test. Scalia asked, "Do you want us to sit here and evaluate the prospects of each condemnation one by one?"[60] Clearly the justices were not satisfied with the prospect of an increased workload akin to the one they had already been facing in gerrymandering cases. Ginsburg asked Bullock, "do you do that [apply the test] area by area?"[61] To which O'Connor chimed in, "do you have to do it parcel by parcel or can it be with the whole—?"[62] Bullock replied that it should only be done where the property was "actually being conveyed."[63] Souter, who asked how the proposed test of Bullock's was any different than the "good faith requirement," finally boiled down the whole argument to an important question of intent.[64] As mentioned in the Superior Court and Connecticut Supreme Court arguments, the good faith requirement was something the courts may already look into. Bullock began to answer, but was cut short by his time constraint and the question was never explored further.

In summation, Bullock's arguments focused chiefly on the necessity of a higher standards test that would increase judicial oversight in takings cases. Most likely for reasons of precedent, he never argued that the Public Use Clause had become radically perverted from the original intent of the Fifth Amendment. By implication he was hinting at this idea, however. He never explicitly said it was his wish, but one can get the sense that this was the ultimate train of logic. Instead of advocating this, he shrewdly devised a test which would place a higher burden on the courts in takings cases. This was, in essence, a reversal of the public use evolution since the Progressive Era, and would create a stronger platform for a narrowed interpretation of the Public Use Clause.

HORTON

Horton's argument on behalf of the City of New London began on an interesting note. He began with the following statement, "The principle purpose of the takings clause was to provide for just compensation."[65] He began to discuss another topic and was immediately cut off by O'Connor, "Well, but it has to be for a public use."[66] Horton agreed but also brought up the defense's theoretical argument by explaining, "the primary purpose of the takings clause was not to regulate legislative determinations of that [public use]."[67]

This opening exchange spelled out one of the key points in the defense's understanding of the Fifth Amendment. As Horton noted, the amendment focused on the government providing just compensation in takings cases, but it was silent on who should define what a public use is. He asserted that the Framers never intended to second-guess a legislature's definition in takings. The assertion struck at the heart of the matter, and it was something that, although not challenged directly, Bullock had attacked in his argument with his desire for a court-imposed "reasonable foreseeability" test for state legislatures and city councils. As soon as Horton established his point that second-guessing was not part of the intent of the Fifth Amendment, he quickly moved on to shore up his flank by arguing against the Bullock test.[68]

As noted previously, Bullock's argument for a reasonable foreseeability test revolved around an overreach of the judiciary, as well as an overturning precedent. When pressed, Horton said he would never impose such a test on takings because that would create a bright line rule that would be the exact argument Bullock was making. Both Scalia and O'Connor asked him if there should be a line drawn for economic redevelopment or not. Or, if there should be one drawn around higher taxes or not. As Scalia pointed out about a taking for a higher share of taxes, "Any city can do it."[69] At this point, Horton said that while there was that possibility, there was still a test for discrimination in cases of this kind.[70] The problem/test Horton referred to was the "*Willowbrook* versus *Olech*" test coming from the case of *Village of Willowbrook v. Olech*. In this case, a petitioner was being singled out and discriminated against by the village regarding an easement to be built on her property. The question revolved around the Equal Protection Clause of the Fourteenth Amendment. In a 9–0 opinion, the justices noted that the Equal Protection Clause did protect an individual against an unwarranted taking discrimination. The *per curiam* opinion noted, "Our cases have recognized successful equal protection claims brought by a 'class of one,' where the plaintiff alleges that she has been intentionally treated differently from others similarly situated and that there is no rational basis for the difference in treatment." Horton used the case to show that because the Fourteenth Amendment applies to discrimination even in takings cases, irrational discrimination based on something such as taxes or partisanship will still be able to be challenged in Court.

The justices began to say that the *Willowbrook* anti-discrimination test notwithstanding, there was still a discrimination problem regarding profitability. Justice O'Connor explained, "For example, Motel 6 and the city thought, well, if we had a Ritz-Carlton, we would have higher taxes. Is that okay?"[71] As repugnant as O'Connor's example was, he had to utter, "That would be okay . . . because otherwise you're in the position of drawing a line."[72]

Political science and legal scholars had long noted the problems of the public use definition. As mentioned in the first chapter, Rubenfeld called it the "doctrine-in-most-desperate-need-of-a-principle prize."[73] Horton's idea was to let the legislatures and cities determine the principle, since any lines drawn by the Court would be infringing upon police powers and legislatorial rights. The Connecticut Supreme Court majority opinion stated: "the economic development plans that the *appropriate legislative authority* rationally has determined . . . constitute a valid public use for the exercise of the eminent domain power under the either the state or federal constitution."[74]

Henry St. George Tucker, in his introduction to an edition of Blackstone's Commentaries in 1803, remarked, "The right of property, with all its train of incidents . . . seemed to have been left exclusively to the state regulations."[75] In the case of *Barron v. Baltimore* (1833), Marshall noted that the state governments were in charge of property and takings in their states and for their states. Strangely, the case was never spoken about during the *Kelo* trial or legal articles afterwards. In *Barron*, Marshall pointed out:

> Had the framers of these [state] amendments intended them to be limitations on the powers of the state governments, they would have imitated the framers of the original constitution, and have expressed that intention. . . . In almost every convention by which the constitution was adopted, amendments to guard against the abuse of power were recommended. These amendments demanded security against the apprehended encroachments of the general government—not against those of the local governments . . . the provision in the fifth amendment to the constitution, declaring that private property shall not be taken for public use, without just compensation, is intended solely as a limitation on the exercise of power by the government of the United States, and is not applicable to the legislation of the states.[76]

Disregarding for the moment the inclusive nature of the Bill of Rights believed to be found in the Fourteenth Amendment's Incorporation Doctrine, Marshall's words on takings in *Barron* pointed to the supremacy of the state when deciding takings issues. He validly asserted that if the Fifth Amendment's Takings Clause was meant to be utilized in the same way by the states, the states would have adopted it into their own constitutions.[77] Interestingly, Connecticut had done so by 1818. As noted in the previous chapter, Article I-11 of the Connecticut Constitution reads, "The property of no person shall be taken for public use, without just compensation therefor [sic]."[78] At the time of the *Barron* case, Maryland's constitution had no such takings provision. As Marshall wrote in his opinion, "they [are] justified under the authority they deduced from the charter of the city, granted by the legislature of Maryland, and under several acts of the legislature conferring powers on the corporation, in regard . . . to the health of the city."[79] The police powers were in force in the case, and Marshall sided with the plaintiffs and their understanding of federalism. Although the Connecticut Constitution had the same basic Takings Clause as the federal constitution, chapter 132 of the General Statutes had further amended the legal understanding of the provision. Chapter 132 specifically gave the power of determining public use to the legislature: "the necessity in the public interest for the provisions of this chapter was hereby declared as a matter of legislative determination."[80] As both Corradino and Norcott pointed out in their opinions, the Connecticut Supreme Court had never struck down chapter 132 as unconstitutional, and therefore according to both the interpretation of the modern federal jurisprudence and the state statutes, the City of New London may determine redevelopment as a legitimate public use. Horton understood that to argue against this would be to redefine police powers under the Tenth Amendment as well as state law.

Horton continued to push for the Court to deny Bullock's test, but began to be questioned by the justices about the redevelopment issue itself. The justices keyed in on this and began to ask him various questions regarding the extent and limitation that siding with New London would produce. The justices first asked Horton if there was a difference in a taking for a common carrier, such as those mentioned in the Utah cases.[81] He noted that there was, and the justices agreed that common carriers were still regulated by specific regulatory rules and regulations that made them public. Regarding Horton's argument, however, the justices pointed out that with no test, there was no regulation of the common carrier kind. This, in effect, transfers from private owner A to private owner B with minimal public benefit. Horton argued that such was the same thing that happened in the *Berman* slum clearance case. At this point Breyer asked, "Could the courts, under this clause, at least review what you've just said [regarding takings in parcels 3 and 4a] for reasonableness?" He then continued, "Reasonableness is a concept that's already in the Constitution in terms of what the legislature can do, but I'm thinking of the stronger kind of reasonableness review that you might have in an administrative action. . . . Is that a possible kind of review that you might find appropriate here?"[82] Horton replied "No, Your Honor, if what you're defining as reasonableness is being higher than rational basis."[83] Unconvinced, Breyer told Horton,

> Well, the reason that you would apply a somewhat higher standard is because the rational basis, with tremendous deference, applies to the power of Congress to act in an economic area in the absence of a particular constitutional provision designed to protect a minority from the actions of the majority. And

> if you read that public purpose doctrine, a section here as having that in mind, you might want a somewhat higher level of review. Now, that's the whole thing spelled out. I'm not advocating it. But I am putting it forward to get . . . to get your reaction.[84]

Horton said that according to this logic, one could also be made about a higher standard of equal protection review. Breyer replied that the courts do already have such a higher standard of equal protection review.

The argument then shifted to another facet of the case that had, thus far, been overlooked. While talking about the possibility of compensation, Scalia put forward a question: "you're taking property from someone who doesn't want to sell it. Does that count for nothing?"[85] Horton acknowledged that it does mean something, but that there are some people who would always want to stay in their homes and on their property and would stymie the public good. Breyer said that the introduction of a reasonableness test would give those people a legal means of defending themselves in cases of losing their homes unreasonably.

Breyer had brought up one of the points that both of the Connecticut opinions focused on. The reasonable test being advocated by Breyer seemed to be in the same milieu as that advocated by Bullock. However, the test was problematic because it was, in essence, the same as the good faith principle. As noted in the previous chapter, the good faith principle was where the courts may intervene and decide whether or not the taking was done with "good faith" to benefit the public or not. As Souter asked Bullock earlier, "why do you think it's necessary to adopt the test you've just articulated as distinct from a good faith requirement?" Breyer could be asked the same question, although it was clear that he, along with Bullock, believed that the good faith requirement was not sufficient. It was a question of degrees at this point—one that Kennedy wrote about in his concurring opinion but Breyer abandoned by joining the majority.

The closing minutes of Horton's argument had the justices bringing up questions of fair compensation including social costs as well as private benefits. Scalia took the last few moments to point out that a private-to-private transfer with "incidental benefits" to the public was a perversion of public use.[86] Picking up on the social costs, undoubtedly a nod the BUILD amicus brief, Horton pointed out that "if a person is without a job and if a person is not able to get basic services that they need from the town because the town can't afford it, that's just as important [as other public uses or public utilities]."[87] Horton connected the Public Use Clause to the notion that the town must provide welfare to citizens in need. This appeal to a social form of justice was mentioned briefly—and dropped just as briefly. It assumed several propositions that came up in the majority opinion, but stood in stark contrast to the other arguments made in Horton's decision.

In his closing statement, Horton revisited the police powers argument and said that the "essence of federalism" was to let the states and state courts decide their own public use standard.[88] Constrained by time, Horton began his final statement but was cut short. He said only, "And so it seems to me the four words I think that this Court should consider . . . and I'm not going to tell you the four words since my red light is on."[89] The Court and gallery then burst into a much-needed fit of laughter and the time was turned over to Bullock.

Horton's arguments are summarized by his attention to the Public Use Clause as it had been interpreted in the modern era. To invoke a higher standard test would be to change the course of takings jurisprudence since *Berman*. Horton believed that if cities were so bound, they would have far less power over their own economies and public welfare, and would become far more ineffectual when dealing with blight and other such issues. According to Horton's arguments, keeping the status quo increases federalism and state power in the face of an overarching federal power. While most people in the public disagreed with this notion, and the backlash in America was enormous, he advocated an adherence to police powers and the federal system by letting New London take Kelo's house.

After Horton alluded to the final four words, the time was given to Bullock who was immediately asked by Kennedy, "Mr. Bullock, do you know those four words?"[90] Bullock replied, "I wish I did. I could respond to it if I . . . if I actually did."[91] The Court has a moment of good-natured laughter, the tension was broken, and Bullock succinctly reiterated what he said in his original argument.

As the session ended, the gallery and lawyers exited the building, only to be greeted by a host of national reporters who began asking Kelo for statements. Completely unsure of what to say, Kelo told the press, "I was very encouraged by today's arguments with the justices. . . . They [the NLDC and City of New London] had more than enough room to develop everything they want to develop. . . . We simply wanted to keep our homes."[92]

CONCLUSION

The amicus curiae briefs and the oral argument represented the refining of the constitutional arguments at issue in the case. In the amici, the sundry approach to the concept of takings and property rights ranged from natural rights to race, and from federalism to heightened scrutiny. As mentioned before, the briefs were far more numerous for the petitioners, and covered a host of legal and social considerations. Taken altogether, the amici proved valuable as a snapshot of American notions of takings at the beginning of the twenty-first century. Blackstone observed: "There is nothing which so generally strikes the imagination, and engages the affections of mankind, as the right of property; or that sole despotic dominion which one man claims and exercises over the external things of the world, in total exclusion of the right of any other individual in the universe."[93] Property has always been valuable to Americans, and it seems, in a somewhat subtle way, the amici in *Kelo* were written to consider the foundation and extent of that right. The imaginations of many legal and academic scholars were struck by the case, and a host of different interpretations of takings and property were found in numerous articles, books, and commentaries afterward.

The oral argument itself was also noteworthy for its myriads of reflections on the modern takings doctrine. Carefully acknowledging precedent, utilizing nuanced arguments, appealing to social concerns, and offering legal solutions, both lawyers Bullock and Horton framed their positions within the legal possibilities of precedent. The larger philosophical questions of property and ownership in general were never directly tackled, but were nonetheless implied throughout the argument. It is ultimately these arguments that were refined even further in the opinions issued from a divided Court several months later.

Both the amici and the oral argument got at the heart of the statement of Gouverneur Morris from the federal convention found at the beginning of the chapter: "property was the main object of Society."[94] As Americans with diverging views argued over the nature of holding property in society, the justices made their decisions on the matter in much the same way. Perhaps this was noteworthy in and of itself. Over the next several chapters, the opinions of the majority, concurring, and dissenting justices will be examined in greater detail.

NOTES

1. James Madison, "Notes (July 5, 1787)," in *The Records of the Federal Convention of 1787*, vol. I, ed. Max Farrand (New Haven: Yale University Press, 1911), 533.
2. Ibid., 533.
3. Alexis de Tocqueville. *Democracy in America*, trans. Harvey C. Mansfield and Delba Winthrop (Chicago: University of Chicago Press, 2000), 228.
4. Salkin, Lucero, and Phillips, "Friends of the Court," 165–66.
5. Salkin, Lucero, and Phillips, "Friends of the Court," 165–66.
6. This argument is directly asked in the oral argument to the lawyer for the respondents, Wesley Horton: *Justice Scalia*: "I just want to take property from people who are paying less taxes and give it to people who are paying more taxes. That would be a public use, wouldn't it?" *Justice O'Connor*: "For example, Motel 6 and the city thinks, well, if we had a Ritz-Carlton, we would have higher taxes. Now, is that okay?" *Mr. Horton*: "Yes, Your Honor. That would be okay." *Susette Kelo et al. v. City of New London, et al.*, Supreme Court Case 04-108, Oral Argument Transcript. Alderson Reporting Company (2005), Supreme Court of the United States Website, accessed March 20, 2012. http://www.supremecourt.gov/oral_arguments/argument_transcripts/04-108.pdf, p. 30, lines 4–12.

7. Brief of Amicus Curiae for the Becket Fund for Religious Liberty, *Kelo v. New London*, No 04-108 FindLaw.com, accessed October 2, 2012, supreme.lp.findlaw.com/supreme_court/docket/2004/February.html#04-108.

8. Brief of Amici Curiae for The American Farm Bureau Federation and the Farm Bureau Federations of the Following States: California, Connecticut, Florida, Indiana, Iowa, Kansas, Louisiana, Michigan, New Haven County, New Jersey, New York, North Carolina, Ohio, Oklahoma, Pennsylvania, Rhode Island, Texas, Utah, and Virginia, *Kelo v. New London*, No 04-108 FindLaw.com, accessed October 2, 2012, supreme.lp.findlaw.com/supreme_court/docket/2004/February.html#04-108.

9. Brief of Amici Curiae for The National Association of Home Builders and the National Association of Realtors, *Kelo v. New London*, No 04-108 FindLaw.com, accessed October 2, 2012, supreme.lp.findlaw.com/supreme_court/docket/2004/February.html#04-108.

10. Brief of Amici Curiae for Develop Don't Destroy (Brooklyn) Inc. and The West Harlem Business Group. *Kelo v. New London*, No 04-108 FindLaw.com, accessed October 2, 2012, supreme.lp.findlaw.com/supreme_court/docket/2004/February.html#04-108.

11. Ibid.

12. Brief of Amicus Curiae for The CATO Institute, *Kelo v. New London*, No 04-108 FindLaw.com, accessed October 2, 2012, supreme.lp.findlaw.com/supreme_court/docket/2004/February.html#04-108.

13. Ibid. It is interesting to note here that the term *police power* is invoked on the side of the petitioners in such a way that would benefit an increase in the city's seizing power. However, there are distinctions in the argument found in Epstein, *Takings*: "Supreme Court cases have repeatedly referred to the control of nuisances as a proper end of the state, and there is no doubt today, as in times past, that this proposition is sound in principle. The other side of the proposition, that the state can act only to control nuisances, is far more controversial," 12. See also pps. 112–21.

14. See chapter 2; see also Philip Nichols' *The Law of Eminent Domain: A Treatise on the Principles Which Affect the Taking of Property for the Public Use*. (Albany: Matthew Bender & Company Incorporated, 1917).

15. Brief of Amicus Curiae for The CATO Institute, *Kelo v. New London*, No 04-108 FindLaw.com, accessed October 2, 2012, supreme.lp.findlaw.com/supreme_court/docket/2004/February.html#04-108.

16. Brief of Amicus Curiae for Claremont Institute, *Kelo v. New London*, No 04-108 FindLaw.com, accessed October 2, 2012, supreme.lp.findlaw.com/supreme_court/docket/2004/February.html#04-108.

17. Ibid.

18. *Van Horne's Lessee v. Dorrance*, 2 U.S. 304 (1795).

19. Brief of Amicus Curiae for Claremont Institute, *Kelo v. New London*, No 04-108 FindLaw.com, accessed October 2, 2012, supreme.lp.findlaw.com/supreme_court/docket/2004/February.html#04-108.

20. Ibid.

21. *Susette Kelo et al. v. City of New London, et al.*, Supreme Court Case 04-108, Oral Argument Transcript. Alderson Reporting Company (2005), Supreme Court of the United States Website, accessed March 20, 2012. http://www.supremecourt.gov/oral_arguments/argument_transcripts/04-108.pdf. O'Connor raised the question of the limits of the heightened scrutiny test several times during the oral argument, and it is clear she wants to explore this reasoning further. However, she ultimately rejects the idea in her dissent, apparently not being convinced of the utility of such a test.

22. Brief of Amici Curiae for David L. Callies, James T. Ely, Paula A. Franzese, Nicole Stelle Garnett, James E. Krier, Daniel R. Mandelker, John Coepland Nagle, John Nolon, J.B. Ruhl, Shelley Ross Saxer, A. Dan Tarlock, Laura Underkuffler, and Edward F. Ziegler, *Kelo v. New London*, No 04-108 FindLaw.com, accessed October 2, 2012, supreme.lp.findlaw.com/supreme_court/docket/2004/February.html#04-108.

23. Brief of Amici Curiae for the Cascade Policy Institute, American Association of Small Property Owners, Grassroots Institute of Hawaii, James Madison Institute, John Locke Foundation, Illinois Policy Institute, Indiana Policy Review Foundation, Oregonians in Action Legal

Center, Pioneer Institute, Sutherland Institute, and Tennessee Center for Policy Research; and Brief for The New London Railroad Company, Inc., *Kelo v. New London*, No 04-108 FindLaw.com, accessed October 2, 2012, supreme.lp.findlaw.com/supreme_court/docket/2004/February.html#04-108.

24. Brief of Amici Curiae for The National Association for the Advancement of Colored People, AARP, Hispanic Alliance of Atlantic County, Inc., Citizens in Action, Cramer Hill Resident Association, Inc., and the Southern Christian Leadership Conference, *Kelo v. New London*, No 04-108 FindLaw.com, accessed October 2, 2012, supreme.lp.findlaw.com/supreme_court/docket/2004/February.html#04-108.

25. *Poletown Neighborhood Council v. City of Detroit*, 410 Mich. 616, 304 N.W.2d 455 (1981).

26. In the *Poletown* case, a section of Detroit known as "Poletown" because of its large concentration of less affluent Polish immigrants, was seized and was to be razed for a General Motors plant to built in its place. The case became a rallying cry for commentators, journalists and academics in their opposition to redevelopment takings. See Abraham Bell and Gideon Parchomovsky "The Uselessness of Public Use," *Columbia Law Review* 106 (2006): 1419-21; See also Epstein, *Takings*, 52–79.

27. *County of Wayne v. Hathcock*, 684 N.W. 2d 455 (Mich. 2004).

28. Brief of Amici Curiae for The National Association for the Advancement of Colored People, AARP, Hispanic Alliance of Atlantic County, Inc., Citizens in Action, Cramer Hill Resident Association, Inc., and the Southern Christian Leadership Conference, *Kelo v. New London*, No 04-108 FindLaw.com, accessed October 2, 2012, supreme.lp.findlaw.com/supreme_court/docket/2004/February.html#04-108.

29. Ibid., quoting both *Berman* and *Kelo* (2004).

30. Ibid.

31. Brief of Amici Curiae for The Connecticut Conference of Municipalities and the State Municipal Leagues of Alabama; Arkansas; California; Colorado; Florida; Georgia; Illinois; Indiana; Iowa; Kansas; Kentucky; Louisiana; Maryland; Massachusetts; Michigan; Minnesota; Missouri; New Hampshire; New Jersey; New Mexico; New York; North Carolina; Ohio; Oklahoma; Pennsylvania; Rhode Island; South Carolina; South Dakota; Texas; West Virginia and Wisconsin in Support of Respondents, *Kelo v. New London*, No 04-108 FindLaw.com, accessed October 2, 2012, supreme.lp.findlaw.com/supreme_court/docket/2004/February.html#04-108; and Brief of Amici Curiae for The National League of Cities, National Conference of State Legislatures, U.S. Conference of Mayors, Council of State Government, National Association of Counties, International Municipal Lawyers Association, and International City/County Management Association, *Kelo v. New London*, No 04-108 FindLaw.com, accessed October 2, 2012, supreme.lp.findlaw.com/supreme_court/docket/2004/February.html#04-108.

32. Ibid.

33. Ibid., footnote 26 reads: "The petitioners contrive to squeeze into three 'categories' cases finding public uses where the condemned property was transferred to another private party."

34. Brief of Amici Curiae for Law Professors Robert H. Freilich, Richard Briffault, Julie Cheslik, Janice C. Griffith, Tim Iglesias, Julian Conrad Jurgensmayer, Anita Miller, Thomas E. Roberts, Patricia E. Salkin, Edward J. Sullivan, Robert R.M. Verchick, Judith Welch Wegner, and Alan Weinstein in Support of the Respondents, *Kelo v. New London*, No 04-108 FindLaw.com, accessed October 2, 2012, supreme.lp.findlaw.com/supreme_court/docket/2004/February.html#04-108.

35. Ibid. This becomes a stickier situation than at first glance with defining the limit and scope of police powers themselves. Police powers being largely undefined and stemming directly from Amendment X of the Constitution in American law, the limits or areas of police powers can be murky. That the professors use lines drawn by the Court in *Berman* (at least in this case) makes sense, as it provides a demarcated line. However, does such a line exist in the original Constitution or constitutional jurisprudence? The answer is anything but clear. They do cite one source: "Phillip A. Talmadge, The Myth of Property Absolutism and Modern Govern-

ment: The Interaction of Police Power and Property Rights, 275 Wash. L. Rev. 857 (2000)," but again focus on the Court's precedent as the defining line of Amendment X powers.

36. Ibid.

37. Brief of Amici Curiae for Brooklyn United for Innovative Local Development (BUILD), Rev. Herbert Daughtry, and the New York City and Vicinity Carpenters Labor-Management Corporation in Support of the Respondents, *Kelo v. New London*, No 04-108 FindLaw.com, accessed October 2, 2012, supreme.lp.findlaw.com/supreme_court/docket/2004/February.html#04-108.

38. Ibid.

39. Ibid.

40. Ibid.

41. Benedict, *Little Pink House*, 314.

42. Ibid., 309–21.

43. Hanoch Dagan, "Takings and Distributive Justice" *Virginia Law Review* 85 (1999): 742–43.

44. *Susette Kelo et al. v. City of New London, et al.*, Supreme Court Case 04-108, Oral Argument Transcript. Alderson Reporting Company (2005), Supreme Court of the United States Website, accessed March 20, 2012. http://www.supremecourt.gov/oral_arguments/argument_transcripts/04-108.pdf, p. 3, lines 12-15. He is drawing here on the amici, especially those of the Beckett Religious Institute, the American Farm Bureau Federation, and Develop Don't Destroy Brooklyn (see above).

45. Ibid., p. 3, line 20-p. 4, line 1.

46. Ibid., p. 4, lines 2–20.

47. Ibid., p. 5, lines 21–23.

48. Ibid., p. 16, lines 14–17.

49. Ibid., p. 18, line 19.

50. Ibid., p. 17, line 17—p. 19, line 6.

51. Ibid., p. 8, lines 7–9; and p. 11, lines 7–9, 17–22.

52. Ibid., p. 13, line 24—p. 14, line 6.

53. Ibid., p. 27, lines 13–18.

54. Ibid., p. 51, lines 21–24.

55. *Clark v. Nash*, 198 U.S. 361 (1905); *Strickley v. Highland Boy Gold Mining Co.*, 200 U.S. 527 (1906).

56. Justice Peckham wrote in *Clark v. Nash*, 198 U.S. 361 (1905): "Where the use is asserted to be public, and the right of the individual to condemn land for the purpose of exercising such use is founded . . . upon or is the result of some peculiar condition of the soil or climate, or other peculiarity of the state, where the right of condemnation is asserted under a state statute, we are always, where it can fairly be done, strongly inclined to hold with the state courts, when they uphold a state statute providing for such condemnation. . . . This court has stated that what is a public use may frequently and largely depend upon the facts surrounding the subject, and we have said that the people of a state, as also its courts, must, in the nature of things, be more familiar with such facts, and with the necessity and occasion for the irrigation of the lands, than can any one be who is a stranger to the soil of the state, and that such knowledge and familiarity must have their due weight with the state courts. . . . We simply say that in this particular case, and upon the facts stated in the findings of the court, and having reference to the conditions already stated, we are of opinion that the use is a public one."

57. *Strickley v. Highland Boy Gold Mining Co.*, 200 U.S. 527 (1906).

58. Ibid.

59. *Susette Kelo et al. v. City of New London, et al.*, Supreme Court Case 04-108, Oral Argument Transcript. Alderson Reporting Company (2005), Supreme Court of the United States Website, accessed March 20, 2012. http://www.supremecourt.gov/oral_arguments/argument_transcripts/04-108.pdf, p. 52, lines 6–11.

60. Ibid., p. 18, 18–20.

61. Ibid., p. 25, lines 3–4.

62. Ibid., p. 25, lines 11–12.

63. Ibid., p. 25, lines 14–15.

64. Ibid., p. 25, line 25—p. 26, line 7.
65. Ibid., p. 26, line 25—p. 27, line 2.
66. Ibid., p. 27, lines 4–5.
67. Ibid., p. 27, lines 8–12.
68. Of course, one could argue here, as scholar Keith Whittington does in *Constitutional Interpretation: Textual Meaning, Original Intent, and Judicial Review* (Lawrence: University Press of Kansas, 1999), that in the absence of a clear definition, the political bodies (i.e., not the Court), should be in charge of defining the provision. This speaks to a certain type of judicial restraint, and in the case of *Kelo*, it would indeed be the argument of the defense for restraint from an inclusive or new test.
69. *Susette Kelo et al. v. City of New London, et al.*, Supreme Court Case 04-108, Oral Argument Transcript. Alderson Reporting Company (2005), Supreme Court of the United States Website, accessed March 20, 2012. http://www.supremecourt.gov/oral_arguments/argument_transcripts/04-108.pdf, p. 29, line 12.
70. *Village of Willowbrook v. Olech,* 528 U.S. 562 (2000).
71. *Susette Kelo et al. v. City of New London, et al.*, Supreme Court Case 04-108, Oral Argument Transcript. Alderson Reporting Company (2005), Supreme Court of the United States Website, accessed March 20, 2012. http://www.supremecourt.gov/oral_arguments/argument_transcripts/04-108.pdf, p. 30, lines 3–5.
72. Ibid., p. 30, lines 6–8. In his closing statement, Bullock singles this out and says, "I think the key to understanding their argument is the answer to the question of, can you take a Motel 6 and give it to a fancier hotel? Their answer is yes. And that's really what's at stake here."
73. Bell and Parchomovsky, "Takings Reassessed," 278.
74. *Susette Kelo et al. v. City of New London et al.*, 2004 Conn. LEXIS 54, italics added.
75. St. George Tucker, "*Blackstone's Commentaries: With Notes of Reference to the Constitution and Laws of the Federal Government of the United States and of the Commonwealth of Virginia,*" 5 vols, Philadelphia, 1803. Reprint. South Hackensack, N.J.: Rothman Reprints, 1969, in Philip B. Kurland and Ralph Lerner, eds., *The Founders' Constitution* (Chicago: University of Chicago Press, 1987), accessed February 28, 2010, http://press-pubs.uchicago.edu/founders/.
76. *Barron v. City of Baltimore*, 32 U.S. 243 (1833).
77. Scholar William Baude noted, "We all know that the Fifth Amendment was not intended to restrain the states." Cf. William Baude, "Rethinking the Federal Eminent Domain Power," *The Yale Law Journal* 122 (2013): 1791–93.
78. *Constitution of the State of Connecticut*, Art. I, § 11.
79. *Barron v. City of Baltimore*, 32 U.S. 243 (1833).
80. *Connecticut General Statutes*, chapter 132, § 8, §§ 186.
81. *Strickley* and *Nash*.
82. *Susette Kelo et al. v. City of New London, et al.*, Supreme Court Case 04-108, Oral Argument Transcript. Alderson Reporting Company (2005), Supreme Court of the United States Website, accessed March 20, 2012, http://www.oyez.org/cases/2000-2009/2004/2004_04_108, p. 37, lines 4–19.
83. Ibid., p. 37, lines 20–22.
84. Ibid., p. 37, line 25—p. 38, line 12.
85. Ibid., p. 39, lines 2–3.
86. Ibid., p. 53, line 10.
87. Ibid., p. 53, line 25—p. 54, line 5.
88. Ibid., p. 54, line 12.
89. Ibid., p. 54, line 22–25
90. Ibid., p. 55, lines 5–6.
91. Ibid., p. 55, lines 7–8.
92. Benedict, *Little Pink House*, 320.
93. Sir William Blackstone, *Commentaries on the Laws of England* (A Facsimile of the First Edition of 1765-1769), vol. II (Chicago: University of Chicago Press, 1979), 2.
94. Madison, "Notes," 533.

Chapter Four

The Evolving Public Use Clause

The Majority Opinion

In early May 1907, Republican lawyer and newly minted Governor of New York, Charles Evans Hughes, arrived in Elmira, New York, to deliver a speech. The speech was an answer to public corruption charges, brought forth by his political enemies because he had vigorously tried to remove the superintendent of insurance. Instead of winning his appeal, he lost in the state senate, and the Elmira speech was to be the first public reply on the matter. By some accounts, over 2,000 people, as well as his public opponent Democratic lawyer John B. Stanchfield, had arrived to hear the governor. Stanchfield rose and verbally attacked the character of Hughes by saying, "I stand before you with no man's retainer in my pocket," the railroad lawyer proclaimed before launching into a vigorous attack on Hughes's bill. "I represent no corporation or combination of men, but appear simply as a citizen interested in the growth and prosperity of Elmira."[1] This attack prompted Hughes to lay aside his prepared remarks and respond directly, "In distinction from my learned friend, I am here under a retainer. I am here retained by the people of the State of New York, to see that justice is done."[2]

As Hughes began to deliver his speech, he gave his views on the corruption of the court system in America. He said:

> I have the highest regard for the courts. My whole life has been spent in work conditioned upon respect for the courts. I reckon him one of the worst enemies of the community who will talk lightly of the dignity of the bench. We are under a Constitution, but the Constitution is what the judges say it is, and the judiciary is the safeguard of our liberty and of our property under the Constitution.[3]

As he noted, the judges existed to interpret the Constitution for the citizens. This view was consistent with a variety of interpretational approaches.[4] However, the most important gem for the *Kelo* case was that Hughes found that the judiciary was the safeguard of property in America. In his eyes, it became the specific role of the judiciary to guard the ability to hold private property from those "arbitrary powers" seeking to take it away under some sort of scheme or plan. Hughes continued his speech by pointing out how the judiciary could possibly lose popular esteem:

> I tell you, ladies and gentlemen, no more insidious assault could be made upon the independence and esteem of the judiciary than to burden it with these questions of administration . . . . Let us keep the courts for the questions they were intended to consider. When questions of property rights are involved, the constitutional right to hold property and not to be deprived of it without due process of law is involved; when, under the guise of regulation or authority . . . there is an assumption of arbitrary power not related to public convenience; when there is a real judicial question let the courts have it and every good citizen will stand aside and hope to see it decided fairly and with even-handed justice.[5]

If the courts descended to the level of second-guessing and regulating public administration, they would stray from what Hughes called "the questions they were intended to consider." Managing administrative affairs was not a "real judicial question"—it was a Trojan horse best left alone. According to Hughes, the courts should stick to questions that belong in the realm of jurisprudence, not day-to-day administration that wasn't high-minded law. The majority opinion in *Kelo* reflected this same sentiment: it was not the role of the courts to involve themselves in administrative questions. Quoting *Berman* in the majority opinion of *Kelo*, Justice Stevens wrote, "Once the question of the public purpose has been decided, the amount and character of land to be taken for the project and the need for a particular tract to complete the integrated plan rests in the discretion of the legislative branch."[6]

Hughes's reasoning portended to the future disposition of the Court in both *Berman* and *Kelo*. Stevens' opinion solidified the principle and the notion of the proper realm of the courts in takings matters was more specifically defined. This chapter will analyze the majority opinion and several aspects of the decision that Stevens presents.

BACKGROUND

Before an examination of the opinion, it is useful to understand what was going on outside the courtroom in the personal narrative of Susette Kelo and her neighbors. After the oral argument, Susette Kelo and company had approximately four months to await a decision from the Supreme Court. The decision was finally handed down on June 23, 2005. It was reported that when Kelo heard the news, she began to cry. As she put down the phone after hearing about the decision, she began to wonder where she would end up. With her home being taken, and the fair market value for the area far below the sentimental value and sweat equity, Kelo knew the future was uncertain. She began to grow angry. As author Jeff Benedict explained, "She had gone to America's ultimate source of justice and found none."[7] As she began to think about what the decision personally meant to her and her neighbors, including eighty-seven-year-old Wilhelmina Dery, she grew disgusted. She developed an even stronger attitude of defiance. "I know you won, you assholes. . . . Now come get us out."[8]

The defiance Kelo showed became newsworthy the very same day. Scores of people began calling her and offering their support. Author Carla T. Main documented much of the more noteworthy responses. She noted that one individual called Kelo and told her that he had a boat and an Uzi and offered to sail up to her shorefront and protect her if she desired.[9] Headlines began publicizing the event around the nation. In an MSNBC website poll, a staggering 98% of Americans disagreed with the decision.[10] Main also noted that many of the Founding Fathers reacted to the decision "by turning over in their graves at an alarming speed." Thomas Jefferson apparently spun over, as did George Mason (who helped draft the Fifth Amendment) rolled over, and even James Madison himself who wrote a memorandum to Stevens, excoriating him for the decision.[11] Citizens and the media were visibly angry, but so was the House of Representatives. On the day following the announcement of the decision (June 24th), the House introduced a resolution stating, "*Resolved,* That the House of Representatives disagrees with the majority opinion in Kelo et al. v. City of New London et al. and its holdings that effectively negate the public use requirement of the takings clause."[12] The resolution received bipartisan support and passed six days later by a vote of 365–33.[13]

It seems the words of Justice Scalia uttered during the oral argument were embraced by the public far more than the broad interpretation of public use. He said, "She [Kelo] is living in this house . . . and she does not want to move . . . it seems to me that's . . . an objection in principle, and an objection in principle that the public use requirement of the Constitution seems to be addressed to."[14] The public increasingly made its outrage known by various demonstrations and vociferous reactions to the case. The City of New London reacted by issuing a bill to the plaintiffs for unpaid "rent" since they had been living on city property for the past six years.[15] As the city council met to discuss evictions, large vitriolic crowds formed outside of city hall led by Bullock himself. They chanted and yelled at the legislators inside, expressing their hatred of the "plague of eminent domain." City Attorney Tom Londregan, who had defended New London in the case, became instantly aware of the situation. He said, "I thought I won. But nobody cares. America doesn't accept what the Supreme Court said."[16] However, one might argue that Londegran and the City Council eventually won. The fervor, although sincere, was short-lasted as author Ilya Somin noted in his article "The Limits of Backlash: Assessing a Political Response to *Kelo*" (2010).[17] Political scientists, historians, and philosophers have long noted the often confused and short-lived reactions of the masses. Since Ancient Greece, democratic masses have often been fickle and passionate. While this is a subject for another book (or perhaps many volumes of work), the *Kelo* case was yet another example to be added to the evidence. The public uproar turned into a whimper as public memory rapidly grew stale.

What exactly Stevens said in the decision was nothing radically different from the opinions of the Connecticut Superior Court and the Connecticut Supreme Court. The major difference in the Stevens' decision compared to the previous opinions was its brevity, and its focus on the modern history of the Public Use Clause. Stevens eschewed hypothetical situations and statistics, and instead focused on the legal interpretation of public use as found in both precedent and the nation's history. The decision made a strong argument in favor of the Progressive view of the administrative process as well as a strong deference to federalism and police powers. Relying almost exclusively on *Berman* and *Midkiff*, Steven's short opinion read like a short primer on public use and how it had been modified to correctly fit into an interpretation of the Fifth Amendment. The concurring and dissenting opinions delved into deeper philosophical and historical territory, but the majority opinion was admittedly brief and to the point. Whether or not it was the worst decision of Justice Stevens, as *The Economist* called it, was open to interpretation, it certainly created an overwhelming public outcry.[18]

PUBLIC WELFARE

The majority opinion was, more or less, an explanation of the last century of takings jurisprudence. It focused on a string of four public use cases, with the most attention and weight being given to the two cases of *Berman* and *Midkiff*, which Stevens saw as the natural evolution of the Public Use Clause. The dissenting opinions also used the cases, but looked farther into precedent from other sources. Drawing heavily from these *Berman* and *Midkiff* gave Stevens a strong legal precedent to decide *Kelo* for the respondents because the cases focused on the limited role of the courts and well as the Court's deference to a state's police powers.

Stevens laid out the opinion in three major parts: (1) the current accepted meaning of the Public Use Clause, (2) the precedents set by *Missouri Pacific Railroad v. Nebraska* (1896), *Berman*, *Midkiff*, and *Ruckelshaus v. Monsan-*

to, Co., and (3) the problem of introducing a new test for takings. The combination of these three parts delineated the modern interpretation of the Takings Clause. Interesting to note throughout all of this, was that Stevens himself was not present at the oral argument. He was, as was mentioned in the last chapter, stuck at an airport and unable to make it back to the session.[19]

In the first part of the opinion, Stevens focused on the evolving and changing notion of the Public Use Clause in relation to society. He opened with an observation to frame the opinion: "The question presented is whether the city's proposed disposition of this property qualifies as a 'public use' within the meaning of the Takings Clause of the Fifth Amendment to the Constitution."[20] Scholar Steven J. Eagle noted in his article "Assembling Land for Urban Redevelopment: The Case for Owner Participation" (2010) that for many progressives such as Stevens, eminent domain no longer took its cue from a close reading of the original principles at work in the Fifth Amendment. Instead, it was an understanding more closely linked to the Preamble of the Constitution, specifically the section reading "in Order to . . . promote the general Welfare." The general welfare became a way to shift and change constitutional meaning to fit the purposes of society when they required a change.[21] The Congressional Research Service wrote candidly in their 1992 report on the Constitution: "For 'public use,' then, it may well be that 'public interest' or '*public welfare*' was the more correct phrase."[22]

Heavily ensconced in the judicial philosophy of "living constitutionalism," this Progressive notion of an evolving constitutional interpretation to further the changing ends of society made its claim as far back as Oliver Wendell Holmes in the late nineteenth century. Indeed, much of what Holmes believed can be gleaned from his 1897 essay in the Harvard Law Review entitled *The Path of the Law*. He noted, "primary rights and duties with which jurisprudence busies itself again are nothing but prophecies."[23] The "prophecies" set down in law are only guides to demonstrate the path the law should and will take in society. He also noted regarding natural rights and principles, "In regard to the law, it is true, no doubt, that *an evolutionist will hesitate to affirm universal validity for his social ideals*, or for the principles which he thinks should be embodied in legislation."[24] Holmes's theory was such that "natural" and "inalienable" rights, such as those found in the Declaration of Independence or Bill of Rights, are not universal truths. For anyone to continue to follow the strict and original understanding of the Constitution's enumerated rights as unchangeable in an ever-changing society was to revert to a tyrannical form of government which worked against the general welfare.[25]

Stevens based his argument on this theory. Note his citation of Holmes in *Strickley*: "Justice Holmes' opinion for the Court stressed 'the inadequacy of use by the general public as a universal test.'"[26] Both of the previous *Kelo* decisions stressed the same definitional idea, and kept it consistent with both state and federal law. The Public Use Clause had moved away from a strict "use by the public" interpretation. Stevens wrote, "For more than a century, our public use jurisprudence has wisely eschewed rigid formulas and intrusive scrutiny in favor of affording legislatures broad latitude in determining what public needs justify the use of the takings power."[27]

He pointed out that this evolution had been legal precedent for over a century. Congruent with this precedent of "eschew[ing] rigid formulas and intrusive scrutiny" was the legislature's determination of public needs and takings. The "general welfare" was to be promoted by the legislatures of America as well as the states. The states specifically were able to exercise this power because of practicality. He noted, "our jurisprudence has recognized that the needs of society have varied between different parts of the Nation, just as they have evolved over time in response to changed circumstances."[28] Police powers are again deferred to here as they were in previous opinions.

Even though the narrow view had "steadily eroded over time," Stevens wrote that there were two structures that remained in place.[29] The first was that no sovereign might take private property from private owner A and give it to private owner B for a public purpose even if just compensation was paid; and the second was that a sovereign may transfer private property from private owner A and give it to private owner B if a "future 'use by the public'" was the purpose of the transfer.[30] As to the second point, he cited the historic railroad cases as such takings which included common-carrier duties along with them. This line of reasoning was something Justice Scalia took up near the end of the oral argument when he pointed out to Horton, "You can give it to a private entity, you can give it to a railroad, to some public utility. . . . But the use that it's put to by that railroad and public utility is a public use. . . . That's why it's a public utility."[31] Scalia then further noted that "It's quite different to say you can give it to a private individual simply because that private individual is going to hire more people and pay more taxes. . . . That . . . just washed out entirely the distinction between private use and public use."[32] Horton, more in the vein of Stevens' opinion, believed that it was "just as important" as railroads or other public utilities if "a person was not able to get basic services that they needed from the town because the town couldn't afford it."[33] Here, then, was the major distinction between the theories on display, with the majority opinion siding more with the Progressive notion of "general welfare" as a public use justification.

The problem of private-to-private transfer was still in the forefront, however. Stevens dispelled these notions using several steps. The first was that since redevelopment plans were comprehensive, they must be looked at as a whole, and not as individual parts.[34] It was not the job of the Court to scrutinize every redevelopment plan in minute detail, for such a thing would be far beyond the role of the Court. This would create the administrative court feared by Hughes in his Elmira speech. It would also fundamentally cause a large problem with federalism concerns. Since the plan was adopted and characterized as a whole, and the plan "unquestionably serves a public purpose," the Court must agree that the Public Use Clause was met.[35] As for the claim that private individuals would be enriching themselves on a taking which benefits them, Stevens noted, "Quite simply, the government's pursuit of a public purpose will often benefit individual private parties."[36] It was not the private-to-private transfer that worried him, but instead the nature of the redevelopment plan as a whole. To adopt such a stance "would unquestionably impose a significant impediment to the successful consummation of many such plans."[37]

Stevens' overall understanding of the Public Use Clause can be summed up as follows: the Public Use Clause must be broadly interpreted to mean "public purpose" which was to be defined by pertinent legislatures, and instead of a close scrutiny of such definitions or takings by the courts, it must be deferred to towns, cities, and states, who ultimately know the most pressing public needs.

THE BUILDING BLOCKS OF PRECEDENT

According to Stevens, precedent heavily fortified the opinion. As mentioned before, precedent had been specifically tied to a small string of cases beginning in the late nineteenth century and ending in 2005.[38] The first case chronologically, was the famous 1896 railroad case *Missouri Pacific Railroad Co. v. State of Nebraska*. The opinion in *Missouri Pacific Railroad* was one of the examples cited by Kennedy and Scalia, as well as Horton, in the oral argument.[39] Justice Horace Gray, who served on the Court for twenty years at the end of the nineteenth century and was the predecessor to Oliver Wendell Holmes, wrote the majority opinion of the case. The case itself was only cited once in the opinion by Stevens, but quite a lot hung on the reasoning of the case, as the oral argument made clear. The case itself was a disagreement between several farmers and growers who claimed that the State of Nebraska had restricted building on all land near the new railroad (held as state land) in order to set grain prices. The petitioners claimed there was discrimination at work since Nebraska had purposefully stifled competition from a co-op of farmers. In a brief opinion, Gray made it clear that the case was to be decided in favor of the State of Nebraska. Since the state had clearly taken the railroad to be of benefit to the entire public, it would be against the public to force the state to permit a private group of farmers to enrich themselves at the expense of public land. In other words, the public purpose in the case would not hold up to the farmers' private ownership.

Gray noted in the conclusion of the opinion, "The taking by a state of the private property of one person or corporation, without the owner's consent, for the private use of another, was not due process of law, and was a violation of the fourteenth article of amendment of the constitution of the United States."[40]

The reason the *Missouri Pacific Railroad* case was remarkable was because it struck down a private group seeking to benefit from eminent domain. To reexamine the case using the rationale from the *Kelo* opinion, a different opinion might actually be reached. As the State of Nebraska had taken the land in order to facilitate greater use by the public, denying the public the use of such land, even if, as Gray said, "The petitioners were merely private individuals voluntarily associated together for their own benefit," would be denying the public a benefit from the tax revenue of the private individuals.[41] However, in the *Kelo* case, ironically, the city was allowed to take land from a private individual and transfer it to another private individual or corporation (i.e., Pfizer, Inc.) specifically for the tax revenue gained. Stevens only mentioned the *Missouri Pacific Railroad* case once in his opinion as a further explanation of *Midkiff*'s explanation of private-to-private transfers.

The second case in the chronology that Stevens cited was *Berman v. Parker* (1954). Up to this point, the specter of *Berman* had been hanging around the entire proceedings of the *Kelo* case. Brought up in every opinion since the first hearing in the superior court, *Berman*'s rationale buttressed the shift in the Public Use Clause. The case itself was often cited for good reason: it was demonstrative of the Court's understanding of takings regarding redevelopment.

In 1954, the Supreme Court, under Chief Justice Earl Warren, heard perhaps the most famous case ever decided in the Court's history: *Brown v. Board of Education.*[42] The Warren Court had been known almost exclusively by that case alone to many, both inside and out of, academia. However, in the same year another case came to the Court that did as much to establish a new direction for constitutional interpretation. The case of *Berman v. Parker*, which established the precedent that influenced the interpretation of the Public Use Clause for the next half-century, had largely been forgotten except by legal scholars. In fact, the case continued the shift that had already occurred with Holmes in *Strickley* by using the term "public purpose" instead of public use. Almost exactly fifty years later, *Berman* was cited by Stevens as the case that launched the Court into the modern era of deference to cities and state legislatures regarding their designations of public use as well as proper takings actions surrounding redevelopment plans.

In 1945, the District of Columbia was in bad shape, much as the City of New London had become in the last decade of the twentieth century. Slums, crime, and other problems had pervaded the city in several areas, and living conditions were becoming increasingly shocking and deplorable. The United

States Congress, who oversaw the District, passed a law entitled "The District of Columbia Redevelopment Act of 1945," which allowed for the creation of a redevelopment agency to clean up the city.[43] The Act granted the redevelopment agency the power to use eminent domain in part for the necessity of clearing out the numerous slum districts littering the area. The principal owner of a department store, Berman, and several other owners, had their stores condemned as part of a grand redevelopment plan. He objected to his store being taken for no other purpose than beautification, since this type of taking did not fall under the realm of public use as the Fifth Amendment requires, nor did it meet the requirements of the Fourteenth Amendment which stated that no citizen "may be deprived of life, liberty, or property without due process of law."

In a brief opinion, Justice William O. Douglas found that the Act was constitutional and that the delegation of such takings authority was also constitutional. Douglas first explained that thanks to the necessary and proper clause, Congress did have the power to delegate such takings authority to the agency, and that the claim to violation of the Fourteenth Amendment was invalid. Just as Congress might delegate authority to other agencies, it had the same power in this case, and if takings occurred, it was simply part of the agency's prerogative. He wrote, "The power of eminent domain is merely the means to the end."[44] Regarding the definition of the Public Use Clause, Douglas established much the same reasoning as Stevens in *Kelo*. Since slum clearance was necessary in order to protect the "public health, safety, morals, and welfare," the police powers governing the district (as well as states in general according to the Tenth Amendment) could be used. In other words, slums created dangerous conditions for many people in the community, and therefore eradication by means such as redevelopment were completely within the police powers.

Interestingly enough, this opinion had a far different take on police powers than the other famous case mentioned earlier that same year, *Brown v. Board of Education*. In *Brown*, the states were far more restricted in their ability to handle the police powers due to racism as well as rampant inequality stemming from corrupt state governments. However, in *Berman*, the states were seen as competent protectors of the same police powers. Also interesting to note was that the targeted slums contained a population which were approximately 97% black. Perhaps racial policy was also a consideration here, but it hardly had the intended consequences.[45]

Douglas also found that the *Berman* case was useful in pointing out how narrowly the role of the Court was when interpreting the Public Use Clause. As noted before, the term public purpose was already being used: "The role of the judiciary in determining whether that power is being exercised for a public purpose is an extremely narrow one."[46] It was a narrow role because "the legislature, not the judiciary, was the main guardian of the public needs."[47] The legislature in this case, or legislatures generally as the police powers assume, were free to decide how and where public needs arise, but the Court played a very limited role. By so doing, as long as they followed a very broad interpretation of the Fifth Amendment, they were able to make decisions involving eminent domain when the public needs it (or they conclude, as a legislature, that the public needs it). Delegation merely stems from this principle. However, Douglas was cementing the Progressive notion first annunciated by Holmes in *Strickley* ("the inadequacy of use by the general public as a universal test") by stating that the strict interpretation of public use had been rendered inadequate in the new era of city planning and urban development.[48] When dealing with the thorny issue of a private-to-private taking in such cases, Douglas noted "the means by which it [the taking] will be attained is also for Congress to determine."[49]

While the *Berman* opinion tread new ground, it also retained some of the older caveats that might be difficult to justify in the *Kelo* opinion. According to Douglas, a legislature must pass the public purpose test before it can devise the means to deprive someone of their property. However, Douglas pointed out, that does not include depriving someone of their property to develop a "better balanced" community. He noted about the District Court's interpretation, "To take for the purpose of ridding the area of slums is one thing; it is quite another, the argument goes, to take a man's property merely to develop a better balanced, more attractive community."[50] The question then followed, could Susette Kelo's house, as well as the other petitioners' houses, be classified as slums? To put it another way, was condemning such houses in order to invite the prospective Pfizer Corporation and other businesses to the area, taking property for "a better balanced, more attractive community?" Or, was it akin to the *Berman* idea of eliminating a slum district in the name of the greater good? Was Kelo's house a casualty in the war against poverty and dearth of urban welfare? While Douglas had drawn his line, he also seemed to open the door for legislative leeway by stating later in the opinion,

> The concept of the public welfare is broad and inclusive. . . . The values it represents are spiritual as well as physical, aesthetic *as well as monetary*. It is within the power of the legislature to determine that the community should be beautiful as well as healthy, spacious as well as clean, well-balanced as well as carefully patrolled.[51]

Douglas conceded that the public welfare portion of the police power included an appeal to monetary value. He also noted that taking for a well-balanced community was also part of the police power, in contradistinction to the "better balanced" community he mentioned before. The argument was never fleshed out between the two purposes, but suffice it to say, Douglas had noted that economic concerns were part of the police powers, and that deference must be paid to the legislature after they had determined a public purpose was the ends of a taking.

Where *Berman* left the public purpose limitations broad, the case of *Hawaii Housing Authority v. Midkiff* (1984) sought to further elucidate the public purpose requirements. Stevens cited *Midkiff* the same amount of times as *Berman* (8), placing it on an equal footing. The opinion was authored by Justice O'Connor, who was joined by a unanimous Court in the decision, with one abstention.[52] The circumstances surrounding *Midkiff* could not have been more different than the other cases. Instead of a redevelopment plan, the case dealt with a land oligopoly in the state of Hawaii.

Early in Hawaii's history, the high chiefs of the island had owned and distributed the land to a small number of landowners. Holding fee simple, the owners, seventy-two of them by the time of the case, owned 47% of all of the land in the state. In order to promote equality, the state legislature passed an act (The Land Reform Act of 1967) which would allow the state to exercise eminent domain in order to break up the land and redistribute it to new, private owners. Such an act was to take several years, and in 1977 the proceedings began against the landowners. Bringing suit against the state, the owners claimed that this was simply a land transfer from a private individual to another private individual with no public use allotment. The 9th Circuit Court ruled in favor of the petitioners, stating, "a naked attempt on the part of the state of Hawaii to take the private property of A and transfer it to B solely for B's private use and benefit."[53] In the case, the Court focused on the claims of a private-to-private transfer, as well as the jurisdictional issue faced by the Courts in eminent domain procedures.

O'Connor began *Midkiff* by noting that the starting place for the public use understanding was *Berman*. She pointed out that *Berman* established the Court's deference principle regarding a legislature's definition of public use. That case set up the precedent that defining public use was "coterminous with the scope of a sovereign's police powers."[54] She noted, "There is, of course, a role for courts to play in reviewing a legislature's judgment of what constitutes a public use, even when the eminent domain power is equated with the police power. But the Court in *Berman* made clear that it is 'an extremely narrow' one."[55]

Briefly restating the reasoning in *Berman*, O'Connor then began to visit other cases that tangentially framed the deference argument, such as *Thompson v. Consolidated Gas Corp.* (1937) among others.[56] Where exactly the line was to be drawn over Court intervention in the case of takings seemed to be around the conceivable public purpose. She wrote, "the Court has made clear that it will not substitute its judgment for a legislature's judgment as to what constitutes a public use 'unless the use be palpably without reasonable foundation.'"[57] She also pointed out that as long as just compensation was paid, the Court had no reason to interfere so long as the public use requirement was "reasonable." This reasoning placed the Court's role somewhere along the lines of an intent overseer. As long as legislatures could produce a reasonable foundation for their definition of public use, the Court had no business interfering.

Part of the police powers included "Regulating oligopoly and the evils associated with it was a classic exercise of a State's police powers," according to the opinion.[58] This became a difficult proposition to adequately defend against in the Constitution. Police powers are necessarily vague, and the only real reference to them is in a vague way through the Tenth Amendment. The accepted police powers often fall under the four categories mentioned in *Berman* ("public health, safety, morals, and welfare"). Where O'Connor's appeal to regulating land oligopoly and market malfunctions fell under the police powers is up for debate, but it is most likely found in the welfare power. However, the opinion did not dwell on the issue, but quickly moved on, citing that this public purpose was sufficient, and that the legislature's means were of its own concern.[59]

The other issue that O'Connor treated in the opinion, albeit extremely briefly (one paragraph), was the private-to-private transfer question. The petitioners held that their property was not being taken for a public use since the public would not ultimately benefit from the private ownership of different individuals. The opinion sidestepped the issue by noting that the issue was not about to whom the transfer was being made, but rather from whom. She wrote,

> The Hawaii Legislature enacted its Land Reform Act *not to benefit a particular class of identifiable individuals, but to attack certain perceived evils* of concentrated property ownership in Hawaii—a legitimate public purpose. Use of the condemnation power to achieve this purpose is not irrational. Since we assume for purposes of these appeals that the weighty demand of just compensation has been met, the requirements of the Fifth and Fourteenth Amendments have been satisfied.[60]

In other words, benefitting a certain class of individual private owners was not the point of the Act. The issue was to "attack certain perceived evils" which had occurred since before Hawaii was a state. This begged the question of where, in fact, the line was drawn around public purpose. The Court said that the legislature determined it by having a "reasonable foundation." This spoke to Stevens in *Kelo*, and he used this precedent when he wrote, "Because that [redevelopment] plan *unquestionably* serves a public purpose, the takings challenged here satisfy the public use requirement of the Fifth Amendment."[61] Bullock challenged the broad deference precedent by advocating a new "reasonable foreseeability" test which would force the legislatures to prove that such a plan, or public use definition, would actually work, but Stevens dismissed the argument by saying that the Court "had wisely eschewed rigid formulas and intrusive scrutiny" in determining legislative intent.[62] His line of reasoning made sense according to precedent in *Midkiff* Quoting *Midkiff*, he wrote, "'[I]t is only the taking's purpose, and not its mechanics,'" we explained, that matters in determining public use."[63]

The final case Stevens briefly relied upon for the meat of the *Kelo* opinion was one from the same term as *Midkiff*. In 1984 the Court decided the case of *Ruckelshaus v. Monsanto, Co.*, a case involving pesticides and just compensation.[64] Stevens used the case as an example of public use being defined in terms of economic matters under congressional authority. The petitioners in that case had submitted secrets regarding a new form of pesticide to the Environmental Protection Agency in hopes of obtaining a patent for their work. Congress ruled that certain new discoveries which would eliminate "a significant barrier to entry in the pesticide market" and thereby save research time and ultimately enhance competition would be a boon to the market.[65] *Ruckelshaus* ultimately focused on economic and patent issues, but tangentially touched on public use. The opinion in the case, written by Justice Blackmun, stated, "It is enough for us to state that the optimum amount of disclosure to the public is for Congress, not the courts, to decide," and that because of this deference, "any taking of private property that may occur in connection with EPA's use or disclosure of data submitted to it . . . is a taking for a public use."[66] Not much other relevant law for *Kelo* was referred to in the *Ruckelshaus* case, but it was indicative of Blackmun's attention to established precedent to legislatures when defining public use. Property, even intellectual property, was something subject to the legislatures when determining public use. While not many takings cases had given *Ruckelshaus* more than a glance, Stevens showed that the idea of deference had been a thread running throughout the Court for over half of a century.

These four cases all shared the common ideas of (1) deference to a legislature regarding public use, (2) using a broad interpretation of the Public Use Clause, and (3) emphasizing a state's police powers. In *Berman*, the plan was to eliminate slums; in *Midkiff* the plan was to break up a market failure; in *Missouri Pacific Railroad*, the plan was to expand commerce to the general public and not a co-op of private owners; and in *Ruckelhaus*, the plan was to benefit the public by seizing intellectual property which would produce a more beneficial pesticide for the public. *Kelo*'s contribution to the corpus was to firmly state that a plan involving economic redevelopment of a financially depressed city was a viable public use.

A NEW TEST

A new test, or bright-line rule, played a major role in the proceedings of *Kelo*. As noted before, several amici advocated it, as well as the petitioners in the oral argument.[67] Justices Kennedy, Breyer, and O'Connor all discussed the possibility (or impossibility) of a new test for takings with both sides over the course of the debate. Bullock began his argument hoping to create a new bright-line rule for takings that would include redevelopment projects, and at the same time would not necessarily be overturning *Berman* or *Midkiff*. Breyer began to entertain the notion of a new test by telling Bullock, "you're getting to what I think is a possible realm of reason here."[68] Bullock only brought up vague ideas of "reasonable foreseeability" and proving economic possibilities, and his test seemed to fall apart because of vagueness. Perhaps he was hoping the justices would further flesh out such a test (as Kennedy attempted to do in his concurring opinion—see chapter five). Horton fought against it, stating that such a new test would be strangely categorical and apart from *Berman*, *Midkiff*, and *National Railroad Passenger Corporation v. Boston and Maine Corp.*[69]

Perhaps because the idea of a new test had been thrown around so much, Stevens devoted several short paragraphs to it. He rejected the notion that a new test was advisable for redevelopment takings. As he saw it, precedent rejects such an action because it would cause the Courts to suddenly draw an arbitrary line through the police powers and reinterpret over a century's worth of Public Use Clause evolution. As noted previously in this chapter, he wrote "It is not for the courts to oversee the choice of the boundary line nor to sit in review on the size of a particular project area . . . the integrated plan rests in the discretion of the legislative branch."[70]

As noted before, Stevens believed that the Court was not in the position to create a line for public use takings *ex nihilo*. As precedent pointed out, this was something the legislatures were tasked with. He wrote that if such a test were to be created, matching every single redevelopment plan to the test "would unquestionably impose a significant impediment to the successful consummation of many such plans."[71] This would overburden the Courts with the new problem of city planning, which was, as *Lingle v. Chevron U.S.A. Inc.* noted, substituting a Court's unlearned judgment over that of experts and designated agencies.[72] Such an assumption of Court power would not only erode the role of administrative experts, but it would also erode federalism.

In a final nod to federalism, Stevens pointed out that while the opinion had given a very open hand to the legislatures in interpreting the Public Use Clause, it in no way kept states from exercising a more stringent interpretation. States had already been doing this, he said, and nothing in the opinion closed the door on the debate once public use had been established. The logic was perhaps not altogether sound. It is hard to believe that if the only requirements at the federal level were (1) meeting a broad interpretation of public use, and (2) meting out just compensation, a bevy of states would suddenly strive to become much stricter on their own agencies and legislatures. Fulfilling such a notion, Somin pointed out that, at first, states made a fuss about the Court's overbroad interpretation, but in the end did nothing to limit legislatures to a stricter interpretation of the Public Use Clause.[73]

CONCLUSION

The majority opinion laid out the fundamental premise that the Public Use Clause had evolved over time through a string of cases (*Missouri Pacific Railroad—Berman—Midkiff—Ruckelshaus*). These cases demonstrated that public use was something the state agencies and legislatures were permitted to define by virtue of their inherent police powers. To wipe away such an inherent state power would be dangerous to federalism and embroil the courts in far more problems than necessary. Adding a new test or rule to the already-existing precedent would be just as problematic.

At the end of the opinion, Stevens wrote, "we do not minimize the hardship that condemnations may entail."[74] He made it known that the Court was not oblivious to the hardships of being forced out of one's own home in the name of redevelopment. However, because of precedent and sound adherence to strict constitutional principles found in the Fifth Amendment, Susette Kelo and her neighbors must accept the sometimes-odious conditions of losing a takings case in a constitutional republic. The majority, as slim as it was, had critics both inside of, and outside of, the Court. Three other justices penned their own responses to the case, and it became clear that the takings doctrine was not as settled as Stevens describes.

Looking back at Governor Hughes's speech in Elmira in 1907, it was obvious the courts were beginning to determine their role in the minute affairs of administration. Hughes roundly rejected a heavy involvement as something beneath the purview of the Court, and if it were to become a new reality, the courts would lose all prestige and power. They were to function at a higher level to be "the safeguard of our liberty and property." Stevens' opinion in *Kelo* attempted to follow the same logic of high-mindedness. If the courts began to get involved with takings legislation by creating a new test and departing from well-established precedent, they would be subjected to the petty squabbling and a notoriousness that Hughes foresaw. Such a role for the courts, especially the Supreme Court, would be detrimental to their continued role in the American regime.

NOTES

1. Charles Evans Hughes, *Addresses of Charles Evans Hughes: 1906–1916* (2nd Ed.) (New York: G.P. Putnam's Sons, 1916), 179.
2. Ibid., 179.
3. Ibid., 277
4. Hughes has become popularly quoted among legal scholars for his approach. For a further explanation of this, including an examination of the quote and its relation to legal approaches in general, see Ralph A. Rossum and G. Alan Tarr, *American Constitutional Law* (Vol. I) (Boulder: Westview Press, 2010), 1–24.
5. Hughes, *Addresses*, 186.
6. *Kelo v. New London*, 545 U.S. 469 (2005).
7. Benedict, *Little Pink House*, 324.
8. Ibid., 324.
9. Ibid., 325.
10. Main, *Bulldozed*, 174.
11. Ibid., 177.
12. H.R. 340, 109th Cong. (2005)
13. Main, *Bulldozed*, 174.
14. *Susette Kelo et al. v. City of New London, et al.*, Supreme Court Case 04-108, Oral Argument Transcript. Alderson Reporting Company (2005), Supreme Court of the United States Website, accessed March 20, 2012. http://www.supremecourt.gov/oral_arguments/argument_transcripts/04-108.pdf, p. 51, lines 10–20.
15. Main, *Bulldozed*, 180.
16. Benedict, *Little Pink House*, 330.
17. Somin, "The Limits of Backlash," 101–49.
18. Lexington, "The Worst Decision of Justice Stevens."
19. See chapter 3.
20. *Kelo v. New London*, 545 U.S. 469 (2005).
21. Steven J. Eagle. "Assembling Land for Urban Redevelopment: The Case for Owner Participation," in *Property Rights: Eminent Domain and Regulatory Takings Re-Examined*, ed. Bruce L. Benson's (New York: Palgrave Macmillan, 2010): 7–27.
22. *The Constitution of the United States of America: Analysis, and Interpretation*. ed. Congressional Research Service (Washington, D.C.: Government Printing Office, 1992), 1466 (italics added), http://www.gpo.gov/fdsys/pkg/GPO-CONAN-1992/pdf/GPO-CONAN-1992.pdf.
23. Oliver Wendell Holmes, "The Path of the Law" *Harvard Law Review* 457 (1897), accessed July 11, 2009, http://constitution.org/lrev/owh/path_law.htm.
24. Ibid., italics added.
25. For more on this, see all of Watson, *Living Constitution, Dying Faith*.
26. *Kelo v. New London* 545 U.S. 469 (2005). Justice Thomas notes that this comes from the opinion in *Fallbrook* (Cf. chapter Seven).
27. *Ibid.*
28. Ibid. Here, then, we have the rationale or understanding of a facet of federalism which sees states and regions as best governed by local circumstances and needs. Instead of a way in which the populace might feel closer to the elective franchise and their own government, federalism becomes a way to govern practically and without fear of overarching federal laws.
29. Ibid.
30. Ibid.
31. *Susette Kelo et al. v. City of New London, et al.*, Supreme Court Case 04-108, Oral Argument Transcript. Alderson Reporting Company (2005), Supreme Court of the United States Website, accessed March 20, 2012. http://www.supremecourt.gov/oral_arguments/argument_transcripts/04-108.pdf, p. 53, lines 14–18.
32. Ibid., p. 53, lines 19–24.
33. Ibid., p. 54, lines 1–5.
34. *Kelo v. New London* 545 U.S. 469 (2005).

35. Ibid.
36. Ibid.
37. Ibid.
38. See note 19 in this chapter.
39. Cf. *Susette Kelo et al. v. City of New London, et al.*, Supreme Court Case 04-108, Oral Argument Transcript. Alderson Reporting Company (2005), Supreme Court of the United States Website, accessed March 20, 2012. http://www.supremecourt.gov/oral_arguments/argument_transcripts/04-108.pdf, pps. 14–15 (Kennedy); p. 53 (Scalia), and pps. 27, 42 (Horton).
40. *Missouri Pacific Railroad Corporation v State of Nebraska*, 164 U.S. 403 (1896).
41. Ibid.
42. *Oliver Brown, et al. v. Board of Education of Topeka, et al.*, 347 U.S. 483 (1954).
43. *Berman v. Parker*, 348 U.S. 26 (1954).
44. Ibid.
45. Brief of Amici Curiae for The National Association for the Advancement of Colored People, AARP, Hispanic Alliance of Atlantic County, Inc., Citizens in Action, Cramer Hill Resident Association, Inc., and the Southern Christian Leadership Conference, *Kelo v. New London*, No 04-108 FindLaw.com, accessed October 2, 2012, supreme.lp.findlaw.com/supreme_court/docket/2004/February.html#04-108.
46. *Berman v. Parker*, 348 U.S. 26 (1954).
47. Ibid. It is quite interesting to contrast this with Hughes's statement about the courts being the "safeguard" of property in the Elmira speech.
48. Stevens quoting Holmes in his *Kelo* opinion, *Kelo v. New London* 545 U.S. 469 (2005).
49. *Berman v. Parker*, 348 U.S. 26 (1954).
50. Ibid.
51. Ibid., italics added.
52. The case was unanimous for the Justices taking part, except for Justice Thurgood Marshall who did not participate.
53. *Hawaii Housing Authority v. Midkiff* (1984).
54. Ibid.
55. Ibid.
56. She cited *Thompson v. Consolidated Gas Corp.*, 300 U.S. 55, 80 (1937); *Cincinnati v. Vester*, 281 U.S. 439 (1930); *Madisonville Traction Co. v. St. Bernard Mining Co.*, 196 U.S. 239 (1905); *Fallbrook Irrigation District v. Bradley*, 164 U.S. (1896).
57. Ibid., O'Connor is quoting *United States v. Gettysburg Electric R. Co.* (1896) here.
58. Ibid.
59. Cf. Epstein, *Takings*, chs. 9–12.
60. *Hawaii Housing Authority v. Midkiff* (1984), italics added.
61. *Kelo v. New London* 545 U.S. 469 (2005), italics added.
62. Ibid.
63. Ibid.
64. *Ruckelshaus v. Monsanto Co.*, 467 U.S. 986 (1984).
65. *Kelo v. New London* 545 U.S. 469 (2005).
66. *Ruckelshaus v. Monsanto Co.*, 467 U.S. 986 (1984).
67. Several amici who advocated such a test are mentioned and explored in chapter 3.
68. *Susette Kelo et al. v. City of New London, et al.*, Supreme Court Case 04-108, Oral Argument Transcript. Alderson Reporting Company (2005), Supreme Court of the United States Website, accessed March 20, 2012. http://www.supremecourt.gov/oral_arguments/argument_transcripts/04-108.pdf, p. 17, lines 18–19.
69. Ibid., p. 27, lines 8–18. He is referring in the railroad case to *National Railroad Passenger Corporation v. Boston & Maine Corp.*, 503 U.S. 407, (1992), a case involving seizing of freight rails by Amtrak, which was made legal under the Rail Passenger Service Act of 1970. This case is only made mention of once more in O'Connor's concurring opinion. Most likely because the majority opinion in *National Railroad*, written by Kennedy, focuses more on the definition of "required" under the Act and not the public use question. It seems less relevant to the question in *Kelo*.
70. *Kelo v. New London* 545 U.S. 469 (2005).

71. Ibid.

72. Ibid. He quotes the contemporary unanimous case *Lingle v. Chevron U.S.A. Inc.*, 544 U.S. 528 (2005), written by O'Connor, in his opinion.

73. Somin, "The Limits of Backlash," 101–49.

74. *Kelo v. New London* 545 U.S. 469 (2005).

Chapter Five

At a Loss What Expedient to Substitute

The Concurring Opinion

On August 15, 1787, at the Constitutional Convention, delegate John Dickinson from Delaware voiced his concern of the problems of giving too much power to the judiciary. While discussing the proposed Council of Revision, which was to be made up of members of the judiciary and the executive branches and have a rudimentary form of judicial review, Dickinson began to grow uneasy. Several of the delegates, including Charles Pinckney, Nathaniel Gorham, and Gouverneur Morris, were all growing uneasy with mixing the executive and the judiciary power, but Dickinson saw a different threat. He was himself no stranger to either power, having been a practicing attorney since age twenty-two, and having served terms as President in both Delaware and Pennsylvania. He knew the problems both types of power brought with them. In an almost unheard of questioning of the judicial power, he is one of the few delegates who brought up the problem of judicial ascendancy.

Responding to a comment of fellow delegate John F. Mercer of Maryland, he was recorded by Madison as saying:

> [He] was strongly impressed with the remark of Mr. Mercer as to the power of the Judges to set aside the law. He thought no such power ought to exist. He was at the same time at a loss what expedient to substitute. The Justiciary of Aragon he observed became by degrees the lawgiver.[1]

The remark had gone largely unnoticed by all but the most ardent of legal scholars. The Justiciary of Aragon is largely unknown to modern scholarship, but to lawyers who had studied medieval law in England, such as Dickinson, the reference was all too telling. In 1769, William Robertson translated and published a description of the Justiciary of Aragon:

> [T]he Aragonese had recourse to an institution peculiar to themselves, and elected a justiza, or supreme judge. This magistrate, whose office bore some resemblance to that of the ephori in ancient Sparta, acted as the protector of the people and the comptroller of the prince. The person of the justiza was sacred, his power and jurisdiction almost unbounded. He was the supreme interpreter of the laws. Not only inferior judges, but the kings themselves, were bound to consult him in every doubtful case, and to receive his responses with implicit deference. . . . It was the prerogative of the justiza to inspect the conduct of the king. He had a title to review all the royal proclamations and patents, and to declare whether or not they were agreeable to law, and ought to be carried into execution. He, by his sole authority, could exclude any of the king's ministers from the conduct of affairs, and call them to answer for their mal-administration.[2]

The body set up as the safeguard of the people's liberty and property, the judiciary, became, as Robertson shows, the most powerful body in the kingdom. This did not occur all at once, but instead "by degrees." Scholars had shown that the timeline of the ascendance of the *Justiza* was roughly between the twelfth and fifteenth centuries.[3] Dickinson feared an ascendant judiciary that could usurp political power by becoming the "supreme interpreter of the laws" as the Justiciary of Aragon had done.[4] The comment he made was food for thought about the role of the judiciary, and the argument over the Council of Revision was eventually dropped.

Dickinson's fear was implicitly reflected in the logic of Kennedy's concurring opinion. Kennedy voiced the tension which had existed at the heart of the Takings Clause for almost a century. He wrote in a previous opinion, "The concept of a taking under the Clause has become a term of art."[5] Ultimately, Kennedy was proposing, or rather reinforcing, a rational-basis review in cases such as *Kelo*—a review that he believed already operated unwittingly in most takings cases. However, he feared that if the line demarcating the boundaries of the review was drawn too narrowly, it would lead to the creation of a new Court-mandated and government-centered takings doctrine. He briefly cited the problem of the doctrine of regulatory takings, created by the Court in the Progressive Era, as an example of a way to draw arbitrary lines where none exist at all.

Kennedy believed his proposed rational-basis review was a more honest approach. It was something he felt the Court should annunciate since it had already been engaging in it with Due Process cases for over half of a century. He brought up the idea of the review, but never fully fleshed it out. Much like Dickinson at the Convention, Kennedy in *Kelo* seemed to be completely "at a loss what expedient to substitute." He feared a judiciary that created arbitrary lines, and by degrees, interpreted the Constitution in a way only familiar to itself. When such arbitrariness and interpretation occurs at the highest Court of the land and becomes law, he would most likely argue that it had become the "lawgiver."

AGREEING WITH THE MAJORITY

Where Stevens' opinion devoted a small portion to the reasons a new test would not be feasible, Kennedy's concurring opinion expressed reservations, pointing to reasons a new test or review should be embraced by the Court. He argued a review already was being used, albeit in a watered-down form and unaware to the Court. He pointed to a subtle problem that had existed in the takings doctrine for over a century. Where the limits to public use were defined, and even where they were defined in the Court-created doctrine of regulatory takings, was something that deeply troubled him. The Court had ceased to come up with a definitive limit and Kennedy used the opportunity to express the need for a bright-line rule and rational-basis review of the definition of public use As with many concurring opinions, Kennedy believed the case was correctly decided, but he forecasted problems for the future of takings jurisprudence. Without a rational basis review, both the legislatures and the courts would be going too far in either direction.

In order to understand how important Kennedy's opinion was to the case, it is important to understand how different it was from the majority. The decision was split 5–4, and it was obvious that Kennedy was the member who tipped the balance, but not without a caveat. His opinion agreed largely with the majority on almost every aspect. He said numerous times that in *Kelo*, the rational basis review had been met.[6] He also took time to examine the superior court and state supreme court decisions and their thoroughness. He praised the superior court which "conducted a careful and extensive inquiry" into the case.[7] By running through the actions of the superior court, Kennedy was pointing to the opinion's reasoning about the relative merits of the case regarding a rational basis test. As he seemed to say, nothing further was necessary in this case, because from the beginning there was no violation of the public use test.

In a nod to the majority opinion, Kennedy pointed out that it was not the business of the courts to second-guess a legislature regarding public use definitions. He implicitly agreed with the majority that this was a role of the police powers of the state, but it was not an unbounded power. Where Kennedy's opinion distinguished itself was in its attitude towards a standard which should be put in place to limit dangerous abuse. He did not advocate overturning any previous cases, but he did believe "a more stringent standard of review than that announced in *Berman* and *Midkiff* might be appropriate for a more narrowly drawn category of takings."[8] He spent only a little time of his short opinion advocating a new "rational-basis test," but this was the focus of his opinion. The Court should think it over, but not in the present case.

With these agreements, his concurring opinion brought up a valuable idea which was present in the dissenting opinion in the Connecticut Supreme Court as well as the oral argument.[9] The rest of the chapter will consider the review as Kennedy presented it.

RATIONAL-BASIS REVIEW

The concurring opinion began with a reminder to the Court that a rational basis test had always been part of takings precedent since *Midkiff*. A rational purpose had to exist as had been explicitly stated in the case. He then drew a parallel to the economic rational-basis test and the takings cases of *Berman*, *Midkiff*, and *Kelo*. He wrote, "This deferential standard of review echoes the rational-basis test used to review economic regulation under the Due Process and Equal Protection Clauses."[10] Relying on the decisions of *Williamson v. Lee Optical* (1955) and *FCC v. Beach Communications* (1993), he found that the Court had accepted a more rational approach to federalism.

In *Williamson*, the Court was facing the end of the era of economic due process where, as Justice William O. Douglas wrote in the opinion, "The day is gone when this Court uses the Due Process Clause of the Fourteenth Amendment to strike down state laws . . . because they may be unwise, improvident, or out of harmony with a particular school of thought."[11] The era of economic due process occurred from the late nineteenth century until the mid-twentieth century and was marked by the Court's interpretation of economics and the Fifth and Fourteenth Amendments' Due Process Clauses. Believing the Amendment to point to a substantive as well as procedural part, the Economic Due Process Era allowed for the Court to strike down state laws which were believed to violate economic rights inherent in the doctrine of natural rights. A much longer and much richer discussion had been made on the economic due process approach, but for the present work it is enough to explore the two cases Kennedy refers to specifically.[12]

A more deferential attitude towards the states, even when upholding ridiculous laws (as in the case of *Williamson* according to Douglas in the opinion), was taken. In *FCC v. Beach Communications, Inc.*, the modern deferential approach was more fully explained by Justice Clarence Thomas who wrote, "Whether embodied in the Fourteenth Amendment or inferred from the Fifth, equal protection is not a license for courts to judge the wisdom, fairness, or logic of legislative choices."[13] In the opinion, Thomas spelled out the modern way in which the Court had moved from economic regulations of legislatures to more deference to their judgment. Federalism became more important to protect, even in the face of bad laws, and the Court should allow such decisions to be made at the polls. As Chief Justice Morrison Waite wrote in his opinion in the early Due Process case of *Munn v. Illinois* (1877), "For protection against abuses by legislatures the people must resort to the polls, not to the courts."[14] Interestingly, the *FCC* decision was unanimous, with only Justice Stevens issuing a concurring opinion. In his short opinion, he stayed consistent with his rhetoric in *Kelo* by noting, "Freedom is a blessing. Regulation is sometimes necessary, but it is always burdensome."[15]

Stevens' discussion of freedom aside, the *FCC* case was, for Kennedy, an example of how to solve the public use problem. As both *Williamson* and *FCC* show, legislatures should be given a mostly-free hand over takings, which is a police power. However, Kennedy quickly noted, this deference did not mean the Constitution can be trampled on by private corruption at the state level. He wrote that such deference "does not . . . alter the fact that transfers intended to confer benefits on particular, favored private entities, and with only incidental or pre-textual public benefits, are forbidden by the Public Use Clause."[16] Like the rational-basis review in economic legislation since the mid-twentieth century, a rational-basis review should be applied to state legislature's takings actions.

The rational-basis review (or test) was congruent with precedent on several fronts. First, Kennedy was borrowing the review standard famously delineated in footnote four of the *U.S. v. Carolene Products* (1938) case.[17] The Court saw the distinction between strict scrutiny and rational-basis review focused on "discrete and insular minorities," and their relation to political processes, but rational-basis review was the more lenient review in which the burden of proof was on the petitioner against legislature-made law.[18] For decades, the rational-basis test had upheld in Court as a way of preserving federalism. The Court needed to simply admit it and outline it.

Second, citing *Midkiff*, Kennedy said the Court had already created the boundaries of takings review by saying, "This Court has declared that a taking should be upheld . . . as long as it is 'rationally related to a conceivable public purpose.'"[19] Those boundaries were never fully fleshed out, but some were given regarding favoritism. He wrote that the Court must treat each charge of private corruption in takings seriously, but faith must be given to the government as acting in a correct manner. In the majority opinion, Stevens rejected such review as too invasive and too burdensome on the legislatures. Stevens bluntly wrote in the opinion, "Just as we decline to second-guess the City's considered judgments about the efficacy of its development plan, we also decline to second-guess the City's determinations as to what lands it needs to acquire in order to effectuate the project."[20] Rational-basis review would prove to be the problem of the Court replacing the judgment of legislatures and agencies, which would lead to an improbable mess of guessing and second-guessing every taking.[21]

REDEVELOPMENT REVIEW

It was worth contrasting this to the oral argument, where this idea in the form of a test was mentioned but never fleshed out. Kennedy argued with Bullock, who was trying to draw the line of rational-basis review at economic redevelopment:

> **Justice Kennedy:** Well, suppose an economist or even the judge might say, well, it's very clear that if this economic depression continues for another five years we are going to have blight. Blight is in the eye of the beholder, I know that.
> **Mr. Bullock:** Exactly. And I think that that is really one of the dangers of the majority opinion here [in the Connecticut Supreme Court decision] is that it puts any property up for grabs. Under the blight statutes, they actually have to—governments have to meet a certain objective criteria to satisfy that this is actually a blighted area.
> **Justice Kennedy:** Why isn't it an objective criteria to say that we are going to have economic revival, avoid economic downturns?[22]

Kennedy was foreshadowing his rational-basis review in the exchange. Bullock believed that if the line of the new test was drawn beyond economic development, developers and legislatures might use takings to favor private individuals and skirt the public use requirement. Kennedy, as noted, said that development could be a very necessary public use, which in turn, created objective criteria that could be used according to a rational-basis test. He more fully fleshed out the idea: "And this seems to be really essential for the purpose of developing industrial property to increase the tax base. . . . There isn't another practical way to do it. And there is a public benefit at the end, and that ought to qualify it as a public use."[23]

Kennedy connected public use with "the rationale for the railroads," which were public utilities. For Kennedy there was no distinction between public utility condemnations and redevelopment condemnations because the reason behind each was essentially the same: public purpose. In his opinion, he wrote that even though there was private benefit occurring from the taking, there was also a valid public use occurring from it. Near the end of his opinion, he wrote that to make a test that cuts out economic development would be harmful to the public essentially as harmful as if the railroad cases were reversed. He wrote, "A broad *per se* rule . . . would prohibit a large number of government takings that have the purpose and expected effect of conferring substantial benefits on the public at large."[24] To Kennedy, the rational-basis review was the strictest the Court should go, and in order to see how well this worked, the Court should be turning to the example of the review in economic cases since *Williamson*.

Since this test was often being hinted at in most of the takings cases, including *Berman* and *Midkiff*, Kennedy said it would be a mistake to limit such a review at economic development in the case of *Kelo*. After pointing out how well the superior court judge did in his analysis of the case, he wrote, "This case, then, survives the meaningful rational basis review that in my view was required under the Public Use Clause."[25]

Since Kennedy agreed with the majority, but also with the idea of a narrower set of limits on takings, he felt the urge to demonstrate how *Kelo* passed the test, but other similar cases might not. For this, he turned to one of his own opinions issued in *Eastern Enterprises v. Apfel* (1998).[26] Before examining his opinion however, it should be remembered that Kennedy did not believe that economic takings, which could benefit a private individual, should be a reason to doubt the intent of the taking. He noted, "This demanding level of scrutiny, however, is not required simply because the purpose of the taking is economic development."[27] To start drawing lines in gray areas was hazardous, he concluded, and presented a particularly messy problem for takings. His concurring opinion in *Apfel* demonstrated why.

In 1998, the Court was faced with the case of *Apfel*, which dealt largely with coal employees' pension plans. The underwriters of the employee benefit plan were the victims of a national law aimed directly at them and mandated that the company pay retiree benefits to the retired miners. The problem arose from the fact that the company had sold its shares several years before the Act was written, and was therefore being subjected to a government taking of their money to be issued to the miners.[28] In a plurality opinion, O'Connor wrote that the Act was unconstitutional, as there was a problem with a *post facto* law, as well as a taking that was improperly construed. Stevens dissented, arguing that the unconstitutionality of the Act was not sufficiently proven. Breyer dissented, claiming that the issue was not a takings at all, but "fundamental fairness" which was violated by the underwriters. Kennedy concurred in part and dissented in part, but made a valuable observation into takings in general.

As an opinion writer, Kennedy has been known to write some very succinct and memorable lines.[29] He opened his opinion by writing, "The concept of a taking under the [Takings] Clause had become a term of art, and my discussion begins here."[30] The "art" was as problematic as any in American jurisprudence. It was an area where the natural right of property and the right of the majority begin to uneasily coexist. Kennedy sensed the tension and pointed out that when the size of government began to grow, and the role of the administrative state began to take a more important role, especially in the Progressive Era, the line became even more difficult to draw. He wrote, "As the role of Government expanded, our experience taught that a strict line between a taking and a regulation is difficult to discern or to maintain."[31] As the line became increasingly difficult to discern and maintain, the Court began creating even slighter and subtler categories to cope with the nuances. One of these newfound nuances in the law was the now-ubiquitous regulatory takings doctrine found in *Pennsylvania Coal Co. v. Mahon* (1922).[32]

In *Mahon*, the Court suddenly created a new hybrid doctrine which contained the ability of the state to regulate with the power of the state to take property. This new doctrine created an even more confusing and government-empowering gray area that has permitted the government to get away with takings "so long as it pays the charge."[33] However, "paying the charge," or just compensation, was only one part of the Fifth Amendment. In this regulatory fashion, government actors had been able to bypass the public use part of the test in the name of government oversight. This bypassing had served to weaken citizens against the government. He wrote, "The imprecision of our regulatory takings doctrine does open the door to normative considerations about the wisdom of government decisions."[34]

Such a doctrine as regulatory takings was precisely what Kennedy saw in the problem of drawing a line at economic takings. Since the Court had been using regulatory takings for so long, and with such a detrimental effect, he did not want to see yet another takings doctrine pop up, which undoubtedly would if the Court began drawing lines arbitrarily regarding the public use.[35] It was for this reason that Kennedy believed a line drawn around economic takings, even when they might benefit the public at large, was something to avoid.

Kennedy admitted that he would seek to avoid economic takings as a per se limit to public use, but he never explicitly expressed where the line should be drawn. He wrote, "This is not the occasion for conjecture as to what sort of cases might justify a more demanding standard, but it is appropriate to underscore aspects of the instant case that convince me no departure from *Berman* and *Midkiff* is appropriate here."[36] In other words, *Berman* and *Midkiff* met the rational basis review, and so did *Kelo*, but there might be other cases in which a stricter basis of review should be used. Kennedy did not attempt to draw such a line, but used the opinion as a platform to express his uneasiness about the evolving, legislature-friendly public use interpretation.

CONCLUSION

The concurring opinion Kennedy wrote portends a troubling time for the public use doctrine after *Kelo*. Even though he agreed with the logic of the majority opinion, he could not help but see a problem with such a deference-friendly public use interpretation. On one hand, he wanted the Court to consider establishing a review, or a test, which would place the Takings Clause in a more definite sphere of operation. On the other hand, he did not wish the Court to draw arbitrary lines concerning where the limits of defining public use are and are not. He feared the Court's possible rising power if such a line is drawn, but he realized that unless a review was made, the legislatures or future Courts would begin to interpret the Constitution in an unnatural way.

His opinion was useful because it demonstrated the need for clarification. O'Connor, Kennedy, and Breyer discussed this with Bullock in the oral argument, and the idea was picked up by O'Connor in her dissenting opinion, to be discussed in the next chapter. While it was impossible to say where exactly Kennedy would draw the line, it was plain to see that takings for economic redevelopment would not be it. To draw the line would be a degree that Dickinson spoke about. He believed the *Kelo* case was correctly decided, but only because

> [T]here may be categories of cases in which the transfers are so suspicious, or the procedures employed so prone to abuse, or the purported benefits are so trivial or implausible, that courts should presume an impermissible private purpose, [but] no such circumstances are present in this case.[37]

If the Court was going to strike down a taking, it must have a compelling interest in doing so. Such cases will arise, however *Kelo* was not the case. Just how far the Court was going to go without defining the limits of rational-basis review was something Kennedy feared, but as he wrote, he was self-aware that he had no immediate solution. Like Dickinson at the Convention, he was "at a loss what expedient to substitute."

NOTES

1. Madison, "Notes," 299.
2. William Robertson, *The History of the Reign of Emperor Charles V With A View of the Progress of Society in Europe from the Subversion of the Roman Empire to the Beginning of the Sixteenth Century*, (New York: J&J Harper, 1829), 71. For a further explanation of the meaning of the Justiciary of Aragon, consult Lynn D. Wardle's "The Judicial Imposition of Same-Sex Marriage: The Boundaries of Judicial Legitimacy and Legitimate Redefinition of Marriage," *Washburn Law Journal* 50 (2010), 88–91.
3. Wardle, "The Judicial Imposition of Same-Sex Marriage," 91.
4. Robertson, *History*, 71.
5. *Eastern Enterprises v. Apfel*, 524 U.S. 498 (Kennedy, J. concurring) (1998).
6. *Kelo v. New London*, 545 U.S. 469 (2005) (Kennedy, J., concurring).
7. Ibid.
8. Ibid.
9. See chapter Two for Zarella's test.
10. *Kelo v. New London*, 545 U.S. 469 (2005) (Kennedy, J., concurring).
11. *Williamson v. Lee Optical, Inc.*, 348 U.S. 483 (1955).

12. For a concise explanation, see Ralph A. Rossum and G. Alan Tarr's *American Constitutional Law*, vol. I, (Boulder: Westview Press, 2010), 528–36; and for a more lengthy discussion on the subject, see Christopher Wolfe, *The Rise of Modern Judicial Review: From Constitutional Interpretation to Judge-Made Law*, (New York: Rowman and Littlefield Publishers, 1994); Robert G. McCloskey, "Economic Due Process and the Supreme Court: An Exhumation and Reburial," *The Supreme Court Review* 1962 (1962), 34–62; and "The Rise and Fall of Economic Substantive Due Process: Overview," Justia.com, accessed June 1, 2013, http://law.justia.com/constitution/us/amendment-14/07-economic-substantive-due-process.html; among many others.

13. *FCC v. Beach Communications, Inc.*, 508 U.S. 307 (1993).

14. *Munn v. Illinois* (1877), 94 U.S. 113.

15. *FCC v. Beach Communications, Inc.*, 508 U.S. 307 (1993), (Stevens, J., concurring).

16. *Kelo v. New London*, 545 U.S. 469 (2005) (Kennedy, J., concurring).

17. *United States v. Carolene Products Company*, 304 U.S. 144 (1938).

18. Ibid., footnote four. The complete text of Justice Stone's footnote is as follows: There may be narrower scope for operation of the presumption of constitutionality when legislation appears on its face to be within a specific prohibition of the Constitution, such as those of the first ten amendments, which are deemed equally specific when held to be embraced within the Fourteenth. See *Stromberg v. California*, 283 U. S. 359, 283 U. S. 369-370; *Lovell v. Griffin*, 303 U. S. 444, 303 U. S. 452.It is unnecessary to consider now whether legislation which restricts those political processes which can ordinarily be expected to bring about repeal of undesirable legislation is to be subjected to more exacting judicial scrutiny under the general prohibitions of the Fourteenth Amendment than are most other types of legislation. On restrictions upon the right to vote, see *Nixon v. Herndon*, 273 U. S. 536; *Nixon v. Condon*, 286 U. S. 73; on restraints upon the dissemination of information, see *Near v. Minnesota ex rel. Olson*, 283 U. S. 697, 283 U. S. 713-714, 283 U. S. 718-720, 283 U. S. 722; *Grosjean v. American Press Co.*, 297 U. S. 233; *Lovell v. Griffin*, supra; on interferences with political organizations, see *Stromberg v. California*, supra, 283 U. S. 369; *Fiske v. Kansas*, 274 U. S. 380; *Whitney v. California*, 274 U. S. 357, 274 U. S. 373-378; *Herndon v. Lowry*, 301 U. S. 242, and see Holmes, J., in *Gitlow v. New York*, 268 U. S. 652, 268 U. S. 673; as to prohibition of peaceable assembly, see *De Jonge v. Oregon*, 299 U. S. 353, 299 U. S. 365.

Nor need we enquire whether similar considerations enter into the review of statutes directed at particular religious, *Pierce v. Society of Sisters*, 268 U. S. 510, or national, *Meyer v. Nebraska*, 262 U. S. 390; Bartels v. Iowa, 262 U. S. 404; *Farrington v. Tokushige*, 273 U. S. 284, or racial minorities, *Nixon v. Herndon*, supra; *Nixon v. Condon*, supra: whether prejudice against discrete and insular minorities may be a special condition, which tends seriously to curtail the operation of those political processes ordinarily to be relied upon to protect minorities, and which may call for a correspondingly more searching judicial inquiry. Compare 17 U. S. Maryland, 4 Wheat. 316, 17 U. S. 428; *South Carolina v. Barnwell Bros.*, 303 U. S. 177, 303 U. S. 184, n 2, and cases cited.

19. *Kelo v. New London*, 545 U.S. 469 (2005) (Kennedy, J., concurring).

20. *Kelo v. New London*, 545 U.S. 469 (2005).

21. It is interesting to consider how the superior court judge, Norcott, views the problem of experts vs. judges. As noted in chapter 2, it is his belief that while scholars and academics have erroneously feared the new interpretation of the Public Use Clause and its propensity toward legislative abuse, Norcott believes the judges to be the safeguards of the people regarding takings. As quoted in the chapter, he writes, "We, however, conclude that responsible judicial oversight over the ultimate public use question does much to quell the opportunity for abuse of the eminent domain power." It is not altogether clear whether he means the current interpretation of the Public Use Clause and the rational-basis review, or whether judges correctly and more fully understand public use corruption over and above agencies and legislatures. However, he finds judges, much as Governor Hughes wrote, "safeguards of liberty and property." Stevens seems to want judges out of this racket by trusting in the legislatures and agencies, and Kennedy wants them to create a solid perimeter to define how they will protect the people from state corruption.

22. *Susette Kelo et al. v. City of New London, et al.*, Supreme Court Case 04-108, Oral Argument Transcript. Alderson Reporting Company (2005), Supreme Court of the United States Website, accessed March 20, 2012. http://www.supremecourt.gov/oral_arguments/argument_transcripts/04-108.pdf, p. 13, lines 9–23.

23. Ibid., p. 14, line 22—p. 15, line 8.

24. *Kelo v. New London*, 545 U.S. 469 (2005) (Kennedy, J., concurring).

25. Ibid.

26. *Eastern Enterprises v. Apfel*, 524 U.S. 498 (1998).

27. *Kelo v. New London*, 545 U.S. 469 (2005) (Kennedy, J., concurring).

28. Explained in the first part of O'Connor's plurality opinion in *Apfel*.

29. For a good example of this, his opening line in *U.S. v. Alvarez* 567 U.S. ___ (2012): "Lying was his habit."

30. *Eastern Enterprises v. Apfel* (Kennedy, J., concurring).

31. Ibid.

32. *Pennsylvania Coal Co. v. Mahon*, 260 U. S. 393 (1922). Of course, where the line is drawn around regulatory vs. physical takings has been something the Court has struggled to define. In *Tahoe-Sierra Preservation Council, Inc. v. Tahoe Regional Planning Agency* 535 U.S. 326 (2002), Stevens wrote, "In subsequent opinions we have repeatedly and consistently endorsed Holmes' observation that 'if regulation goes too far it will be recognized as a taking.' *Id.*, at 415. Justice Holmes did not provide a standard for determining when a regulation goes 'too far,' but he did reject the view ex- pressed in Justice Brandeis' dissent that there could not be a taking because the property remained in the possession of the owner and had not been appropriated or used by the public. After *Mahon*, neither a physical appropriation nor a public use has ever been a necessary component of a 'regulatory taking.'"

33. Ibid.

34. Ibid.

35. For a further example of the problems of regulatory takings doctrine, see Epstein, *Takings*, chapters 5–10, 17.

36. *Kelo v. New London*, 545 U.S. 469 (2005) (Kennedy, J., concurring).

37. Ibid.

Chapter Six

Merely Incidental Benefits

O'Connor's Dissenting Opinion

The neighborhood of Poletown in the City of Detroit received its name from the large numbers of Polish immigrants who immigrated there in the late nineteenth century. After the Polish immigrants arrived, various groups of people and cultures, including Filipinos, African-Americans, Albanians, and Ukrainians began to populate the city in the wake of World War II when the automobile industry was booming. Although Poletown was never a homogenous group of citizens, they all shared a common goal: they came for the jobs the "big three" (Chrysler, Ford, and General Motors) were bringing to the area. Jobs were to be found in large numbers, and thanks in large part to the work of United Auto Workers Labor Union, the benefits were some of the best in the nation.[1] The neighborhood had been largely spared of the effects of the increasing Detroit problems that began to occur in the 1950s and 60s, including the race riots of 1967 that killed forty-three people and injured thousands.[2] However, rapid economic decline began to take hold once the big three had begun to face stiff competition from international automakers that did not have to deal with "outdated plants and expensive labor forces."[3] The neighborhood's population and economy steadily declined, and when the major automotive plants began to leave in the late 1970s, Poletown was left with a depressed economy mirroring that of the rest of Detroit.

Newly-elected Detroit Mayor Coleman Young, whose impressive list of civic involvement included service as a former officer in the Tuskegee Airmen, an executive director of the National Negro Labor Council, and being elected the first black Democratic National Committeeman, made rescuing Poletown a part of his economic redevelopment plan.[4] Young asked GM what it needed to build a new plant in the area and help revitalize jobs and grow the tax base. They replied that they needed a "500-acre site, with adequate road and rail transportation, other improvements, and tax abatements," and to compound matters, they needed it "in a short time frame."[5] Young began to push for the neighborhood to accept a redevelopment plan, which would use eminent domain to displace an area that included over 6,000 residents, 1,400 houses, and 144 businesses.[6] With the backing of the Union, the sitting United States President Jimmy Carter, and the Roman Catholic Archdiocese of Detroit, plans for the removal of the residents began to go into effect in 1980. Protestors in the neighborhood began to make their case known, and before long the case began to garner national attention. Major social and political figures, including a young Ralph Nader, began to make headlines as they protested in Poletown. The neighborhood council brought suit and the case made it to the Michigan Supreme Court.

In the case of *Poletown Neighborhood Council v. Detroit* (1981), the question is almost identical to the one asked in *Kelo*: "Can a municipality use the power of eminent domain . . . to condemn property for transfer to a private corporation to build a plant to promote industry and commerce, thereby adding jobs and taxes to the economic base of the municipality and state?"[7] The justices took up the question, and in a 5–2 decision sided with the City of Detroit. Using Michigan case law, the per curiam opinion noted that it was for the legislature to determine what a valid "public purpose" was, and citing *Berman*, wrote, "The United States Supreme Court has held that when a legislature speaks, the public interest has been declared in terms 'well-nigh conclusive.'"[8] Foreseeing the next question regarding a good faith test, the opinion also said, "The power of eminent domain is to be used in this instance primarily to accomplish the essential public purposes of alleviating unemployment and revitalizing the economic base of the community. The benefit to a private interest is merely incidental."[9]

The Poletown neighborhood was cleared out, relocating 3,400 people, and razing over 1,500 homes, businesses, and churches, and GM's automotive plant was built and put into operation.[10] The case became a rallying cry in the same way *Kelo* did. The case was so odious that one of the justices who sided with the majority in the case later said, "I think if I had it to do over again, I wouldn't vote the way I voted in that case . . . I overstepped the bounds there. I think I was probably wrong on *Poletown*."[11] The case was eventually overturned in 2004 in the Michigan Supreme Court case of *County of Wayne v. Hathcock*.[12] Scholars and legal professionals have largely decried the overzealous use of eminent domain and the misreading of the Public Use Clause in *Poletown*, and the case has become synonymous with the evils of economic takings.

Justice Sandra Day O'Connor's dissent in *Kelo* called forth the specter of *Poletown* that was put to rest by *Hathcock* only one-year prior. She mentioned the "infamous decision" of *Poletown* twice in her opinion, and noted that the decision had put every piece of property in danger of being taken by a larger and more promising economic benefit.[13] Her fear and disgust was largely based on the limitless possibility of takings that *Kelo* represented, and by attacking Stevens' logic in the opinion, she hoped to point out how dangerous it would eventually become. *Kelo* was *Poletown* for O'Connor, and her dissent proclaimed what she believed to be the last rites of the Public Use Clause.

THE WRATH OF O'CONNOR

The majority opinion represented the most progressive of notions on the public use interpretation. Kennedy's concurring opinion took the argument and tried to add a subtle, if not foreboding, air to the optimism and limitless character of what Kennedy saw in Steven's reasoning. Kennedy ultimately stopped short of a complete vision of the new takings doctrine, and O'Connor's dissenting opinion roundly criticized Kennedy for it. It also rejected the entire premise of the majority opinion in a very direct style and left little doubt that the dissenting justices foresaw calamities of a tyrannical proportion after the decision in *Kelo*.

O'Connor, who was joined by Chief Justice William Rehnquist, and Justice Antonin Scalia, called for a halt to the evolving public use interpretation. The opinion also called for a return to the original intent. O'Connor stated in the opinion, "When interpreting the Constitution, we begin with the unremarkable presumption that every word in the document has independent meaning, 'that no word was unnecessarily used, or needlessly added.'"[14] The dissent included appeals to both precedent as well as the text of the Constitution. Justice Clarence Thomas's dissent, filed separately, was much more focused on exploring the original intent of the Fifth Amendment, and much more consideration was given to the philosophical and historical underpinnings of property rights in general. That being said, O'Connor did have an eye for originalism in her opinion, but she focused on a critique the evolution of public use after her own opinion in *Midkiff*.

The opinion focused on several issues. The public use interpretation was the regnant concern in the opinion, which she addressed accordingly. Stemming from this was her discussion of the proper role of police powers, where she pointed out that the states are not allowed to simply define constitutional terms on their own. If this was allowed, she argued, anything expressed in the Constitution is mere "hortatory fluff."[15] Her third problem was that of the NLDC's delegated authority. She found it troubling that a private entity, which was isolated from the political process, was able to enact condemnations on its own. Such a problem bypassed the political (and therefore democratic) process and created a regime where property existed only at the whim of insulated administrative bodies.

PUBLIC USE PROBLEMS

O'Connor's largest problem with the majority opinion was its misinterpretation of the Public Use Clause which seemingly included the limitless category of redevelopment takings. In her opening lines she wrote:

> To reason, as the Court does, that the incidental public benefits resulting from the subsequent ordinary use of private property render economic development takings "for public use" is to wash out any distinction between private and public use of property - and thereby effectively to delete the words "for public use" from the Takings Clause of the Fifth Amendment.[16]

Redevelopment taking resulted from a skewed understanding of private and public use, she reasoned. Before this, each of the cases on takings had focused on a strict public benefit to the citizens. This new addition to takings made the mistake of conflating "incidental public benefits" with public use. Stevens explained the majority's rationale: "Quite simply, the government's pursuit of a public purpose will often benefit individual private parties."[17] O'Connor argued that such reasoning blurred the line between public and private. She rhetorically asked that if a private benefit would often occur from such takings, and would produce public benefits all the same, "why should it matter . . . what inspired the taking in the first place?"[18]

There is a strong argument made by O'Connor about how determining the disposition of the property is the major determining factor. She wrote that if a taking has the ultimate goal of employing the property in "ordinary use," it has lost all credibility under the Fifth Amendment. In other words, to take from a private citizen and give to another private citizen for his or her own choice of how to employ the land (making it a wholly private endeavor), is simply to transfer from one owner to another for no public purpose. For O'Connor, public use meant "use by the public" (rejecting Holmes' idea in *Strickley*), not simply transfer of ownership.[19] Falling outside one of the three categories of takings, she rejected the notion that a private transfer that would result in an "ordinary use" is a valid taking. As she pointed out in both the oral argument as well as in the opinion, "Nothing is to prevent the State from replacing any Motel 6 with a Ritz-Carlton, any home with a shopping mall, or any farm with a factory."[20]

The reason the doctrine had become so perverted, according to O'Connor, was that the public purpose rule was something the Court had not yet settled. She referred to the definitional problem as a "hard question," which only popped up from time-to-time (in this case twenty years).[21] The line of cases to *Kelo* was slightly longer in the twentieth century than Stevens made it out to be in his opinion, but regardless, economic takings was something the Court had not had to confront in a major opinion until *Kelo*. It was remarkable for that reason alone—it needed to answer the question of where "public purpose" extends and how far the evolution of public use will go. She wrote that Stevens and Kennedy got it all wrong, and because of that, "nearly all real property is susceptible to condemnation."[22]

PUBLIC USE AS IT SHOULD BE: THE TWO PRONGS

The majority opinion was also troubling to O'Connor because it represented the Court's latter-day wandering in the wilderness of precedent and Progressive political philosophy. As she saw in the opinion in *Kelo*, the Court was more focused on a state trying to correct an economic problem than respect the natural rights of citizens. As noted before, she bluntly wrote, "When interpreting the Constitution, we begin with the unremarkable presumption that every word in the document has independent meaning, 'that no word was unnecessarily or needlessly added.'"[23] O'Connor's approach was decidedly a textual one. Scholars Ralph Rossum and Alan Tarr defined textualism as the view that "primacy must be accorded to the text, structure, and history of the document being interpreted, and . . . that the job of the judge is to apply the clear textual language of the Constitution or statute, or the critical structural principle necessarily implicit in the text."[24] O'Connor largely followed this interpretative approach and focused heavily on the phrase "public use."

She wrote an exposition on how the Court should have viewed the Takings Clause. She wrote "In keeping with that presumption [following the text of the Constitution], we have read the Fifth Amendment's language to impose two distinct conditions on the exercise of eminent domain: 'the taking must be for a "public use" and "just compensation" must be paid to the owner.'"[25] The amendment created a two-prong test which she said the majority was not following. Explaining this a bit further, she wrote "Together they ensure stable property ownership by providing safeguards."[26] It is interesting to note the use of the word "safeguard" in the same sense the Governor Hughes used it in his Elmira speech about the courts and property. Only by following both parts of the Takings Clause could the Court be a safeguard of property as it is instructed to be by the Constitution. By not following the Public Use Clause, the majority became complicit in a doctrine of tyrannical takings. After *Kelo*, O'Connor reasoned, the Court could not be trusted to be a safeguard any longer.

O'Connor believed the Court should have used a strict interpretation of the Takings Clause if it was to remain a safeguard. Not only did she fear an arbitrary government agency (as in the NLDC) making tyrannical and corrupt decisions, but she also feared that without a safeguard, property owners "may be unable to protect themselves in the political process against the majority's will."[27] She was referring to the sadly ironic and historically shown propensity of democracies towards a majority tyranny. In *Democracy in America*, Alexis de Tocqueville noted the very real problem democracies faced when they were ruled by a tyranny of the majority. In an entire section of his work, he related the problems of majority tyranny on the thoughts and mores of the people, on their moderation, on their excesses, on their laws, and on other political areas. He wrote:

> There is therefore no authority on earth so respectable in itself or vested with a right so sacred that I should wish to allow to act without control and to dominate without obstacles. Therefore, when I see the right and the ability to do everything granted to any power whatsoever, whether it is called people or king, democracy or aristocracy, whether it is exercised in a monarchy or a republic, I say: there is the seed of tyranny, and I seek to go live under other laws. What I most reproach in democratic government, as it has been organized in the United States, is not, as many people in Europe claim, its weakness, but on the contrary, its irresistible force. And what is most repugnant to me in America is not the extreme freedom that reigns there; it is the lack of a guarantee against tyranny.[28]

Others in American political thought also expressed the same concern. Publius, who O'Connor quoted at the end of her dissent, also raised a concern when he wrote, "It is of great importance in a republic not only to guard the society against the oppression of its rulers, but to guard one part of the society against the injustice of the other part."[29] If the safeguard of the people's right to property simply turn the definition and, by association, the power of takings to the popularly-elected legislatures, the rights of the minority are completely insecure. O'Connor argued that this is what was being done in *Kelo*. While tyranny had not flooded the system yet, it easily would because of "the lack of guarantee against tyranny." Majority tyranny would creep in, O'Connor asserted, and the right of owning property, guarded by the Fifth Amendment, would vanish in the interpretation.[30]

In her examination of the two-prong test of the Fifth Amendment, she briefly covered the just compensation clause, noting that it existed as a way to help share the burden of takings amongst all citizens.[31] However, her main thrust in the dissent was focused on public use. She wrote that the requirement imposed a basic limitation on government as well as "circumscribing the very scope of the eminent domain power."[32] This circumscription was drawn around forfeiting property for public use and "not for the benefit of another person."[33] By adhering to the strictly narrow definition of the Public Use Clause, the Court should be promoting "fairness as well as security."[34] However, O'Connor believed that in the majority opinion, the Court failed to follow the text and instead had provided a private benefit for a private person who wished to use the land for "ordinary use." O'Connor bluntly asserted that only by rejecting the "ordinary use" principle, and reinforcing the correct interpretation of public use, could the Fifth Amendment have been correctly applied.

PUBLIC USE AS IT SHOULD BE: THREE CATEGORIES

In order to help the Court ascertain the correct form of public use, it had, through precedent, created three categories for correct public use definitions. The first was the commonly held and understood concept of use by the public. This included such transfers as those for "a road, a hospital, or a military base."[35] This idea is without question the most straightforward and popularly accepted when referring to takings. It is the second and third categories in which O'Connor found much more obfuscation.

The second category the Court had created was where transfers were made to private owners for public purposes. For examples, O'Connor offered the term "common carriers," which always "make the property available for the public's use—such as a railroad, a public utility, or a stadium."[36] The issue of common carrier is one that has been explored by the Court at different times to different effects.

One such case was *Fallbrook Irrigation District v. Bradley* (1896).[37] The facts of the case surrounded a group of citizens in the small town of Fallbrook, California, in the semi-arid area just north of San Diego. Many of the citizens desperately needed water for their own crops, and came together to vote for an irrigation project to be created which would include a system of canals for water flow. When landowner Mrs. Maria King Bradley, herself a British citizen and wife of a British Colonel, received her bill for the project, which included being forced to give up pieces of her property for irrigation purposes in Fallbrook, she refused to pay. When the county offered her land for sale because of her refusal, the case went to the Supreme Court. In his consideration of the case, Justice Rufus Wheeler Peckham considered the nature of public use and common carriers, such as those associated with private citizens building irrigation ditches for the public. Peckham considered the necessity of public water in an arid land as part of the common carrier doctrine.[38] Transfers of necessities, such as water for irrigation in dry lands, has commonly been borne by those around the necessity. In this instance, the person is a carrier of the public purpose, the water, and the public is benefitted in common with a necessity. Therefore, the Public Use Clause was validated in *Fallbrook* by virtue of the public necessity rooted in the ground water. Without it, the land would be untenable, and the area's population would suffer and leave. Other examples include railroads being built across people's lands by third parties, or aerial buckets for coal being hauled across someone's property in order to complete a vital function of coal mining.[39]

This second category revolves around things necessary for the public, thereby serving a valid public purpose. However, these things may not go too far. Although not exactly circumscribed in the takings literature, there is precedent at several levels detailing when something is necessary and when it is not. Using the *Fallbrook* example, Justice Peckham made sure to note a limit on such common carrier justifications:

> To provide for the irrigation of lands in states where there is no color of necessity therefor [sic] within any fair meaning of the term, and simply for the purpose of gratifying the taste of the owner or his desire to enter upon the cultivation of an entirely new kind of crop, not necessary for the purpose of rendering the ordinary cultivation of the land reasonably remunerative, might be regarded by courts as an improper exercise of legislative will, and the use might not be held to be public in any constitutional sense, no matter how many owners were interested in the scheme.[40]

A self-gratifying owner such as Peckham described, would not be using the water for an "ordinary use" of land, and would flunk the public use test according to the reasoning of the category. Peckham also wrote in *Clark v. Nash* (1905) that often a public purpose and a common carrier stems from the area and conditions themselves.[41] The definition of necessity may be unique to time and place, and the safest route was to let the state legislatures determine it.

The first and second categories described, O'Connor then wrote about the troubling third category:

> But "public ownership" and "use-by-the- public" are sometimes too constricting and impractical ways to define the scope of the Public Use Clause. Thus we have allowed that, in certain circumstances and to meet certain exigencies, takings that serve a public purpose also satisfy the Constitution even if the property is destined for subsequent private use.[42]

This category is troubling and hazy, but is not left without a qualifier. She noted that a public purpose could still be valid, even if it was going to a private use, if, as she said before, it was not going to fulfill an "ordinary use." She wrote that *Berman* and *Midkiff* were examples on this head.

In *Berman,* the Court decided the department store was not blighted, but allowed the taking. This was because the Court did not need to go lot-by-lot through each takings case and decide which lot's disposition met the public use requirement and which did not. In the case of *Berman,* it was not the transfer of the lot (after the store was replaced by apartments) to another owner which met the public purpose, but instead it was the destruction of blight in the area. That is to say, the effect of destroying the store along with the blighted areas was the public purpose itself, not the disposition of the lot after the demolition.[43] *Midkiff*, on the other hand, was more difficult to explain. Attempting to explain the decision, she wrote, "The Hawaii Legislature had concluded that the oligopoly in land ownership was skewing the State's residential fee simple market, inflating land prices, and injuring the public tranquility and welfare."[44] Accordingly, it became a possible public use justification to correct the skew in the "residential fee simple market," because the effects of ownership by the oligopoly were "injuring the public tranquility and welfare." This is far more difficult to prove, and leaves a host of unanswered questions. For example, what are the limits on "public tranquility" and "welfare"? More importantly, can a textualist interpret such terms broadly? The terms are echoed in the Preamble to the Constitution, but this is often not cited as concrete law since it is open to such broad interpretation. She never approached this overbroad definition problem in her opinion. Instead, she fell back on the larger notion that "courts are ill-equipped to evaluate the efficacy of proposed legislative initiatives."[45] This hearkens back to Peckham's deference principle in *Fallbrook* and *Nash* about time and circumstance.

The third category became the catchall for difficult cases that did not lend themselves to easy interpretations. Interpreting this the third category, a constitutional law professor remarked that all you need now was "a really, *really* good reason" for the taking to be a public use.[46] One cannot help but draw this distinction when examining O'Connor's validations of the third category. For all of her defense of *Berman* and *Midkiff*, it is difficult to discern between her justifications in those cases and her sudden shift in *Kelo*. Law professor D. Benjamin Barros has gone back to the *Berman* and *Midkiff* conference notes and has pointed out that it's difficult to assume, as Justice O'Connor does, that the broad language granting such eminent domain powers to the states was the result of "errant language in *Berman* and *Midkiff*" which misled the majority.[47] Barros noted in his article, "A more compelling dissent by Justice O'Connor therefore would have argued not that *Berman* and *Midkiff* contained loose language, but that with the benefit of hindsight *Berman* and *Midkiff's* deference to the legislature was a mistake that should be corrected by overruling the prior cases."[48] The line becomes razor-thin between something like correcting a problem with a state land market (*Midkiff*) and correcting a citywide depression (*Kelo*). Throughout the opinion, she maintained that tax benefits to a city are only "incidental" benefits, whereas those in the other categories were for a legitimate public purpose.[49] When something becomes an incidental benefit, the correct definition of public use is all but negated because of the lack of intent. She wrote,

> But nearly any lawful use of real private property can be said to generate some incidental benefit to the public. Thus, if predicted (or even guaranteed) positive side-effects are enough to render transfer from one private party to another constitutional, then the words "for public use" do not realistically exclude any takings, and thus do not exert any constraint on the eminent domain power.[50]

While explaining her understanding of the third category, she noted that no public good could come from taking away parcels 3 and 4a in the NLDC plan in the case. Taking a house away from Kelo, Dery, and their neighbors, would not produce any public good, nor was it intended to do so beyond the hope of higher taxes. A hope was not good enough for O'Connor, and neither was the charge of incidental public benefits. Where *Berman* and *Midkiff* took something for a public purpose, *Kelo* took for something that was set up strictly as a private benefit. If the businesses failed or were sold, and no taxes were raised, the only party benefitted was the private owner of the new land. For O'Connor, this negated the entire idea of public use. It is reminiscent of Bullock's proposed test offered during the oral argument where he argued for a reasonable foreseeability test to be put in place by the Court. He said, "if this Court accepts that economic development can be a public use, then we advocate a test of reasonably foreseeable uses and minimum standards in order to counter the dangers posed by such private involvement in the use of eminent domain power."[51] O'Connor's third category used this idea as well, and went clearly against Kennedy's answer to Bullock regarding the test: "I think it's pretty clear that most economists would say this development wouldn't happen unless there is a foreseeable chance of success."[52] O'Connor would draw the line at economic development, and Kennedy would draw the line at having legislatures proving success because it would be redundant.

Later in the decision, she directly criticized Kennedy's concurring opinion as being too vague and not drawing a discerning line anywhere. One can sense that she was, more or less, criticizing Kennedy for not drawing the line at economic takings, as she and her cohorts on the bench had done. She wrote, "Whatever the details of Justice Kennedy's as-yet-undisclosed test, it is difficult to envision anyone but the 'stupid staff[er]' failing it."[53] The majority got it all wrong she thought, but Kennedy got it mostly wrong for not drawing the line at economic takings. She foresaw a litany of economic takings stemming from the Court's reasoning, to which only "stupid staffer[s]" would not be able to take advantage of *Kelo*.

O'Connor saw the majority opinion as one that completely destroyed the meaning of public use. She predicted a large amount of problems for property owners in the modern era of administrative planning and urban development. She never turned against takings precedent, no matter how thin that precedent was, but found this a bridge too far. The new definition was the death of the Public Use Clause.

THE PROPER ROLE OF POLICE POWERS

The second major problem O'Connor had with the majority was over the proper role of police powers. She felt as though the majority had given an overbroad definition power to state and federal legislatures. Her opinion becomes much more interesting when one remembers that an argument against giving more power to the states was being waged by the conservative members of the Rehnquist Court. In 2001, law professor Steven G. Calabresi wrote, "Perhaps the most striking feature of the Rehnquist Court's jurisprudence has been the revival over the last 5–10 years of doctrines of constitutional federalism."[54] When the article was written, the pro-federalism concerns of the Rehnquist Court were still active when *Kelo* was decided in 2005. He wrote that the usual suspects were often "Chief Justice Rehnquist and Justices O'Connor, Scalia, Kennedy, and Thomas."[55] These justices upheld state-empowering decisions during their tenures on the Court, including such cases as *United States v. Lopez, City of Boerne v. Flores, U.S. v. Morrison, New York v. United States,* and *Printz v. U.S.*, among many others.[56] Although championing the states in almost all major issues that conceivably fell under a Tenth Amendment question, all except Kennedy rejected the majority's holding strengthening state power. Even Kennedy, who went along with the majority opinion, expressed his disturbance at the possibility of an unrestrained eminent domain doctrine.

O'Connor indirectly attacked the majority's understanding of police power in her opening remarks by how she categorized the NLDC. In the majority opinion, the NLDC was viewed as "a private nonprofit entity established some years earlier to assist the City in planning economic development."[57] O'Connor viewed it somewhat differently. She initially agreed with the majority's description, but, she continued, "It is not elected by popular vote, and its directors and employees are privately appointed."[58] She described the "ambitious plan" which the NLDC created, emphasizing the private, or at least non-democratic nature, of the plan itself.[59] She then turned to the petitioners who had sued the NLDC for Fifth Amendment infringement. O'Connor's words make it clear how the two opinions diverged. She saw the NLDC as something private in nature, insulated from the political process.[60] However, she never wrote a formal condemnation of the NLDC in the opinion. O'Connor stayed focused on the issue of public use and police powers, but did not hesitate to point out the private nature of the body.

Aside from the private nature of the NLDC, O'Connor had an even more explicit disagreement with the representation of police powers in the case.

Beginning by quoting Justice Samuel Chase from the 1798 Supreme Court case *Calder v. Bull*, she wrote: "[A] law that takes property from A. and gives it to B: It is against all reason and justice, for a people to entrust a Legislature with SUCH powers."[61] For a legislature to rise above "the great first principles of the social compact" is to render the Constitution itself meaningless.[62] It was against all reason, she believed, to think that a legislature (state or federal) should have the power to override the Constitution without a formal amendment, but, as she argued in her opinion, this is exactly what Stevens and the majority allowed.

Exactly how the legislature had been given such powers was shown in her attack on the definition power. In Stevens' opinion, the legislatures were given the police powers over such public use determinations because states (1) are in charge of health, safety, morals, and welfare, and (2) know the conditions of the area and peoples better than the federal government.[63] These encompassed the federalism component that the conservative members of the Rehnquist Court often upheld. This was also the understanding of the majority opinion in *Midkiff* regarding the state's power to determine when a taking was a public use. In *Kelo*, however, O'Connor understood that deferring the definition of public use to the very entity involved in the taking was like putting the fox in charge of the henhouse. As she wrote, "anyone but the stupid staffer" would fail to pull a taking off.

The definition problem is far too easy for any legislature, made up largely of lawyers, to overcome. To allow for a private-to-private transfer with the promise (but not assurance) of increased taxation allowed for any number of corrupt dealings. She wrote that by this logic, it did not matter "what inspired the taking in the first place" because "How much the government does or does not desire to benefit a favored private party has no bearing on whether an economic development taking will or will not generate secondary benefit for the public."[64] Stevens had written, "Quite simply, the government's pursuit of a public purpose will often benefit individual private parties."[65] Directly refuting this notion, O'Connor notes that using the new analysis of "incidental" public benefits, a private party's interest would almost always benefit the government. She mentioned that it didn't matter anymore since crafty legislatures will always be able to find a way to prove a public benefit in some taxable way.

She rejected the notion of the allowing legislatures to determine what is a valid public use, and instead reinforced the role of the courts in determining the definition. The majority believed that courts still had a role, albeit a very narrow one—namely that of determining the good or bad faith of the taking. This was practically impossible for O'Connor because courts are never given details as to how to accomplish this new understanding of takings that blurs the lines. In the past, it had been the two-prong test and three categories she mentioned before, but now the problem was expanded to a much larger scope that courts are unable to deal with. She wrote, "Even if there were a practical way to isolate the motives behind a given taking, the gesture toward a purpose test is theoretically flawed."[66] It is flawed because of the notion of an incidental public benefit. It becomes impossible for courts to define the motives of legislatures when they cannot tell the difference between ultimate ends.

Kennedy's musings were not sufficient for her either. His pining for a stricter test was nothing more to O'Connor than utter confusion. She challenged his alleged new scrutiny test:

> For his part, Justice Kennedy suggests that courts may divine illicit purpose by a careful review of the record and the process by which a legislature arrived at the decision to take—without specifying what courts should look for in a case with different facts, how they will know if they have found it, and what to do if they do not.[67]

She reemphasized her point that even if they were strictly scrutinizing an economic takings case, judges, who are not experts in the field of urban redevelopment or city planning, would never be able to discern what a malicious motive was. In other words, it is the judges who would be on trial to prove any sort of malicious behavior by a city. Judges would from now on have an added burden that they will not be fully prepared for.

This limited role of a judge in an economic takings case was not novel in the majority or concurring opinions. As pointed out in chapter 2, Corradino wrote that the role of judge in a takings case was to "discover whether it [the legislature] has acted unreasonably or in bad faith, or has exceeded its powers."[68] In the Connecticut Supreme Court decision, Norcott wrote that the burden of finding this "bad faith" in the legislature was up to the plaintiff. While a judge might adjudicate, the burden of proof in such cases was on the person bringing suit.[69] The Connecticut Supreme Court's dissenting opinion by Zarella tackled the problem in a wholly different way. As noted previously, he would make the scrutiny of economic development cases a four-part test that would shift the burden of investigation and proof to both the legislature and the plaintiff.[70]

All of these different opinions, as well as "Kennedy's gloss," left O'Connor with the larger question of how judges are to discern bad faith in economic takings with any sort of uniformity.[71] The judges' role was far simpler when public use was more strictly adhered to, but now that the Court has allowed for (1) legislatures to define public use, and (2) the judges to mystically divine the thoughts and intents of a takings rationale, the judges' role has become infinitely more complex. For O'Connor, it has become unworkable. She concluded, "The Court rightfully admits, however, that the judiciary cannot get bogged down in predictive judgments about whether the public will actually be better off after a property transfer. In any event, this constraint has no realistic import."[72]

The police power would ultimately fail to protect citizens in economic takings cases because legislatures and cities will always be looking for ways to increase tax revenue. Since property is finite, it will become too tempting for a city to pass up the improvement of land for tax revenue purposes. They will always fall prey to the idea of a better use of the land: "The logic of today's decision is that the eminent domain may only be used to upgrade, not downgrade, property."[73] Citing a slew of cases, she pointed to the Court's decisions in other economic takings cases where the bad faith was ferreted out by a more textual approach to the Fifth Amendment.[74] She also cited the specific amicus curiae brief for the Becket Fund for Religious Liberty which stated: "Religious institutions will always be targets for eminent domain actions under a scheme that disfavors non-profit, tax-exempt property owners and replaces them with for-profit, tax-generating businesses."[75] She also cited a member of the petitioner's legal team, Dana Berliner, who wrote an article for the Institute of Justice examining abuses of eminent domain (2003).[76]

Even more problematic in the case *Kelo* was the allowance of the city to use an administrative agency such as the NLDC to create and execute the plan. As mentioned before, she never explicitly critiqued the use of the agency, but an implicit fear is easy to find in her reasoning. If legislatures are able to enact eminent domain proceedings on behalf of a legislature, where are the limits to such actions? One such related case dealing with the issue of the proper delegation of authority is *Mistretta v. U.S.* (1989).[77] The ruling held that it was constitutional to delegate authority from Congress to an independent agency if said agency has strict guidelines written by the legislature that it must follow. Using this, combined with the new broad interpretation of public use, agencies will now be able to exercise eminent domain under some guidelines. How strict the guidelines must or shall be is open for debate, which is a major concern itself, but the Court recognized that its role does not include examining plans and guidelines in detail, or as O'Connor put it, "lot-by-lot."[78]

O'Connor believed that such deference to legislatures to delegate the amount of taking authority to a non-government entity, was the beginning of "an abdication of our responsibility."[79] Even if the Court allowed states to be stricter, as it did in the closing paragraphs of the majority opinion, that alone does not protect citizens as the Bill of Rights was meant to do. She believed that the role of judges was to enforce the provisions of the Federal Constitution. As John Marshall wrote in *Marbury v. Madison* (1803), "it is apparent that the framers of the Constitution contemplated that instrument as a rule for the government of *courts*, as well as of the legislature. . . . Why otherwise does it direct the judges to take an oath to support it?"[80] When federal judges shirk their duty in enforcing the Constitution by deferring interpretations and definitions to legislatures, even in the face of federalism, they have failed in their duty. She ended her discussion on judicial duty soberly, "States play many important functions in our system of dual sovereignty, but compensating for our refusal to enforce the Federal Constitution . . . is not among them."[81]

CONCLUSION

O'Connor's dissenting opinion ended with what she would have done if she had decided the case. She expressed bluntly, "the takings in both Parcel 3 and Parcel 4a are unconstitutional."[82] As for the rest of the plan, she would have remanded "for further proceedings."[83] Why she would remand for further proceedings is not made clear, but she would no doubt hold the lower courts to her more textual interpretation of the Public Use Clause. Perhaps more interesting was her examination of the plan in detail (i.e., "lot-by-lot") which was something she said judges were not equipped to do. This, most likely, had something to do with the petitioners filing the suit, but it is worth noting

Her opinion is directed squarely at the problems of both a misinterpretation of public use as well as a blatant disregard for the constitutional system of federalism. She saw the Court getting into too much trouble by disregarding these, and foresaw a major problem in the future for takings jurisprudence. By departing from the text of the Constitution, "nearly all real property is susceptible to condemnation on the Court's theory."[84] The Public Use Clause was dead, she implied, and like the case of *Poletown*, almost nothing can now stop a legislature, city, or corporation from taking private property at will. For all of its analysis, O'Connor's opinion does not touch on the history of the Fifth Amendment or property rights in a republic—for that, Justice Clarence Thomas's dissenting opinion stands apart. However, the strength of O'Connor's opinion lay in its textual reasoning and its focus on precedent.

NOTES

1. John J. Bukowczk "The Decline and Fall of a Detroit Neighborhood: Poletown vs. G.M. and the City of Detroit." *Washington and Lee Law Review* 41 (1984). Bukowczyk writes on page 49: "unlike a group such as the Amish, the residents of the Poletown neighborhood were not a homogeneous and highly cohesive group, but were divided by class, race, and ethnicity. Even the Polish element resident in the area contained such divisions. The neighborhood's internal division certainly affected its ability to resist outside forces, and also meant that individuals and groups with different interests would hold widely differing attitudes toward the conflict that ensued."

2. Paul Moreno, "Poletown Neighborhood Council v. Detroit: Private Property and Public Use." *Michigan Bar Journal* 88, (2009): 19.

3. Ibid., 18.

4. Ibid., 19.
5. Ibid., 19.
6. Ibid., 19.
7. *Poletown Neighborhood Council v. City of Detroit*, 410 Mich. 616, 304 N.W.2d 455 (Mich. 1981).
8. The Michigan case the justices refer to is: *Gregory Marina, Inc. v. Detroit,* 378 Mich. 364, 396, 144 N.W.2d 503 (1966). This came on the heels of *Berman*, and had its origins in the rise of urban development as noted in chapter Two.
9. *Poletown Neighborhood Council v. City of Detroit*, 410 Mich. 616, 304 N.W.2d 455 (Mich. 1981).
10. James Risen, "Poletown Becomes Just a Memory: GM Plant Opens, Replacing Old Detroit Neighborhood," *Los Angeles Times*, September 18, 1985, accessed May 13, 2013, http://articles.latimes.com/1985-09-18/business/fi-6228_1_gm-plant.
11. Moreno, "Poletown," 21.
12. *County of Wayne v. Hathcock*, 684 N.W. 2d. 765 (Mich. 2004).
13. *Kelo v. New London*, 545 U.S. 469 (2005) (O'Connor, J., dissenting).
14. *Kelo v. New London*, 545 U.S. 469 (2005) (O'Connor, J., dissenting). The quoted text is from *Wright v. United States*, 302 U. S. 583 (1938).
15. Ibid.
16. Ibid.
17. *Kelo v. New London*, 545 U.S. 469 (2005).
18. *Kelo v. New London*, 545 U.S. 469 (2005) (O'Connor, J., dissenting).
19. Cf. chapter Four where Holmes notes: "the inadequacy of use by the general public as a universal test."
20. *Kelo v. New London*, 545 U.S. 469 (2005) (O'Connor, J., dissenting). In the oral argument, she says, "For example, Motel 6 and the city thinks, well, if we had a Ritz-Carlton, we would have higher taxes. Now, is that okay?" *Susette Kelo et al. v. City of New London, et al.*, Supreme Court Case 04-108, Oral Argument Transcript. Alderson Reporting Company (2005), Supreme Court of the United States Website, accessed March 20, 2012. http://www.supremecourt.gov/oral_arguments/argument_transcripts/04-108.pdf, p. 30, lines 3–5).
21. *Kelo v. New London*, 545 U.S. 469 (2005) (O'Connor, J., dissenting).
22. Ibid. Perhaps not even just "real property," but intellectual as well, such as in the case of *Ruckelshaus v. Monsanto Co.*, (1984) (Cf. chapter Four).
23. *Kelo v. New London*, 545 U.S. 469 (2005) (O'Connor, J., dissenting).
24. Rossum and Tarr, *American Constitutional Law*, vol. I, (Boulder: Westview Press, 2010), 4.
25. *Kelo v. New London*, 545 U.S. 469 (2005) (O'Connor, J., dissenting). The quotes within are from *Brown v. Legal Foundation of Wash.*, 538 U.S. 216 (2003).
26. *Kelo v. New London*, 545 U.S. 469 (2005) (O'Connor, J., dissenting).
27. Ibid.
28. Tocqueville. *Democracy in America*, 241. See also Tocqueville's discussion on majority tyranny in *Democracy in America*, vol. 1, chapter 7 "On the Omnipotence of the Majority in the United States and its Effects", 235–49; and chapter 8 "On What Tempers the Tyranny of the Majority in the United States", 250–64.
29. Publius. *Federalist No. 51* (1788).
30. For further examples of majority tyranny, it is instructive to also consult Plato's *The Apology of Socrates*; Plato's *The Crito*, and various speeches of Abraham Lincoln, examined in chapters 11–16 (275–363) of Harry V. Jaffa, *Crisis of the House Divided: An Interpretation of the Issues in the Lincoln-Douglas Debates* (Chicago: University of Chicago Press, 1959). In reality, you should read the whole book, as it explicitly and implicitly deals with the issue on almost every page—plus it's a great read in its own right.
31. She cites two cases: *Monongahela Nav. Co. v. United States*, 148 U. S. 312 (1893) and *Armstrong v. United States*, 364 U. S. 40 (1960).
32. *Kelo v. New London*, 545 U.S. 469 (2005) (O'Connor, J., dissenting).
33. Ibid.

34. Ibid. Cf. *Tahoe-Sierra Preservation Council, Inc. v. Tahoe Regional Planning Agency*, 535 U.S. 302 (2002) and *Palazzolo v. Rhode Island,* 533 U.S. 606 (2001) (O'Connor, J., concurring).

35. *Kelo v. New London,* 545 U.S. 469 (2005) (O'Connor, J., dissenting). She cites *Old Dominion Land Co. v. United States*, 269 U. S. 55 (1925) and *Rindge Co. v. County of Los Angeles*, 262 U. S. 700 (1923). Justice Clarence Thomas explores this basic and original understanding of the Public Use Clause much further in his dissenting opinion (chapter 7).

36. Ibid. She cites *National Railroad Passenger Corporation v. Boston & Maine Corp.*, 503 U. S. 407 (1992) and *Mt. Vernon-Woodberry Cotton Duck Co. v. Alabama Interstate Power Co.*, 240 U. S. 30 (1916).

37. *Fallbrook Irrigation District v. Bradley*, 164 U.S. 112 (1896). See also Kay Russell's excellent article on the case and its meaning: Kay Russell, "The Fallbrook Irrigation District Case," *San Diego Historical Society Quarterly* 21 (1975), accessed December 15, 2010, http:// www.sandiegohistory.org/journal/75spring/fallbrook.htm.

38. Ibid., 161.

39. Cf. *Missouri Pacific Railway Co. v. Humes*, 115 U.S. 512 (1885) and *Strickley v. Highland Boy Gold Mining Co.*, 200 U.S. 527 (1906).

40. *Fallbrook Irrigation District v. Bradley*, 164 U.S. 112 (1896).

41. *Clark v. Nash,* 198 U.S. 369 (1905).

42. *Fallbrook Irrigation District v. Bradley*, 164 U.S. 112 (1896).

43. *Kelo v. New London,* 545 U.S. 469 (2005) (O'Connor, J., dissenting).

44. Ibid.

45. Ibid.

46. Dr. Michael M. Uhlmann, in a conversation with the author, August 2011.

47. *Kelo v. New London,* 545 U.S. 469 (2005) (O'Connor, J., dissenting).

48. Benjamin Barros, "Nothing 'Errant' About it: The Berman and Midkiff Conference Notes and How the Supreme Court Got to Kelo With its Eyes Wide Open," Widener Law School Legal Studies Research Paper No. 08-30, 2007. Accessed May 23, 2014, http // ssrn.com/abstract=902926 or http://dx.doi.org/10.2139/ssrn.902926, 3.

49. Ibid.

50. Ibid.

51. *Susette Kelo et al. v. City of New London, et al.*, Supreme Court Case 04-108, Oral Argument Transcript. Alderson Reporting Company (2005), Supreme Court of the United States Website, accessed March 20, 2012. http://www.supremecourt.gov/oral_arguments/argument_transcripts/04-108.pdf, p. 17, lines 10-15.

52. Ibid., p. 21, line 25—p. 22, lines 1–2.

53. *Kelo v. New London,* 545 U.S. 469 (2005) (O'Connor, J., dissenting).

54. Steven G. Calabresi, "Federalism and the Rehnquist Court: A Normative Defense," *Annals of the American Academy of Political and Social Science* 574 (2001): 25.

55. Ibid., 25.

56. *United States v. Lopez*, 514 U.S. 549 (1995); *City of Boerne v. Flores*, 521 U.S. 507 (1997); *U.S. v. Morrison*, 120 S. Ct. 1740 (2000); *New York v. United States*, 505 U.S. 144 (1992); and *Printz v. U.S*, 521 U.S. 98 (1997).

57. *Kelo v. New London,* 545 U.S. 469 (2005).

58. *Kelo v. New London,* 545 U.S. 469 (2005) (O'Connor, J., dissenting), italics added.

59. Ibid.

60. The Connecticut courts also discuss the issue of the delegated power of the NLDC. Cf. chapter Two.

61. Ibid., (capitals in O'Connor's opinion). Also, *Calder v. Bull*, 3 Dall. 386 (1798).

62. Ibid.

63. Cf. chapter 4.

64. *Kelo v. New London,* 545 U.S. 469 (2005) (O'Connor, J., dissenting).

65. *Kelo v. New London,* 545 U.S. 469 (2005).

66. *Kelo v. New London,* 545 U.S. 469 (2005) (O'Connor, J., dissenting).

67. Ibid.

68. Ibid., quoting *Graham v. Houlihan* (1960). See chapter 2.

69. See chapter 2.
70. See chapter 2.
71. *Kelo v. New London*, 545 U.S. 469 (2005) (O'Connor, J., dissenting). She noted: "[T]here is nothing in the Court's rule or in Justice Kennedy's gloss on that rule to prohibit property transfers generated with less care, that are less comprehensive, that happen to result from less elaborate process, whose only projected advantage is the incidence of higher taxes, or that hope to transform an already prosperous city into an even more prosperous one."
72. Ibid.
73. Ibid.
74. Ibid. "Cf. *Bugryn v. Bristol*, 63 Conn. App. 98, 774 A. 2d 1042 (2001) (taking the homes and farm of four owners in their 70s and 80s and giving it to an "industrial park"); *99 Cents Only Stores v. Lancaster Redevelopment Authority*, 237 F. Supp. 2d 1123 (CD Cal. 2001) (attempted taking of 99 Cents store to replace with a Costco); *Poletown Neighborhood Council v. Detroit*, 410 Mich. 616, 304 N. W. 2d 455 (1981) (taking a working-class, immigrant community in Detroit and giving it to a General Motors assembly plant), overruled by *County of Wayne v. Hathcock*, 471 Mich. 415, 684 N. W. 2d 765 (2004)."
75. Brief of Amicus Curiae for the Becket Fund for Religious Liberty, *Kelo v. New London*, No 04-108 FindLaw.com, accessed October 2, 2012, supreme.lp.findlaw.com/supreme_court/docket/2004/February.html#04-108.
76. Dana Berliner, "Public Power, Private Gain," 2009, Institute for Justice Website, accessed August 18, 2012, http://www.castlecoalition.org/index.php?option=com_content&task=view&id=312.
77. *Mistretta v. United States*, 488 U.S. 361 (1989).
78. *Kelo v. New London*, 545 U.S. 469 (2005) (O'Connor, J., dissenting).
79. Ibid.
80. *Marbury v. Madison*, 5 U.S. 137 (1803).
81. *Kelo v. New London*, 545 U.S. 469 (2005) (O'Connor, J., dissenting).
82. Ibid.
83. Ibid. She mentions Parcels 3 and Parcel 4a near the beginning of her opinion.
84. Ibid.

Chapter Seven

Something Has Gone Seriously Awry

Thomas's Dissenting Opinion

The original layout for the City of Washington in the District of Columbia was designed by a former major in the Revolutionary War under the direct appointment of President George Washington. Major Pierre L'Enfant was a French artist and engineer who had become friends with Washington during the war, and upon application, Washington allowed L'Enfant to draw up plans for the city.[1] In October 1791, the plans for the new city were largely completed and sent to Congress for approval. L'Enfant hoped to make Washington a "baroque" city, complete with "ceremonial spaces and grand radial avenues," while at the same time "respecting natural contours of the land."[2]

The city itself was to be a monument to the new democratic age. It was to invoke reverence and awe for the heroes of the time, as well as create a visually stunning place for the government to meet. According to L'Enfant, it had to have open spaces and large avenues for effect. A historical tract notes about the plan,

> L'Enfant specified in notes accompanying the plan that these avenues were to be wide, grand, lined with trees, and situated in a manner that would visually connect ideal topographical sites throughout the city, where important structures, monuments, and fountains were to be erected. On paper, L'Enfant shaded and numbered 15 large open spaces at the intersections of these avenues and indicated that they would be divided among the states. He specified that each reservation would feature statues and memorials to honor worthy citizens. The open spaces were as integral to the capital as the buildings to be erected around them.[3]

As beautiful as the city's plans were, L'Enfant was often irksome to work with because he preferred to work on his own, excluding the commissioners of the city which had been appointed by the president. While working on his plan for the city, commissioners ran into the partially completed house of Daniel Carroll. Carroll was a rich man who "owned more land within the boundaries of the Federal City than did any of the other proprietors."[4] Carroll had previously begun construction on his large, sprawling mansion on the site that was later selected by L'Enfant to be part of a grand avenue. After he heard about the proposed plan in 1791, before continuing on his house, Carroll had approached the commissioners to ask if it was possible to complete the construction of his house. Commissioner Ellicot assured him "that L'Enfant had said the width of the street could be reduced from 110 to 100 feet to accommodate the house."[5]

L'Enfant had no such intentions of reducing the grand avenue for the sake of Carroll's house, which was, he explained in a letter to George Washington, "in opposition to the progress of the plan."[6] Regarding the objection of the commissioners who were cut out of the process, he asserted that he did not need permission to tear down a house which had been built in the way of his plan any more than he needed permission to tear down a tree or a bush.[7] Carroll rode to Philadelphia to get an injunction against the demolition, but when he returned he found that L'Enfant had torn his house down brick-by-brick.[8] Outraged, he wrote to Washington, seeking an explanation as well as compensation for L'Enfant's use of eminent domain.

Washington turned to Secretary of State Thomas Jefferson for advice. L'Enfant, surprised at the President's disapproval, wrote Washington a letter in his own defense on November 21, 1791. Both Jefferson and Washington reviewed L'Enfant's letter, and in early December, Jefferson made several observations to Washington about the affair. Jefferson began, "The Majr. [L'Enfant] says he had as much right to pull down a house, as to cut down a tree. This is true, if he has received no authority to do either. But still there will be this difference. To cut down a tree or to demolish a house in the soil of another is a trespass."[9]

L'Enfant did not have the authority to tear down trees or houses, either from the president or the commissioners (whom he did not inform). The president had certainly not given him a *carte blanche* to seize any piece of land necessary for the new city, and the commissioners were unaware of any seizing going on by L'Enfant. Jefferson wrote, "his [L'Enfant's] fault is aggravated by its having been done to gratify private resentment against Mr. Carrol, and most palpably not because it was necessary."[10]

Jefferson also expressed his sentiments on property that would have been shared by most citizens in the new rights-based republic. Cutting down a tree would hardly have been noticed or punished. However, demolishing someone's house where a plan had yet to be finalized was repugnant. He wrote,

"But the demolition of a house is so gross a trespass, that every man would prosecute it; if civilly, a jury would give great damages; if criminally, the judge would punish heavily by fine and imprisonment."[11] Republican government was not supposed to enact such tyrannical land grabs, even if conducted by a federal official, and it was an overwhelming sense of embarrassment for the new government to be caught up in the affair. Washington wrote, "The conduct of Majr L'Enfant and those employed under him, astonishes me beyond measure!"[12] Jefferson went to dinner with L'Enfant to discuss the issue, but the Major was obstinate about his personal control over the plan of the new city. After months of trying to work with L'Enfant, Washington eventually terminated him in February 1792.[13]

Although the affair dealt with a rogue federal officer (L'Enfant), the words and outrage expressed by Jefferson and Washington help to encapsulate the foundational doctrine of property rights in early America. The Founders believed that private property, and the disposition of that property, was a sacred right, one that roughly followed the English tradition stretching back to the *Magna Carta*. It could only be taken for a strict public use, and even then only if it followed the strict due process of law. Jefferson and Washington were appalled by L'Enfant's blatant disregard for the rights associated with property.

Justice Clarence Thomas took the early notions of the Founders on property and takings as a guide in his opinion. He wrote a separate dissent from O'Connor because he felt that the Court had long ago abandoned the original idea of property rights, and by so doing had gone too far afield. He felt the need to issue his own opinion and to correct past precedent and focus on the original understanding of property and takings. His dissent considered the case from an originalist point of view and was full of historical, legal, philosophical, and textual analyses.

CONSTITUTIONAL HERESY

Thomas's dissenting opinion was a scathing review of the Court's departure from the principles underlying the Constitution. He wrote about the majority opinion, "Something has gone seriously awry with this Court's interpretation of the Constitution."[14] Rhetorical flourish aside, he was voicing his larger concern that the Supreme Court had largely, in a little over a century, strayed from the principles of the Constitution. *Kelo* was dangerous because it set yet another incorrect precedent.

Contrasted with the other opinions in *Kelo*, Thomas's differed significantly. The most significant difference concerned his approach to interpreting the Constitution. As mentioned earlier, he espoused a judicial philosophy that believed in a strict interpretation of the Constitution at the time of the Framing of the document. He wrote, "In my view, it is 'imperative that the Court maintain absolute fidelity to' the Clause's *express limit* on the power of the government over the individual, no less than with every other liberty expressly enumerated in the Fifth Amendment or the Bill of Rights more generally."[15]

Rossum and Tarr noted that originalism "must proceed on the basis of what the Constitution was understood to accomplish by those who initially drafted and ratified it."[16] It is little wonder that the dissent was full of appeals to the Framers of the Constitution, as well as legal texts surrounding the Founding Era. Thomas uses such luminaries as Sir William Blackstone, James Kent, John Marshall, and James Madison. Rossum and Tarr pointed out, "it [originalism] relies heavily on documentary evidence of the original understanding of the Constitution . . . to identify what ends the Framers sought to achieve, what evils they sought to avoid, and what means they used to achieve these ends and avert these evils."[17]

The other opinions in *Kelo* were more heavily focused on precedent and evolving interpretations of law. Thomas went back to history to inform him on the case. He left little confusion on the point with his opening line, "Long ago, William Blackstone wrote that 'the law of the land . . . postpone[s] even public necessity to the sacred and inviolable rights of private property.'"[18] Thomas ultimately rejected the majority opinion for its departure from history and text. He wrote that the Constitution contained very definite phrases and that the Court had turned public use into "public welfare"—which it clearly was not since the wording itself was different.[19] For the majority, these two clauses were the same, but Thomas noted "The Framers would have used some such broader term if they had meant the Public Use Clause to have a similarly sweeping scope."[20] It is interesting to contrast the majority's interpretation of the Public Use Clause with Thomas's originalism. The majority never explicitly claimed to adhere to a strict interpretation of the Constitution. While they upheld the written text, they focused more on precedent, which they believed was set by the "diverse and always evolving needs of society."[21]

In the opening paragraphs of the majority opinion, Stevens wrote that the Court had "embraced the broader and more natural interpretation of public use as 'public purpose.'"[22] He later continued, "We have repeatedly and consistently rejected that narrow test ever since."[23] After such salvos aimed squarely at an originalist or textualist approach, the onus fell on the dissenters to prove why their approach was valid in the face of positive law. It was most likely because of the majority's challenge that Thomas gave such a passionate defense of the original Constitution's text and meaning. Ignoring strict construction and original principles, Thomas pointed out, would produce dire consequences for the Public Use Clause and police power in the future.

Thomas's dissent was also written in contrast to O'Connor's dissent, which focused on precedent of former cases as well as a strict textual interpretation of the Public Use Clause. O'Connor's dissent did not go far enough for Thomas and he had no choice but to take issue with the very cases both Stevens and O'Connor had brought up: *Berman* and *Midkiff.* Every member of the Court except Thomas accepted these cases, and he spent a significant portion of his dissent proving why they should be overturned.

EARLY PROPERTY RIGHTS

Both Thomas and O'Connor expressed their displeasure at the "evolving" public use interpretation. However, it was only Thomas that did an in-depth analysis of the history and philosophy of the clause itself. He began with an interpretation of early English jurists including Blackstone and Kent, and built his foundation on their reasoning.

Early English common law was heavily built around property and ownership. The *Magna Carta* recognized the beginnings of modern property rights and limited what the king and his sheriffs might take.[24] Sir Frederick Pollock and Frederic William Maitland devoted a considerable amount of time tracing property rights in the different incarnations of English common law. Medieval law was focused on the King and his ownership of the whole of England, including all of the land that existed. They explained, "All land in England must be held of the king of England, otherwise he would not be king of all England. . . . To wish for an ownership of land that shall not be subject to royal rights is to wish for the state of nature."[25] Since the sovereign owned the land, law cropped up around the possession and disposition of land. During this time ownership law and feudal theory came about, which created an intricate system of ownership, wills, hierarchy, and taxes. Scholars William B. Stoebuck and William Baude have both asserted that after the medieval period in England, the king's right to take "possessory estate in land" was eliminated.[26]

In America, the English philosopher John Locke's theory of property began to take hold in a greater capacity than anywhere else. Surveying the abundance of land in the North American colonies, Locke wrote, "Thus in the beginning all the world was America."[27] By living in America and far away from the King, ownership was taken even more seriously. The colonists had, as Locke pointed out, worked and cultivated the land, and therefore owned it because "As much land as a man tills, plants, improves, cultivates, and can use the product of, so much is his property."[28] Rights were recognized regarding property—rights which protected a man from a government that might take it away.

By the time of the American Revolution, jurists such as Sir William Blackstone wrote that property rights were vital, and that no man could be stripped of his land even for a public use:

> So great, moreover, is the regard of the law for private property, that it will not authorize the least violation of it; no, not even for the general good of the whole community. If a new road, for instance, were to be made through the grounds of a private person, it might perhaps be extensively beneficial to the public; but the law permits no man, or set of men, to do this without consent of the owner of the land.[29]

Land, by the time of Blackstone, had become "sacred and inviolable."[30] Examples of the early conceptions and protections of property can be multiplied, but it is enough to say that Thomas understood the legal theories and laws of property from the time of the common law's inception throughout the American Founding.

Aside from English legal theory (which highly influenced the American legal theory), Thomas also explored the words of the Founders and Framers. Foremost on the issue was the author of the Fifth Amendment, James Madison. Quoting Madison from the *National Property Gazette*, "[He] argued that no property 'shall be taken *directly* even for public use without indemnification to the owner.'"[31] Interestingly, the article he quoted from was written in March 1792, immediately after the L'Enfant affair, and most likely had something to do with property owners' worries about eminent domain.[32] Scholars have noted that Madison might have even included the Takings Clause because "entrenching rights in the Constitution would help to reinforce their importance in the public mind."[33]

In his book *Vindicating the Founders*, scholar Thomas G. West wrote that Lincoln viewed slavery in conjunction with the deprivation of private property: "To enslave a person is to deprive him of his own right to property. That is why Lincoln, following the Founders, often spoke of the heart of slavery as the denial of property rights: 'It is the same tyrannical principle,' said Lincoln."[34] Thomas never contended that Kelo or her neighbors were slaves, but the reasoning of the Founders, as well as the customs of the early English jurists, made it clear that injustice was being meted out.

Thomas's dissent asserted that the Founders thought a tyrannical government with unlimited takings power was an affront to the idea upon which America was based.[35] By following the Public Use Clause strictly, as he noted the majority should have done, he believed that they would have reached the same conclusion. He wrote, "The Public Use Clause, in short, embodied the Framers' understanding that property is a natural, fundamental right, prohibiting the government from 'tak[ing] property from A. and giv[ing] it to B.'"[36]

Looking at both the early English tradition and the Founders, it was little wonder that eighteenth and nineteenth century state and Federal courts followed the same path. He wrote, "Early American eminent domain practice largely bears out this understanding of the Public Use Clause . . . [and] therefore shed[s] light on the original meaning of the same words contained in the Public Use Clause."[37] To further reinforce the idea, he offered a host of cases which reached the same basic conclusion about public use: *Calder v. Bull* (1798), *Wilkinson v. Leland* (1829), *Vanhorne's Lessee v. Dorrance* (Pa. 1795), *Barron v. Baltimore* (1833), and *Head v. Amoskeag Mfg. Co.* (1885).[38] For Thomas, the Court's respect for the original interpretation of the Public Use Clause ended in *Fallbrook Irrigation District v. Bradley* (1896). O'Connor's dissent had not explicitly mentioned the case itself, although in her categorical breakdown it fell into the third category.[39] However, the majority cited it as the beginning of the "more natural" interpretation of public use as "public purpose" for the Court.[40] Thomas noted that from that point forward, the Court consistently made bad rulings by adopting Peckham's "public purpose," and it was easy to see where twentieth century jurisprudence began to grow apart from the original intent of the Constitution.[41]

All of the other opinions' reliance on *Berman* and *Midkiff* was in error, Thomas concluded. The cases were badly decided and set dangerous precedents that resulted in *Kelo*. He wrote that "The Court adopted its modern reading blindly."[42] While precedent was often important in Supreme Court cases, in this case the Constitution was being left behind in favor of erroneous case law. In other words, when the Constitution had a plain and simple principle to be followed, no case law should be consulted or adhered to which would cast a new interpretation. Since the Court had begun to do this, the most important thing to be done was to refute the precedent that was antagonistic to the correct interpretation.

Thomas described *Berman* and *Midkiff* as "boundlessly broad and deferential [in their] conception of public use."[43] The delegation doctrine to which the Court ascribed in those cases did not hold up to judicial scrutiny. More will be discussed on Thomas's aversion to the delegation of takings later in this chapter, but it is important to note that he believed the two cases gave an unhealthy amount of power to legislatures to determine public use. About *Berman* specifically, he wrote:

> That reasoning was question begging, since the question to be decided was whether the "specific constitutional limitation" of the Public Use Clause prevented the taking of the appellant's (concededly "nonblighted") department store . . . *Berman* also appeared to reason that any exercise by Congress of an enumerated power (in this case, its plenary power over the District of Columbia) was per se a "public use" under the Fifth Amendment. . . . But the very point of the Public Use Clause is to limit that power."[44]

The reasoning in *Berman* was circular, as Thomas pointed out. To assume that the legislature represented the entire public, and thereby anything they did was for the public, was to deny the basis of the Public Use Clause. Public use existed to protect citizens from a greedy and unrestrained government, which included the legislature. Simply being a more populous branch was no indication of justice or the mind of the public. Justice Thomas would have agreed with Thomas Jefferson who said, "173 despots would surely be as oppressive as one."[45]

Both *Berman* and *Midkiff* left the Court without a "principled manner"[46] for the Public Use Clause. Thomas wrote that when the Court assumed the rationale in those cases, it was left with an empty Public Use Clause that meant "public utility, public interest, common benefit, general advantage or convenience."[47] In other words, dress it up as the Court might, the clause became meaningless when it was not interpreted as it was originally intended to be. Stevens' opinion ended by examining *Midkiff*, "'[I]t is only the taking's purpose, and not its mechanics,' we explained, that matters in determining public use."[48] For Thomas, the mechanics of the Fifth Amendment mattered more than a taking's purpose. He wrote about the public purpose reasoning in *Fallbrook*: "This is no statement of constitutional principle: Whatever the utility of irrigation districts or the merits of the Court's view that another rule would be 'impractical given the diverse and always evolving needs of society.'"[49] Even if the principle was a good one, the language of the Fifth Amendment must be obeyed strictly. It is the mechanics that keep the citizens safe, not simply the charitable or correct thinking on an issue. If followed strictly, Thomas's originalism, while perhaps letting some well-meaning laws fall through the cracks, ultimately would take a safer route by providing a repeatable and consistent line of precedent adhering to the plain language of the Constitution. Following his logic, *Berman* and *Midkiff* should be rejected and overturned.

PUBLIC USE PERVERSITY

The majority opinion made the unforgiveable mistake of misinterpreting the Public Use Clause. Thomas noted that the Fifth Amendment was written to limit the Federal government (or, eventually, any state government) to takings involving a public use not simply a public necessity.[50] In other words, even if the public claimed it needed something, the taking would not be justified without the public being able to use it expressly. He went further and claimed that the Public Use Clause had been replaced with the vague term public purpose, which came from *Fallbrook*. He said it should perhaps be changed to the "*Diverse and Always Evolving Needs of Society Clause*."[51]

To prove his point about the incorrect interpretation, Thomas examined the plainness of the language in the Constitution. He broke down everything to the very word, and spent a considerable time examining the word compared to other uses of the same word in the Constitution in other places. This type of interpretation took the justice to a whole new level of the sentiment O'Connor described when she wrote, "When interpreting the Constitution, we begin with the unremarkable presumption that every word in the document has independent meaning, 'that no word was unnecessarily used, or needlessly added.'"[52] To take every single word as seriously as Thomas did required far more than simply reading the text as O'Connor did. It also required a deep historical understanding of how the words used were understood by the Founders and Framers. As he did so, he found that the new interpretation was different from anything the Founders would have known.

Remarkably, Thomas began with the etymology of the word "use." He started with a survey of the dictionaries available at the time and found that it meant "the act of employing any thing to any purpose."[53] After that, he wrote that the word had a Latin root which came from *utor*, meaning "to use, make use, avail one's self of, employ, enjoy, etc."[54] Coupled with "public" (which he did not define), the clause led to the creation of a use, or employment, by the public. He wrote: "When the government takes property and gives it to a private individual, and the public has no right to use the property, it strains language to say that the public is 'employing' the property, regardless of the incidental benefits that might accrue to the public from the private use."[55] In other words, the "incidental benefits" that Stevens allowed, and O'Connor railed against, made no sense. If one followed the originalist interpretation with the notion that "no word was unnecessarily used, or needlessly added," the strict interpretation of the clause is the only interpretation that could make sense. However, Stevens and Kennedy did not claim to be originalists at all, and more closely adhered to Justice Oliver Wendell Holmes who wrote, "an evolutionist will hesitate to affirm universal validity for his social ideals, or for the principles."[56] Thomas knew this, and delivered a jab at the majority when he said that the Public Use Clause should instead be called the "Diverse and Always Evolving Needs of Society Clause."

Thomas also considered the meaning of use as it stood compared to other usages in the Constitution. If use meant one thing in the Fifth Amendment (ratified in 1791), it must also have meant the same thing in other places in the Constitution (ratified in 1789). The Constitution employed the term use in two different areas: Article I, section 10, Clause 2, and Article I, section 8, Clause 12. The former was regarding the disposition of "net Produce of all Duties and Imposts . . . on Imports and Exports," and how they were all to go directly to Treasury for "Use of the Treasury." Thomas wrote that the Treasury was to use it for the taxes and "not use it to any beneficial end."[57] The latter informed Congress that they had power "to raise and support Armies," but "no Appropriation of Money to that Use shall be for a longer Term than two Years." Thomas noted that the money was meant to be strictly used for raising and support armies, "not anything directed to achieving any military end."[58] The way he saw it, the word use was a governmental *limiter*, not a governmental *liberator* as the majority had interpreted it. In both clauses, the word denoted the strict use of funds, which were not to be simply changed by Congressional fiat. For example, in the second case, if the money were allowed to be infinitely extended to the military, specific operations and wars could always be going. As Publius in *Federalist No. 8* wrote, "The means of revenue . . . have produced an intire [sic] revolution in the system of war, and have rendered disciplined armies, distinct from the body of the citizens, the inseparable companion of frequent hostility."[59] The clause in the Constitution existed to limit the use of the revenue, which Congress had, to plans of no longer than two years. Thomas's argument about the word use in the Constitution informed his notion of it as a strict limiting agent in the clause. Any use beyond the strictly public (i.e., enjoyed by everyone), would make the clause malleable and worthless. After he pointed out the Constitution's uniformity in language, Thomas spelled it out more plainly: "The Constitution's text, in short, suggests that the Takings Clause authorizes the taking of property only if the public has a right to employ it, not if the public realizes any conceivable benefit from the taking."[60]

He continued his explanation of the plainness of the language and reasoning behind the legislature's proper employment of public use. He wrote, "The Takings Clause is a prohibition, not a grant of power . . . the Government may take property only when necessary and proper to the exercise of an expressly enumerated power."[61] He reasoned that "For a law to be within the Necessary and Proper Clause . . . it must bear an 'obvious, simple, and direct relationship to an exercise of Congress' enumerated powers.'"[62] The taking in *Kelo* must have been obviously, simply, and directly related to some use by the public, or else it was not justified under the Fifth Amendment. An incidental public benefit, realized from the ordinary disposition of a private owner of property, was not a valid claim of public use. Instead, it "subvert[ed] basic principles of constitutional design."[63] The majority erred yet again when it confused an incidental (or peripheral) public benefit as an obvious, simple, and direct relationship to public use.

Thomas's dissent differed from that of O'Connor's in one key element regarding public use: that of common carriers. O'Connor was careful to create three categories for public use that the Court had identified in the past. These categories had created precedent for the Court to follow in cases such as *Berman* and *Midkiff*. Although not entirely clean and delimited, the categories provided a general overview of the proper evolution (i.e., not *Kelo*) of the clause. Where O'Connor stuck to the categories and explained them (see chapter 6), Thomas recognized no such categories and instead insisted there were incorrectly decided cases and needed to be overturned. Common carriers, the only gray area that Thomas potentially foresaw in the public use interpretation, were perfectly justified. He cited such common carriers as "public roads, toll roads, ferries, canals, railroads" and "grist mills" as examples of common carriers. However, they did not need their own subcategory under public use because they were, quite simply and obviously, used by the public. He wrote, "Those early grist mills 'were regulated by law and compelled to serve the public' . . . and therefore were actually used by the public."[64] He quickly noted that some early states misinterpreted common carriers and went too far, but that did not matter, as the trials eventually led back to the strict interpretation of the clause.[65] There was no need to excessively complicate the Public Use Clause as O'Connor had done with her categories.

The simplicity of interpreting the Public Use Clause as Thomas did in his dissent certainly made the question a much clearer one. While not rejecting O'Connor, he did take issue with her needless complication of the clause, and implicitly rejected it. Of course, Thomas disagreed with the majority's interpretation as well, but seeing his critique of O'Connor's dissent perhaps spoke louder about his approach. Thomas did not write a partisan piece pushing for a conservative outcome—instead he was remaining a strict originalist who believed in the simplicity of the Constitution no matter where it led. In *Kelo*, it happened to lead to rejecting the majority and overturning a century's worth of legal reasoning on public use. However, he also devoted a small portion to the unwarranted enlargement of police power used by the majority opinion.

QUIS CUSTODIET IPSOS CUSTODES?[66]

Perhaps one of the most under-discussed parts of the *Kelo* case was the role of the police powers. Almost an afterthought, the discussion of police power was something briefly discussed in the majority, the concurring opinion, or O'Connor's dissent. Thomas spent more time on the concern than any of the other opinions, but he still did not fully explore the theme. It was not sufficient for Thomas to make the statement (as the majority did) that part of the police power was control over the definition of public use.

The police power question is problematic when dealing with issues such as those in *Kelo*.[67] Police power itself stems largely from the idea of a balanced republic such as that found in *Federalist No. 10*, as well as other places in early American political thought.[68] The genius of the new system was that power could be shared between both the Federal and state governments. Madison wrote,

> The powers delegated by the proposed Constitution to the Federal Government, are few and defined. *Those which are to remain in the State Governments are numerous and indefinite*. The former will be exercised principally on external objects, as war, peace, negociation [sic], and foreign commerce; with which last the power of taxation will for the most part be connected. *The powers reserved to the several States will extend to all the objects, which, in the ordinary course of affairs, concern the lives, liberties and properties* of the people; and the internal order, improvement, and prosperity of the State.[69]

As Madison pointed out, the new Constitution set up a system of shared power that was not strictly defined, but clearly contained such traditional powers as had been in the states immediately after the Revolution. States would to continue to regulate the "lives, liberties, and properties of the people" under the Constitution. The problem became more acute when the Fifth Amendment was formally (or informally) applied to the states by virtue of the Fourteenth Amendment in the latter half of the nineteenth-century.[70] Where exactly the lines of demarcation were drawn after the incorporation of the Bill of Rights became more apparent. Interestingly, the cases the majority based their decisions on all came after the ratification of the Fourteenth Amendment.

Stevens drew the delimiter around a view of takings that granted states the power "to extend to all objects . . . [including the] properties of the people." This view was more consistent with the original understanding of the Constitution as portrayed in *Federalist No. 45*. Thomas, however, by virtue of the Fourteenth Amendment, found that the Fifth Amendment was now the regnant guide for the states. Since property became, or was expressed, as a natural right subject only to the strictest of takings requirements in the Fifth Amendment, it took on a higher role than any police power might assume. The powers expressed in the Fifth Amendment spoke to individual rights protected from the government, not states' rights protected by the government. As the Preamble reads, "We the people" not, as Patrick Henry would have had it, "We the States."[71] Thomas wrote,

> Early American eminent domain practice largely bears out this understanding of the Public Use Clause. This practice concerns state limits on eminent domain power, not the Fifth Amendment, since it was not until the late 19th century that the Federal Government began to use the power of eminent domain, and since *the Takings Clause did not even arguably limit state power until after the passage of the Fourteenth Amendment*.[72]

Originally, states were given the power over eminent domain, and several states even adopted a public use provision the same as in the Bill of Rights. However, the states had also been shown to have interpreted public use in a much more restrained and limited way for over a century.[73] This restraint had led to universality in the public use provision of the law. Thomas further reasoned that "it is most implausible that the Framers intended to defer to legislatures as to what satisfies the Public Use Clause, uniquely among all the express provisions of the Bill of Rights."[74] By following the common law and traditionally held understanding of public use, states had not needed the Fifth Amendment specifically applied to them.

University of Chicago Law School professor William Baude has pointed out that original Fifth Amendment "was not intended to restrain the states."[75] States were given a much more free hand in their takings, but seem to have rarely stepped beyond their authority. Indeed, for the first 100 years of the republic, states rarely, if ever, began making redevelopment or private-to-private transfers (without a common carrier or strict public use qualification). It has been speculated that James Madison foresaw potential eminent domain abuses and sought to make the Fifth Amendment an educative clause for the states to follow. When the Fifth Amendment was ratified, most states did not contain an eminent domain clause.[76] However, with the ratification of the Bill of Rights, the doctrine became law and, by virtue of the Fourteenth Amendment, a law that now controls the states' eminent domain desires. Instead of a state-decided definition (which could be argued it never had in the face of tradition and the common law), it became the realm of judges to protect the original understanding of public use in the Bill of Rights.

Thomas pointed to another provision in the Bill of Rights that fell distinctly into the realm of judicial duty—the searching of homes (Fourth Amendment). By virtue of its placement, the Takings Clause could not simply be one that was "uniquely" deferred to the states. Because of the majority's reasoning, state legislatures could overturn "individuals' traditional rights in real property."[77] It was the natural right of owning property that concerned Thomas, not the unclear federalism question that could destroy it. He wrote, "today the Court tells us that we are not to 'second-guess the City's considered judgments,' . . . when the issue is, instead, whether the government may take the infinitely more intrusive step of tearing down petitioners' homes."[78]

Thomas bluntly rejected the police powers argument the majority had cited: "*Berman* and *Midkiff* erred by equating the eminent domain power with the police power of States."[79] Since the majority had used the erroneous definition of the past two public use cases, it had based its precedent on the false assumption that eminent domain was a police power. *Berman* was misunderstood from the outset. Instead of using eminent domain, as that case had done, the majority should have recognized that slums fell under the state nuisance law.[80] Nuisance laws fell under the proper realm of police powers under the subcategory of welfare.[81] The *Berman* decision had not required an interpretation of takings at all since it was covered under nuisance law. *Midkiff*, however, was beyond all hope. The majority in *Kelo* was not validated under either the Fifth Amendment or *Berman*. Police powers did not include the power to create or shape takings doctrines through legislative interpretation. The conflation of the two set a tyrannical precedent where no property was safe from the state.

In his final statements on police powers, Thomas looked at the problems incorrect takings actions by state legislatures had wrought on different societies. He began by citing the famous Footnote Four of *U.S. v. Carolene Products* (1938).[82] The famous footnote has been recognized as the beginning of the strict scrutiny test. The footnote focused on the Court's scrutiny of minority groups and how to protect them when the political process continually failed. Using this reasoning, Thomas harangued the majority opinion and said, "If ever there were justification for intrusive judicial review of constitutional provisions that protect 'discrete and insular minorities' . . . surely that principle would apply with force to the powerless groups and individuals the Public Use Clause protects."[83]

Changing the Public Use Clause to benefit economic growth would end up harming those who were not economically strong. Often, this discrimination would "fall disproportionately on poor communities."[84] As happened in *Poletown*, those who were not as powerful or influential as General Motors had their neighborhood taken.[85] Thomas wrote that *Kelo* would produce the same effect in many places across the nation, and would often disproportionately harm African-Americans as other instances had shown.[86]

Police power, which can be more easily corrupted at a smaller level (i.e., the state), should not have all power over eminent domain, including defining its limits, especially if the taking presents a real or imagined propensity for economic gain. Thomas soberly wrote, "Regrettably, the predictable consequence of the Court's decision will be to exacerbate these effects."[87]

CONCLUSION

Thomas's dissent in *Kelo* was focused exclusively on the history and original intent of the Fifth Amendment in the Constitution. While the majority relied chiefly upon precedent and an evolving interpretation of the Public Use Clause, Thomas's dissent advocated overturning precedent and restoring the original understanding of the Public Use Clause. His dissent left several questions that were alluded to, but never fully answered.

The questions that were left unanswered could most likely be answered by a more general appeal to the sense of property at the time of the Founding. The L'Enfant affair demonstrated the sacred nature of property rights in the early republic, and showed two of the most famous Founders' reactions. Looking at the words of Sir William Blackstone and James Madison also demonstrated the importance the government placed on preserving property from the state. Thomas sought to channel their mindset, and through his dissent produced a vision of takings much closer to the original understanding at the time of ratification.

The reasoning in Thomas's dissent conveyed the message that the Court was not following the Constitution, as it had sworn to do, and the new precedent in *Kelo* was going to create a mess the Founders had tried to avoid. The same as O'Connor, Thomas foresaw a major calamity in American jurisprudence. It is interesting to note that Kennedy, O'Connor, and Thomas all voiced concern over the decision and rationale in *Kelo*. Kennedy feared it could go too far in the future, O'Connor feared it had already gone too far, and Thomas feared it had gone wrong over 100 years before *Kelo*. He believed that the whole takings doctrine had become perverted and was so far awry from the Constitution that nothing short of an overhaul could save it. In the closing paragraphs, he expressed his fear at the blatant disregard of the Constitution in the Court's opinion:

> It is far easier to analyze whether the government owns or the public has a legal right to use the taken property than to ask whether the taking has a "purely private purpose"—unless the Court means to eliminate public use scrutiny of takings entirely. . . . Obliterating a provision of the Constitution, of course, guarantees that it will not be misapplied.[88]

He echoed Jefferson's sentiment about L'Enfant's authority: "The Majr. [L'Enfant] says he had as much right to pull down a house, as to cut down a tree. This is true, if he has received no authority to do either."[89] As evidenced by his dissent, Thomas felt the same about the Court's grant of authority in *Kelo*.

NOTES

1. "The L'Enfant and McMillan Plans," National Park Service Website, accessed March 3, 2013, http://www.nps.gov/nr/travel/wash/lenfant.htm.
2. Ibid.
3. Ibid.
4. "From Pierre L'Enfant, Editorial Note, 21 September, 1791," *The Papers of George Washington Digital Edition*, ed. Theodore J. Crackel, (Charlottesville: University of Virginia Press, Rotunda, 2008), accessed May 12, 2014, http://founders.archives.gov/documents/Washington/05-09-02-0124.
5. Ibid.
6. Pierre L'Enfant, "From Pierre L'Enfant, George town [Md.], December 7th 1791," in *The Papers of George Washington Digital Edition*, ed. Theodore J. Crackel, (Charlottesville: University of Virginia Press, Rotunda, 2008), accessed May 12, 2014, http://founders.archives.gov/documents/Washington/05-09-02-0124.
7. Ibid.
8. "From Pierre L'Enfant, Editorial Note, 21 September, 1791," *The Papers of George Washington Digital Edition*, ed. Theodore J. Crackel, (Charlottesville: University of Virginia Press, Rotunda, 2008), accessed May 12, 2014, http://founders.archives.gov/documents/Washington/05-09-02-0124.

9. Thomas Jefferson, "Observations on L'Enfant's Letter," in *The Papers of Thomas Jefferson Digital Edition*, eds. Barbara B. Oberg and J. Jefferson Looney, (Charlottesville: University of Virginia Press, Rotunda, 2008), accessed May 12, 2014, http://founders.archives.gov/documents/Washington/05-09-02-0124.

10. Ibid.

11. Ibid.

12. George Washington, "To Thomas Jefferson, Philadelphia, January 18th, 1792," in *The Papers of George Washington Digital Edition*, ed. Theodore J. Crackel, (Charlottesville: University of Virginia Press, Rotunda, 2008), accessed May 12, 2014, http://founders.archives.gov/documents/Washington/05-09-02-0124.

13. "From Pierre L'Enfant, Editorial Note, 21 September, 1791." in *The Papers of George Washington Digital Edition*, ed. Theodore J. Crackel, (Charlottesville: University of Virginia Press, Rotunda, 2008), accessed May 12, 2014, http://founders.archives.gov/documents/Washington/05-09-02-0124.

14. *Kelo v. New London*, 545 U.S. 469 (2005) (Thomas, J., dissenting).

15. Ibid. He is quoting himself in *Shepard v. United States*, 544 U.S. 13 (2005) (Thomas, J. concurring).

16. Rossum and Tarr, *American Constitutional Law*, 12.

17. Ibid., 12–13.

18. *Kelo v. New London*, 545 U.S. 469 (2005) (Thomas, J., dissenting).

19. Ibid.

20. Ibid.

21. Ibid.

22. *Kelo v. New London*, 545 U.S. 469 (2005).

23. Ibid.

24. *Magna Carta*, Constitution.org, accessed May 3, 2013, http://www.constitution.org/eng/magnacar.htm. Of those specific to property were: Clause 9 ("Neither we nor our bailiffs will seize any land or rent for any debt, as long as the chattels of the debtor are sufficient to repay the debt; nor shall the sureties of the debtor be distrained so long as the principal debtor is able to satisfy the debt; and if the principal debtor shall fail to pay the debt, having nothing wherewith to pay it, then the sureties shall answer for the debt; and let them have the lands and rents of the debtor, if they desire them, until they are indemnified for the debt which they have paid for him, unless the principal debtor can show proof that he is discharged thereof as against the said sureties."), Clause 30 ("No sheriff or bailiff of ours, or other person, shall take the horses or carts of any freeman for transport duty, against the will of the said freeman."), and Clause 31 ("Neither we nor our bailiffs shall take, for our castles or for any other work of ours, wood which is not ours, against the will of the owner of that wood."). Granted, 30 and 31 are not about land or houses, but they do focus on property and the taking of it.

25. Sir Frederick Pollock and Frederic William Maitland, *The History of English Law before the Time of Edward I*, vol. 2, (Indianapolis: Liberty Fund, 2010), accessed online May 2, 2013. http://oll.libertyfund.org/index.php?option=com_staticxt&staticfile=show.php%3Ftitle=2314&layout=html#chapter_219571.

26. William B. Stoebuck, "A General Theory of Eminent Domain," *Washington Law Review* 47, (1972): 559-60; William Baude, "Rethinking the Federal Eminent Domain Power," *The Yale Law Journal* 122 (2013): 1798–1800.

27. John Locke, *Two Treatises of Government*, chapter V.

28. Ibid.

29. Sir William Blackstone, *Commentaries on the Laws of England in Four Books. Notes selected from the editions of Archibold, Christian, Coleridge, Chitty, Stewart, Kerr, and others, Barron Field's Analysis, and Additional Notes, and a Life of the Author by George Sharswood. In Two Volumes.* (Philadelphia: J.B. Lippincott Co., 1893), Vol. 1, accessed online May 3, 2013, http://oll.libertyfund.org/index.php?option=com_staticxt&staticfile=show.php%3Ftitle=2140&layout=html#chapter_198690.

30. Ibid.

31. *Kelo v. New London*, 545 U.S. 469 (2005) (Thomas, J., dissenting).

32. See the Introduction to this chapter.

33. Baude, "Rethinking the Federal Eminent Domain Power," 1795–96; see also William Michael Treanor, "The Original Understanding of the Takings Clause and the Political Process," *Columbia Law Review* 95 (1995): 843 n. 308.

34. Thomas G. West, *Vindicating the Founders: Race, Sex, Class, and Justice in the Origins of America* (New York: Rowman & Littlefield Publishers Inc., 1997), 39. Cf. chapter 2 of the same book entitled "Property Rights," 37–70.

35. West, *Vindicating the Founders*, chapter 2. See also the amicus briefs representing the respondents (chapter 3, Table 3.1). West points out that many modern academics have taken issue with property rights at the time of the founding. They call such things "elitist" because only the rich owned property and were looking out for their own self-interest. However, the amici supporting the respondents (New London) make it abundantly clear that redevelopment takings redistribute wealth to lower classes and minority groups since it would never be possible for them to own property otherwise. See especially the amicus for Brooklyn United for Innovative Local Development (BUILD), et al. There are two distinct philosophies at odds in this discussion: private property harms the lower classes or private property gives lower classes "the great fence to liberty" (West, *Vindicating*, 39). Such a divergence of opinions gained popularity during the Progressive Era, and has gained adherents as time has gone on, fundamentally challenging the Founding's views. Thomas was determined to stem the tide.

36. *Kelo v. New London*, 545 U.S. 469 (2005) (Thomas, J., dissenting). The quoted text is from *Calder v. Bull*, 3 Dall. 386 (1798).

37. *Kelo v. New London*, 545 U.S. 469 (2005) (Thomas, J., dissenting).

38. *Calder v. Bull*, 3 Dall. 386 (1798); *Wilkinson v. Leland*, 2 Pet. 627 (1829); *Vanhorne's Lessee v. Dorrance*, 2 Dall. 304 (CC Pa. 1795), *Barron v. City of Baltimore*, 32 U.S. 243 (1833), *Head v. Amoskeag Mfg. Co.*, 113 U.S. 9 (1885).

39. See chapter 6.

40. *Kelo v. New London*, 545 U.S. 469 (2005).

41. *Kelo v. New London*, 545 U.S. 469 (2005) (Thomas, J., dissenting). He also points to *Nash* and *Strickley* accepting this reasoning in their decisions.

42. Ibid.

43. *Kelo v. New London*, 545 U.S. 469 (2005) (Thomas, J., dissenting).

44. Ibid.

45. Thomas Jefferson, *Notes on the State of Virginia*, The Avalon Project, accessed May 24, 2013. http://avalon.law.yale.edu/18th_century/jeffvir.asp.

46. *Kelo v. New London*, 545 U.S. 469 (2005) (Thomas, J., dissenting).

47. Ibid.

48. *Kelo v. New London*, 545 U.S. 469 (2005).

49. Ibid.

50. *Kelo v. New London*, 545 U.S. 469 (2005) (Thomas, J., dissenting).

51. Ibid., italics in original.

52. *Kelo v. New London*, 545 U.S. 469 (2005) (O'Connor, J., dissenting).

53. *Kelo v. New London*, 545 U.S. 469 (2005) (Thomas, J., dissenting).

54. Ibid.

55. Ibid.

56. Holmes, "The Path of the Law." See also chapter 4.

57. *Kelo v. New London*, 545 U.S. 469 (2005) (Thomas, J., dissenting).

58. Ibid.

59. Publius, "Federalist No. 8," Constitution.org, accessed May 28, 2013, http://www.constitution.org/fed/federa08.htm.

60. *Kelo v. New London*, 545 U.S. 469 (2005) (Thomas, J., dissenting).

61. Ibid.

62. Ibid.

63. Ibid.

64. Ibid.

65. Ibid.

66. "*Who watches the watchmen*?"

67. See also chapter 4.

68. Cf. Publius, Federalist Nos. 17–21, 45, 51.

69. Publius, "Federalist No. 45," January 26, 1788, *The Constitution Society*, accessed May 28, 2013, http://www.constitution.org/fed/federa45.htm.

70. Cf. Wolfe, *The Rise of Modern Judicial Review*; Leonard W. Levy, Charles Fairman, and Stanley Morrison, *Fourteenth Amendment and the Bill of Rights: The Incorporation Theory*, (New York: De Capo Press, 1970); and Akhil Reed Amar, *The Bill of Rights: Creation and Reconstruction*, (New Haven: Yale University Press, 2000).

71. Patrick Henry, "Speech at the Virginia Ratifying Convention," June 4, 1788, *The Founders' Constitution*.

72. *Kelo v. New London*, 545 U.S. 469 (2005) (Thomas, J., dissenting), italics added.

73. Baude, "*Rethinking the Federal Eminent Domain Power*," 1791–1800.

74. Ibid.

75. Baude, "*Rethinking the Federal Eminent Domain Power*," 1791; Amar, *The Bill of Rights*.

76. Ibid., 1793–1807.

77. *Kelo v. New London*, 545 U.S. 469 (2005) (Thomas, J., dissenting).

78. Ibid.

79. Ibid.

80. Ibid.

81. For more on this, see the discussion and definition of police powers in chapter 4.

82. *United States v. Carolene Products Co.*, 304 U. S. 144, 152, n. 4 (1938).

83. *Kelo v. New London*, 545 U.S. 469 (2005) (Thomas, J., dissenting).

84. Ibid.

85. Cf. chapter 6.

86. He is worth citing in full here as the research is compelling: In the 1950s, no doubt emboldened in part by the expansive understanding of "public use" this Court adopted in Berman, cities "rushed to draw plans" for downtown development. B. Frieden & L. Sagalayn, Downtown, Inc. *How America Rebuilds Cities* 17 (1989). "Of all the families displaced by urban renewal from 1949 through 1963, 63% of those whose race was known were nonwhite, and of these families, 56% of nonwhites and 38% of whites had incomes low enough to qualify for public housing, which, however, was seldom available to them." Id., at 28. Public works projects in the 1950s and 1960s destroyed predominantly minority communities in St. Paul, Minnesota, and Baltimore, Maryland. Id., at 28–29. In 1981, urban planners in Detroit, Michigan, uprooted the largely "lower-income and elderly" Poletown neighborhood for the benefit of the General Motors Corporation. J. Wylie, *Poletown: Community Betrayed* 58 (1989). Urban renewal projects have long been associated with the displacement of blacks; "[i]n cities across the country, urban renewal came to be known as 'Negro removal.'" Pritchett, *The "Public Menace" of Blight: Urban Renewal and the Private Uses of Eminent Domain*, 21 Yale L. & Pol'y Rev. 1, 47 (2003). Over 97% of the individuals forcibly re- moved from their homes by the "slum-clearance" project upheld by this Court in Berman were black. 348 U. S., at 30. Regrettably, the predictable consequence of the Court's decision will be to exacerbate these effects.

87. Ibid.

88. Ibid.

89. Thomas Jefferson, "Observations on L'Enfant's Letter," in *The Papers of Thomas Jefferson Digital Edition*, eds. Barbara B. Oberg and J. Jefferson Looney, (Charlottesville: University of Virginia Press, Rotunda, 2008), accessed May 12, 2014, http://founders.archives.gov/documents/Washington/05-09-02-0124.

Chapter Eight

More Like a Living Nightmare Than a Dream

The Kelo Backlash

It had been five long years since Susette Kelo had first learned about losing her house. She had worked nonstop since that fateful Thanksgiving Day in 2000, trying to get the courts to overturn the decision and spare her little pink waterfront house. By June 23, 2005, Kelo realized the courts were not going to save her house. She showed defiance at the decision and was determined to fight until the bitter end. She and her legal team at the Institute for Justice, including her attorney Scott Bullock, vowed to fight on using any legal means possible including protests, media appeals, and other popular methods.

All was not lost for Kelo, however. Her case had garnered national attention. Thanks largely to the efforts of the Institute for Justice, the whole nation learned of the case, and newspapers and media outlets reported the facts of the case to an incredulous public. As soon as the media heard the decision, the nation's political bodies began to move decisively against the Court's interpretation of eminent domain. Both state and federal legislatures condemned the decision. A Senate Judiciary Committee hearing was convened under the direction of Senator Arlen Specter. As noted in chapter 4, the House of Representatives officially issued a resolution denouncing the decision.[1] Within a month's time of the decision being handed down, twenty-eight states had introduced more than seventy bills and five constitutional amendments to define or reform eminent domain.[2]

This chapter examines the backlash to the *Kelo* case in four major areas. The first category is the media and political backlash that hit a fever pitch immediately following the case. As noted before, this frenzy did not last long. Democracies tend to have short memories on things, and *Kelo* was no exception. The second category is the precedential use of the case since 2005. While no case regarding private property has yet been as noteworthy as the *Kelo* decision, many cases have cited it as reasoning for takings and public use interpretation. A brief examination of several of the larger examples will be undertaken in the chapter. The third category is the academic commentary since the decision. Academics in both the legal and political science fields have weighed in the on the decision and its consequences for the republic. A large portion of the articles and books post-*Kelo* have criticized the decision. Some are novel, some are not, but a survey of the literature will be undertaken. The final part of the chapter will be a more personal epilogue on the parties involved, including Susette Kelo and her neighbors, as well as the City of New London, the NLDC, and the Supreme Court justices.

St. Petersburg (Fla.) *Times* columnist Howard Troxler wrote shortly after the decision, "The U.S. Supreme Court has basically handed a big pile of crack cocaine to every state and local government . . . and said, 'Try not to get addicted.' The court will be forced to modify this ruling in time."[3] Whether or not the ruling will be overturned sooner or later is yet to be seen. The distance between the prominent public use takings cases (*Nash/Strickley—Berman—Midkiff—Kelo*) has been between thirty and forty years over the past century. To see if this tradition continues will be something for future scholars to explore and debate. However, approaching the tenth anniversary of the decision, no major Court case has overturned *Kelo*, and some of those who originally participated in the case are ending their tenure on the bench.[4]

MEDIA AND POLITICAL BACKLASH

The moment the decision was announced, the media began publicizing the event. Headlines appeared all over the nation: "Property Wrongs: A Supreme Blunder" (California), "Eminent Mistake" (Florida), "High Court Rules on the Side of State Socialism" (Texas), "When 'Public Purpose' Means You Don't Count" (Wisconsin), "For Homeowners, Frustration and Anger at Ruling" (New York), and "Eminent Domain Ruling Has Dire Implications" (Ohio).[5] In an opinion piece entitled, "Stealing Home: Letting Government Take Property for Development Risks Abuse" written a month after the ruling, the author(s) wrote:

> It seems a bizarre anomaly. The government in China or Russia might take private property to hand over to wealthy developers to build shopping malls and office plazas, but it wouldn't happen in the United States. Yet, that is the

> practice the U.S. Supreme Court narrowly approved this week. Local governments, the court ruled, may seize private homes and businesses so that other private entities can develop the land into enterprises that generate higher taxes. The Supreme Court found, 5–4, that *local elected officials are not barred by the Constitution* from condemning whole neighborhoods and small businesses if, in their view, doing so would lead to redevelopment that increases tax collections.[6]

The Roanoke Times wrote, "'This goes against the Founding Fathers' intent,' . . . This is beyond Republicans and Democrats, conservatives and liberals. This deals with everyone right in their homes."[7] Personal stories were also used by the media, including a Boston Globe interview with seventy-nine-year-old Italian immigrant Pasquale Cristofaro who was about to finally be evicted from his home in New London:

> "These people don't have no respect," Pasquale, who immigrated to America from Italy in 1962, told me that day. "You supposed to go like gentlemen—make me a price, ask me a yes or no. I love this house. I pay my bill, I pay the tax. And now they say I should get out? It's not right. It's not right."[8]

Bill Von Winkle, a resident of Fort Trumbull who joined in the case with Kelo, was quoted, "It's desperately hard to believe that in this country you can lose your home to private developers. . . . It's basically corporate theft."[9] Columnist George F. Will spoke out against the case, reminding his fellow conservatives that they "should be careful what they wish for" when advocating state empowerment.[10] *CNN/Money* summed it up, "Public sentiment has been running dead against the decision."[11]

The partisan affiliation of the media also played a role in the coverage. Republicans and conservative-leaning media outlets expressed anger and outrage at the ruling.[12] Conservative talk show host Sean Hannity told Kelo on television, "If they're going to knock your house down so they can build a bigger house with bigger tax revenue . . . that seems like legalized stealing."[13]

Democrats and liberal-leaning media outlets also expressed outrage over the story, but less so than their Republican counterparts. One interesting trend comes from scholar Kyle Scott who noted, "Democratic representatives were not nearly as vocal in their opposition to the *Kelo* decision as the Republican opponents to the decision were."[14] He explained the disparity: "One way to make sense of it is to assume that they hold the same position as those in the Court's majority."[15] Scott also noted the Democratic rejection of the position of the NAACP. As previously noted, the NAACP filed an amicus brief in support of Kelo and her neighbors. In the states that had the most NAACP branches and offices, Democratic legislators often turned against the association on the decision.[16] The overall partisan backlash was not surprising if one looks at the *Poletown* decision that was briefly highlighted in chapter 6.[17] In *Poletown*, the city mayor of Detroit, Coleman Young, was a high-level Democrat, an African American, and an outspoken supporter of the Carter administration. For Young to have used economic eminent domain against Poletown, along with the support of the Carter administration, should make the partisanship on display in the reaction to *Kelo* less surprising.

Polls by the media were also conducted and showed that an overwhelming majority of Americans opposed the decision. 98% of Americans polled in an *MSNBC* poll opposed the decision.[18] A *CNN/Money* poll conducted immediately after the decision found "only one percent of responders thought that the government should be able to seize private homes or businesses for private development."[19] The *Jacksonville Business Journal* found that one year after the decision, 90% of those polled favored restricting eminent domain laws.[20] In a Zogby Survey, 95% disagreed with the outcome of *Kelo*, and in a Saint Index Survey 81% disagreed.[21] Needless to say, most of the country clearly disagreed with the decision.

All of the polls, media, and sheer number of stories show that the case became overwhelmingly important to citizens. Most citizens polled believed that the decision was a bad one and that property rights should be respected more than the ruling had suggested. It seemed (and seems still) that many Americans view property rights in the same vein that Thomas showed the Founders did. The maxim "a man's home is his castle," which always represented the strength of private property against the government, seemed to resonate in most American citizens. After having conducted a fascinating study into the public backlash surrounding the case, scholars Janice Nadler, Shari Seidman Diamond, and Matthew M. Patton appropriately entitled the reaction to *Kelo* the "perfect storm."[22]

The media and national attention represented another avenue for change in a democracy. When Susette Kelo lost her case, she and her team appealed to the citizens themselves through the media. Speaking to the Clark County Bar Association, Stevens said that he thought the public outcry over the *Kelo* decision would bear good political fruit. It would be the politicians and political branches that would change the case—not the Court. He wrote, "I believe that the public outcry that greeted *Kelo* is some evidence that the political process is up to the task of addressing such policy concerns."[23] He was correct that the political bodies would immediately notice the outcry and they, in turn, would begin to write legislation to change the law. How much change actually occurred is a different matter.

In any democracy that enjoys a freedom of the press, politicians take notice of issues that are as salient as *Kelo*. In the *Federalist Papers*, Publius wrote that members of the House of Representatives as well as Senators would necessarily rely on the people for their positions. In *Federalist No. 57*, Publius wrote:

> [Representatives] will have been distinguished by the preference of their fellow-citizens, we are to presume that in general they will be somewhat distinguished also by those qualities which entitle them to it, and which promise a sincere and scrupulous regard to the nature of their engagements . . . the House of Representatives is so constituted as to support in the members an habitual recollection of their dependence on the people. Before the sentiments impressed on their minds by the mode of their elevation can be effaced by the exercise of power, they will be compelled to anticipate the moment when their power is to cease, when their exercise of it is to be reviewed, and when they must descend to the level from which they were raised; there forever to remain unless a faithful discharge of their trust shall have established their title to a renewal of it.[24]

As Publius knew, both the desire for distinction the representatives would have as well as the necessity of reelection would keep them wedded to public sentiment. In the case of *Kelo*, members of Congress immediately began decrying the decision and seeking for a change in eminent domain laws.

In order to understand the decision and the effects on the homeowners, as well as to create a memorable public spectacle, both the House and the Senate invited Kelo (and several neighbors and members of her legal team) to testify, albeit at different times. The Senate rang Kelo first, asking her to testify in September 2005 before the Judiciary Committee. Quite fearful, Kelo agreed to testify because "[she] figured she owed it to millions of other working Americans to do her best to convince the senators that politicians like the one seated next to her [the mayor of Hartford] didn't care about the little guys."[25] She said, "I sincerely hope that Congress will do what judges and local legislators so far have refused to do for me and for thousands of people like me across the nation: protect our homes under a plain reading of the U.S. Constitution."[26] Kelo petitioned the Senate to read the Constitution in a plain and original way. Even Justice Stevens, speaking later about the case, noted that Thomas's plain reading of the Constitution had been "intellectually honest."[27] But Stevens could never accept it because was too "dramatic" and meant going back and overruling a "whole line of cases."[28] Kelo asked the Senate to do just that—follow Thomas's originalism that most Americans believed according to polls, headlines, protests, and state actions.[29]

After she testified, several senators on the committee made official statements at the hearing. Vermont Senator Patrick Leahy addressed the committee and said:

> Ms. Kelo, I am one of probably millions of Americans who were distressed when we learned your story and who are concerned about what happened to you. I intend to work with others on this Committee to fashion some solutions—some better, fairer and more sensible ways for local governments to use, and not use, the significant powers they have over property owners.[30]

Senator John Coryn also spoke and said, "Suffice it to say, the *Kelo* decision was a disappointment."[31] Senators and their staffs rushed forward to meet and congratulate Kelo after the hearing had concluded.[32] Massachusetts Senator Edward Kennedy even offered to personally help her in her struggle.[33]

After the hearing, the Senate introduced bills to change eminent domain and protect property owners. In October of 2005, Republican Senator John Ensign of Nevada introduced a bill entitled: "*Private Property Rights Protection Act of 2005*" (S. 1895). The bill was heavily laden with appeals to the Founders as well as O'Connor and Thomas's dissents. The bill required that no federal funds could be given to a state that engaged in economic takings the way the city had done in *Kelo*.[34] A similar bill passed the House by an overwhelming majority (376–38), but died in the Senate.[35] It was reintroduced the following session but it died in committee.[36] In September 2006, Republican Senator James Inhofe of Oklahoma introduced another similarly titled (but different) bill: "*Private Property Rights Protection Act of 2006*" (S. 3873). The bill contained provisions that would effectively nullify the *Kelo* decision. Bluntly stated in Section 2, Subsection A:

> No State or political subdivision of a State shall exercise its power of eminent domain, or allow the exercise of such power by any person or entity to which such power has been delegated, over property to be used for economic development or over property that is subsequently used for economic development . . .[37]

It also prohibited the federal government from exercising eminent domain for economic development.

In the House of Representatives, things were similar. Republican James Sensenbrenner, Jr. of Wisconsin introduced a similar bill on June 30, 2005—a mere seven days after the *Kelo* decision was handed down. HR 3135 was immensely popular, no doubt due to the national frenzy, and had a total of 136 cosponsors (125 Republicans and 11 Democrats). It also called for the same provisions of economic takings and eminent domain as the Senate version.[38] All of the bills were referred to their respective committees shortly after introduction—and all of them died in committee.[39]

The fervor in Congress began to die shortly after the case had ceased to be popular in the news. After both bills were killed in committee, the popularity stalled, and Congress became less interested in changing perceptions of eminent domain. On the one-year anniversary of the case, President George W. Bush issued Executive Order No. 13406 which allegedly barred the Federal government from any economic development takings. However, as Professor Ilya Somin pointed out, "this language [in the Order] validates virtually any economic development condemnation that the feds might want to pursue."[40]

Somin also pointed out that the Order was itself limited since the states were almost always the culprits in economic takings cases.[41]

In short, the federal government accomplished little, if anything, regarding changing the ruling or sentiment behind *Kelo*. As of June 2013, Representative Sensenbrenner was still trying to change the law, having reintroduced his property rights bill to the 113th Congress, where it was assigned to the House Judiciary Committee. He even had Susette Kelo give a speech before the House Judiciary Committee in April 2013. She largely spoke on the same topics she did before the Senate Judiciary in 2005, but with an updated plea for reform. She said, "the bottom line is, that state legislators have heard the public's outrage over this decision and responded . . . Congress has yet to do so."[42] Kelo's testimony notwithstanding, the grim prognostication on the popular website *GovTrack.us* gave the bill a 32% chance of making it out of committee, and a 5% chance of making it out of the House of Representatives.[43] In a telling comparison, the original bill Sensenbrenner introduced in 2005 had 136 cosponsors, but the 2013 incarnation only had one sponsor.

The state reaction was also large at first, but tapered off in the same way. In an article, Somin described the ardent fervor that greeted state legislatures immediately after the case was decided—and the subsequent lack of change in eminent domain laws that followed. Published in 2010, several years after the public fervor had waned, he noted that most states had enacted little reforms of some sort. He wrote that thirty-five state legislatures had passed "post-*Kelo* reforms."[44] Of those thirty-five, twenty-one "provide little or no protection for property owners against economic development takings."[45] Many of these laws contained major loopholes that were couched in language such as "community development" or other terms left open to cities and agencies to define.[46] By making a show of anti-economic takings legislation, the state legislatures were able to satiate the public's need for legislative action without actually changing much.

Harvey M. Jacobs and Ellen M. Bassett have also shown that the fury by "property rights activists" after *Kelo* did not result in much change. The activists used *Kelo* as way to increase their own power and credibility, including portraying the case negatively in the media, but in the end were perhaps fighting for "solution[s] to a problem that does not really exist."[47] They showed that many landowners voluntarily leave when the city offers to buy their property. In the case of New London 100 of 115 landowners "sold their land without eminent domain action by the city."[48] They have noted that perhaps the public wants more transparency in the planning process, but does not necessarily feel so critical of economic redevelopment takings.

That the legislative reaction had not been grandiose is agreed upon. However, several patterns have emerged regarding legislative reaction. Scholar Kyle Scott noted in his book *The Price of Politics: Lessons from Kelo v. New*

London (2009) that states that have enacted strong post-*Kelo* reform in favor of private property rights were doing better financially than those states that remained with the same or weak reform.[49] Attorney Scott J. Bullock, speaking at a symposium in 2007, noted that engineered cities have had high failure rates. For example, by 2007 in California, there were "395 active redevelopment agencies . . . [which] owned $12.9 billion worth of property" and "had $8.7 billion in revenues."[50] In 2011, redevelopment agencies in California had been curtailed due to budgetary reasons, but author Stephen Greenhut has noted that they are poised for a resurrection.[51]

Reform legislation in the states as well as the federal government has slowed to a crawl. Crusaders still attempt to rally enough votes and attention to change eminent domain laws, but it seems as if most are doomed to fail since the *Kelo* decision has waned in public memory. One scholar noted shortly after the decision, "Sadly, momentum for the issue seems to have waned in most of the country and the initial indignation over the Supreme Court's decision has been met not with a bang, but a whimper."[52] Although the backlash was enormous at first, many states continue to employ takings for economic revitalization with limited results. Perhaps this reflects a deeper insight into the rise of state and urban planning which has been popular since the beginning of the twentieth century and followed Progressive thought.[53] Somin concluded, "the *Kelo* backlash has yielded far less effective reform than many expected . . . the political response to *Kelo* is a striking example of public backlash against an unpopular judicial decision . . . it also shows that backlash politics has its limits."[54]

COURT/LEGAL BACKLASH

In 2011, Justice Stevens spoke about the *Kelo* decision in an interview for *The Wall Street Journal*. He remarked that most people who criticized the ruling simply did not understand the decision or precedent leading up to it. He remarked, "It's the most unpopular opinion I ever wrote, no doubt about it . . . but the legal issue would have been exactly the same if it had been a gas station or a pool hall."[55] Stevens also said he sympathized with Ms. Kelo, but the law was still the law. It took little time for the federal courts to start citing the decision once it had been issued.

The Supreme Court reaction to *Kelo* has been tepid up through 2012. Only two Supreme Court cases have cited it since it was issued, but in the federal district and appellate courts it has been cited 141 times since 2005.[56] Including the state courts, *Kelo* has been used in 344 different cases. Not all of these citations are necessarily based wholly on the decision, and some are simply references to things said peripherally in *Kelo* such as, "It cannot be presumed that any clause in the constitution is intended to be without effect."[57] However, there are several cases that have come up at the federal level that are worth mentioning because of their express connection to *Kelo*. Many of the cases rely more on *Berman* than *Kelo* because the latter is seen as vindicating the former. Stevens believed the decision was based on the precedent set in both *Berman* and *Midkiff*, and it seems that the present Federal courts believe the same.

The two Supreme Court cases where *Kelo* has been mentioned are both in dissenting opinions. The first is from the 2009 case of *Haywood v. Curtis*, and is mentioned in a dissent written by Thomas and joined by Scalia, Roberts, and Alito.[58] The case had nothing at all to do with property rights or eminent domain, but instead revolved around prisoners' rights being infringed upon by the state of New York and the applicability of the Supremacy Clause. Thomas wrote a paragraph where he outlined the necessity of taking the Constitution and its contents seriously. He cited his own commentary from *Kelo* where he said, "It cannot be presumed that any clause in the constitution is intended to be without effect." Two years later, in the case of *Vartelas v. Holder* (2011), Scalia's dissenting opinion mentioned *Kelo*, but not in any takings capacity.[59] The case itself focused on immigration reform and enforcing provisions retroactively. The dissent pushed for a common sense approach to the ruling, and noted that retroactive prohibition was not the issue in the case. He cited cases that should contain such an approach and included *Kelo* as an example.[60] These were the only two cases where the Supreme Court has mentioned the *Kelo* case at all. Perhaps Scalia knows something the Court does not since he quipped in 2011, "I do not think that the *Kelo* opinion is long for this world."[61]

The district and appellate courts have dealt much more with the case in their proceedings since the ruling in 2005. This is to be expected because the caseload of the lower courts is much larger than Supreme Court. Many of the cases only mention *Kelo* in a footnote or as part of a larger appeal to takings or supremacy. Several of them use *Kelo* in a stronger capacity, however, and they bear out the importance of *Kelo* when shaping precedent.

The first noteworthy case to involve the reasoning in *Kelo* was *Whittaker v. County of Lawrence* which began in District Court in 2007 and ended in the Third Circuit Court of Appeals in 2009.[62] In the 2009 opinion, the case was ruled in congruence with the reasoning in *Kelo*. The Lawrence County Economic Development Corporation (or LCEDC) implemented a plan not unlike the NLDC's plan for New London. A new 500-acre industrial park was planned, and like New London, needed space from owners who already lived on the proposed site. Eminent domain was enacted and the owners lost their homes in favor of the plan. The 2009 opinion, written by judge Nora Barry Fischer, cited *Kelo* eighteen times. Setting the tone for the entire opinion, Fischer wrote:

> The broad scope of the term "public use" was further illustrated in *Kelo v. City of New London* . . . in which the Supreme Court held that a government could "take" private property, and pay just compensation to the owner, in order to facilitate private development that was believed to be economically advantageous to the area.[63]

Kelo's broad public use precedent was all that was necessary for the similar case. The opinion also cited Pennsylvania law which agreed with the decision and noted because of the ruling in *Kelo* that economic development was a "traditional and long accepted function of government."[64] Part of the reason the case was not dismissed earlier, Fischer noted, was that it began in state courts before the *Kelo* decision. Now that the case had been decided, *Whittaker* was decided in favor of economic redevelopment takings.

Another important case that relied on *Kelo* was the infamous case of *Goldstein v. Pataki* in 2008. The case began in 2007 when the owner of the New Jersey Nets basketball team offered to build a stadium in Brooklyn, New York, and transfer the team to the location. Such a massive influx of tax revenue would be, the city decided, a boon to both the city and population. The new multibillion-dollar project was to create "a new stadium for the New Jersey Nets, a public open space, the creation of affordable housing units and the redevelopment of an area in downtown Brooklyn afflicted for decades with substantial blight."[65] Fifteen plaintiffs, whose homes and businesses were going to be destroyed, banded together and brought suit against the state (under Governor George E. Pataki) alleging that the economic taking was merely a subterfuge for "enriching the private individual who proposed it [the development plan]."[66] Public use, the plaintiffs contended, was merely a pretext for a development plan. This echoed the sentiment of Justice O'Connor who wrote in her opinion:

> Even if there were a practical way to isolate the motives behind a given taking, the gesture toward a purpose test is theoretically flawed. If it is true that incidental public benefits from new private use are enough to ensure the "public purpose" in a taking, why should it matter, as far as the Fifth Amendment is concerned, what inspired the taking in the first place? How much the government does or does not desire to benefit a favored private party has no bearing on whether an economic development taking will or will not generate secondary benefit for the public. And whatever the reason for a given condemnation, the effect is the same from the constitutional perspective private-property is forcibly relinquished to new private ownership.[67]

Justice Kennedy thought that an economic plan was not necessarily a reason to scrutinize a taking. He wrote, "This [called for] demanding level of scrutiny, however, is not required simply because the purpose of the taking is economic development."[68] Both O'Connor and Kennedy took opposing approaches to economic takings, but because of the ruling in the majority,

Kennedy's approach prevailed. The opinion in *Pataki* by Chief Judge Katzman said:

> But both in doctrine and in practice, the primary mechanism for enforcing the public-use requirement has been the accountability of political officials to the electorate, not the scrutiny of the federal courts. Over the last century, reflecting the direction of Supreme Court case law, federal courts have had a much greater role in addressing what type of governmental action constitutes a taking and what level of compensation is just, leaving to legislatures to determine, in all but the most extreme cases, whether a taking fulfills the public-use requirement.[69]

The opinion pointed out that it was the political and electoral process that was in charge of defining public use—not the judges. This established the broad understanding of public use and the role of the state in the case, and further cemented the *Kelo* ruling. The New Jersey Nets basketball team officially changed its name to the Brooklyn Nets in 2012, and has moved into its new home, the $1 billion Barclay Arena, on Atlantic Ave.[70]

Another case that relied heavily upon *Kelo* was *Fideicomiso de la Tierra del Cano Martin Pena v. Fortuno* (2010), which took place in Puerto Rico. The Land Trust of the Martin Pena Canal had received land from government takings surrounding an old canal that ran through San Juan. Puerto Rican law established that the Trust would develop the canal using the land, and that such a development would "rehabilitate and revitalize the communities along its north and south banks" by implementing a publicly-agreed-to policy of "integrated development based on community empowerment."[71] The law also contained a provision that any land in the canal areas that were owned or managed by public agencies would be turned over to the Trust after 160 days. Five years after the Trust had received the land, little had been accomplished a new party controlled the legislature. As one of its first acts, the legislature passed another law transferring the land away from the Trust and back to the Commonwealth. The Trust sued in federal court, citing Fifth Amendment violations regarding public use. They claimed that lands which had been given to them for the project could not be taken away as there was no public use specified by the new legislature.[72]

The United States First Circuit Court of Appeals considered the matter and came down on the side of the Puerto Rican legislature. The Court came to the same conclusion about the broad interpretation of the Public Use Clause as *Kelo*, *Midkiff*, and *Pataki* had several years earlier. The opinion read:

> "Our review of whether a taking is for 'public use' is necessarily deferential: 'When the legislature's purpose is legitimate and its means are not irration-

> al, . . . empirical debates over the wisdom of takings . . . are not to be carried out in the federal courts.'"[73]

According to the reasoning, the Puerto Rican legislature could not be second-guessed in its assertion of public use. The opinion further pointed out that a taking was possible if a legislature was claiming public use—which by virtue of it being a legislature, could always be claimed a public use:

> This transfer to public ownership reflects the Commonwealth's judgment that the goals of rehabilitating and revitalizing the canal will be better served, and will be consistent with other missions of its public agencies, if these agencies, rather than the [land trust] and the Corporation, again hold and administer the lands in the canal area they once owned. There can be no doubt that [the new law's] transfer to public ownership is for "public use" under the Takings Clause.[74]

This was perhaps the first case to use takings to retake taken land from a development agency that acquired land by takings in the first place. The concurring opinion in the case, written by Judge Torruella, agreed, but clarified that *Kelo* was important to cite because "economic and community redevelopment are legitimate public purposes" according to the Supreme Court.[75]

The *Kelo* reasoning, especially on economic development as a public purpose (or use), has become popular in the courts. As mentioned before, states are beginning to use eminent domain in redevelopment schemes more since *Kelo* was passed. As a study in 2009 has shown, states with high levels of state debt, stronger ties to the Democratic Party, and little-to-no significant post-*Kelo* legislation, have used redevelopment takings than those with fewer.[76] Whether or not states will swing towards or away from *Kelo*-type takings is yet to be seen. Some states seem more prone to takings for economic redevelopment than others. However, it is clear that the issue has been decided in federal as well as state courts, with *Kelo* providing a precedent that so far has yet to be overturned. To overturn it would be, as Stevens said, "a fairly dramatic thing" because the Court would have "go back and overrule this whole line of cases."[77]

ACADEMIC BACKLASH

The use of the *Kelo* precedent has been large, and as with anything so large and popular (or unpopular), the academic backlash has been significant. Many of the articles have sided with Susette Kelo, including many of the law articles which have been written. A brief survey of the relevant literature and scholars in the field will be useful here.

The most vociferous spokesman against the decision in academia has been George Mason Law Professor Ilya Somin. Before the case was heard in the Supreme Court, Somin had written an amicus brief on behalf of legal scholar Jane Jacobs where he denounced economic takings as specifically harmful to minorities in the United States, and only if the Court enacted a categorical ban on economic takings would the clause be meaningful once more.[78] On the popular legal website *The Volokh Conspiracy*, Somin has over 180 articles, posts, and speeches mentioning *Kelo*. He has been a one-man army against the decision, and has traced the effects of the decision in various and sundry ways. In 2007, Somin wrote an article for the *Supreme Court Economic Review* that argued that unless a categorical ban was enacted on all economic takings, abuses would begin to grow and become widespread.[79] Noted previously, Somin also examined the post-*Kelo* legislation and found it to be alarmingly small. He noted the backlash was effectively over before 2009.[80] He continues to blog and give lectures about the dangers of the decision, and as recently as 2013 he gave a lecture at the University of Michigan Law School entitled "Property Rights Since *Kelo*."[81]

Another important scholar in the takings *Kelo* literature is New York University School of Law professor Richard A. Epstein. Epstein has been writing books for many years on legal matters, including a book still often used in law school classes entitled *Takings: Private Property and the Power of Eminent Domain* (1985).[82] The book criticized the Court's evolving understanding of the Takings Clause, and ended with a discussion of *Midkiff* in relation to the public use question. Before the oral argument in *Kelo*, Epstein helped pen the amicus curiae brief for the CATO Institute where he argued for a strict interpretation of the Takings Clause.[83]

Immediately after the decision, Epstein began to post numerous articles and appear in the media offering commentary on the decision. One scholar noted, "No scholar is more responsible than Richard Epstein himself for the national revulsion at New London's treatment of Ms. Kelo."[84] In 2008, he wrote an article entitled, "Public Use in a Post-*Kelo* World," where he argued that the decision would lead to a host of developers enriching themselves at the expense of the public. In the article, he advocated the Court return to a system of restrictions on public use akin to nuisance or restrictive covenants that already exist.[85]

In 2014, Epstein wrote *The Classical Liberal Constitution: The Uncertain Quest for Limited Government* which tackled an array of constitutional topics. He made an example of *Kelo* in his discussion of property law, noting, "The more ambitious systems of land planning cannot coexist with any sensible public use limitation."[86] Examining property cases where he left off in *Takings*, he takes special care to show that *Kelo* got it wrong, and that the Court's deference to state legislatures in determining what is a public use would create intrigue and abuse throughout the nation. It was too easy, he noted, for legislatures and governments to benefit themselves at the expense of the public with such limitless control over a natural right. Since *Kelo* was released, Epstein has once again become synonymous with takings law, and has given numerous lectures and written various entries on legal blogs as well as commenting in popular newspapers and magazines on the subject.[87]

Vanderbilt University law and history professor James W. Ely, wrote that the possibility of eminent domain reform was small at the national level, but that it was much greater at the state level. Although it would be difficult, there were many state avenues that could affect change much more efficiently, such as initiatives. Once legislative changes were made at the state level, judges could feel free to invoke state law. He wrote, "Constitutional challenges to eminent domain are most likely to find success in the state courts where judges are free to invoke state law."[88]

Other authors have noted problems with *Kelo* reform for a variety of different areas. Writing shortly after the decision in 2005, University of Virginia School of Law professor Julia D. Mahoney looked at the public reaction and possibility of reform through the political process. The justices were surrounded by the popular furor over *Kelo*, and this has led others to believe that the political process might be able to correct the problem (as Justice Stevens recommended in a speech to the Clark County Bar Association in 2005).[89] However, Mahoney found "the same forces that lead to dubious eminent domain practices in the first place may impede efforts to curb them."[90] Organized interest groups, wealthy corporations, and political powerful actors often have more political sway with legislators than the general public does, which means they are able to move more efficiently to stop economic redevelopment reform. Several of the amici dealt with this very problem.[91] Because of this, the political process might not produce the results desired by the public outcry, and the Supreme Court might have the chance to reexamine *Kelo* soon.[92]

Scholar Andrew P. Morriss also noticed a stunted state reaction in his 2009 article, and his findings largely agree with Mahoney's. Legislators can use eminent domain as a tool for economic growth, and while this continues, popular reform will not be able to stamp out economic redevelopment takings. He wrote:

> [A]lthough *Kelo* revealed that eminent domain was unpopular with the public at large, there remained an important constituency that supports its use: government officials. Its supporters see eminent domain as a "vital economic development tool" for state and local governments, allowing important redevelopment projects to take place and potentially saving local communities from economic decline or worse.[93]

Bruce L. Benson and Matthew Brown (2010) have argued that many of the arguments and national reforms are moot because it is almost always the state and local governments acting under state law. Since the *Kelo* opinion interpreted heavily on the side of police powers, reforms must be made at that level.[94]

Apart from reaction from, and reform to, several scholars have focused on the philosophy behind the reasoning itself. Scholar Steven J. Eagle (2010) noted that the Court's notion of takings in the decision was rooted in the Progressive notion that redevelopment and urban planning was a better and more effective way to achieve ends of equality over the standard market practice.[95] Attorney Scott J. Bullock, who argued the case before the Supreme Court, has written that state economic redevelopment, although the basis behind the decision, has had a dismal record in almost all states, and is counterproductive to economic reform.[96] Law student Joseph Blocher (2006) demonstrated Bullock's assertion in a case study surrounding a hotel in New Haven, Connecticut in 2004.[97]

Scholars Peter J. Boettke, Christopher J. Coyne, and Peter T. Leeson noted in 2010 that *Kelo* was dangerous because it allowed the government to bypass the market in favor of unfair competition.[98] Proposing an answer to the market problem, scholars Amnon Lehavi and Amir N. Licht (2007) proposed redevelopment reform that would offer the condemned the choice of pre-project fair market value as just compensation, or pro-rata shares in the redevelopment corporation.[99] In other words, the fair market value would be understood more as the function of the land, not simply the price of the structure upon it.

Partisan advocacy groups have also published their reaction. The Institute for Justice has taken up the fight personally after Kelo lost the decision. Attorney Scott J. Bullock who had been employed by the Institute even before the case, has rallied other lawyers and academics around eminent domain reform. In an article entitled "Five Years After *Kelo*: The Sweeping Backlash Against One of the Supreme Court's Most-Despised Decisions" (2010), the Institute described the outrage American citizens had at the decision and how cities around the nation were suffering.[100] The conservative journal *American Thinker* ran an article entitled "The Aftermath of the *Kelo* Ruling" (2006) which highlighted the ongoing abuses of the eminent domain since the decision permitted them to occur.[101] The conservative Heritage Foundation has also released several articles advocating action and tracking changes in eminent domain laws, including an article by Ronald D. Utt entitled: "States Vote to Strengthen Property Rights" (2007).[102] Not every partisan group speaks exclusively for conservatives, however, and author Erik Kain recently wrote in *Forbes*, "Government should not be in the business of cronyism and theft, and liberals should be up in arms when government enriches private corporations at the expense of ordinary citizens."[103]

Several scholars have come out in favor of the decision. Abraham Bell and Gideon Parchomovsky (2006) wrote that the preference for a strict interpretation of public use was the more dangerous threat. Only by enlarging the government's economic development power could citizens be safe from more intrusive takings that the government would employ if stymied by a narrow interpretation. They wrote,

> Paradoxically, therefore, the broad reading of public use affirmed in Kelo is necessary to preserve the best case scenario for private property owners. Limiting the ability of government to use eminent domain to further economic goals will not prevent the government from using its more invasive powers to inflict identical harms on private property rights, but without compensation. Contrary to public sentiment, then, eminent domain should be seen as the least offensive of government's property-related powers.[104]

Pace University School of Law professor John R. Nolon published an article in 2007 called "The Mighty Myths of *Kelo*." His argument centered on the popular myth that *Kelo* was a *carte blanche* to all cities to simply employ takings as they pleased. He argued that instead of helping legislators, the public reaction, bad press, and more stringent laws which were introduced in some states, would prove harmful to most cities. Specifically in the areas of land management, environment, and disaster relief, the states would now be forced to think of other, more dangerous and invasive means to accomplish their tasks.[105]

Considering federalism and eminent domain laws after *Kelo*, Yale Law School professor Robert C. Ellickson (2009) noted that increased power to the states in a federal system would create a market for eminent domain laws (competitive federalism) and citizens could vote with their feet. In other words, viewing the federal system as a market, experimental to produce the greatest goods, would be useful in the case of economic takings because if citizens did not like the eminent domain laws of the state, they were free to leave or vote to change the laws. In this way, states would act as laboratories, and citizen reaction would help states better understand their citizens' preferences on the limits of the takings power.[106]

Published in the *Yale Law Journal* in 2014, several scholars addressed the shifting interpretations and meaning of federalism in the modern era. While these scholars did not focus on property rights, they addressed the larger concerns over the interpretation of federalism in the modern era. In her summary article, Heather K. Gerken of Yale Law School noted that federalism has indeed shifted towards a stronger national government, but that federalism had evolved and states now work towards the national ends of democracy and popular deliberation. Although state sovereignty has become much weaker than national power, it is still able to be instrumental in helping the federal government achieve its ends. Instead of lamenting the loss of sovereignty, scholars and citizens should understand the new federalism as a system in which states are able to participate with the federal government in fostering democratic decision making with an eye towards national debates.[107]

Each of these authors' articles contained much more information than such a short literature review could possibly provide. Indeed, the amount of scholarship and ideas could fill several volumes While much of the literature is against the *Kelo* decision and the problems it has created, each of the articles, and many more not listed here, are helpful in gauging academics' varied reactions to the case. Academics represent a specific type of commentator, and to take them seriously might produce solutions to problems yet to come. Each of these articles contains a unique way to examine the case, and as future economic takings cases arise, they will likely continue to be useful.

PERSONAL BACKLASH

The case took the hardest toll on those personally involved. Unlike the academics, politicians, and journalists, those who were on the front lines of the fight were deeply affected. Some were more affected than others. Justice Stevens has been continually lambasted by his friends and the media over the ruling until he retired in 2011. He spoke candidly in an interview after his retirement: "I had people at a bridge game stop me and ask, 'How could you have written that opinion? We thought you were a good judge, but we learned otherwise.'"[108] As mentioned before, he acknowledged that the *Kelo* decision was the most unpopular decision he had ever made. The *Economist* called it the *worst* decision he ever made.[109] Stevens said that although the case gave stronger police powers to redevelopment forces, he ultimately believed that market forces would produce better results when dealing with a depressed city. In a speech given to the Clark County Bar Association in 2005, he said:

> My own view is that the allocation of economic resources that result from the free play of market forces is more likely to produce acceptable results in the long run than the best-intentioned plans of public officials. But, as Justice Holmes famously observed in his dissent in the *Lochner* case, the Constitution did not enact Mr. Herbert Spencer's "Social Statics." Time and again judges who truly believe in judicial restraint have avoided the powerful temptation to impose their views of *sound economic theory* on the policy choices of local legislators.[110]

Stevens has never backed down and has always stuck by his ruling as the correct one.

Other justices have continued to speak out against the decision, such as Scalia, or have since left the Court, such as O'Connor and Souter. Interestingly, shortly after the decision was released in June 2005, a group of angry citizens began a grassroots campaign to tear down Justice Souter's New Hampshire barn in order to put a more economically viable hotel in its place. The hotel was to be called the "Lost Liberty Inn" and would have featured a museum devoted to eminent domain abuse. Although popular at the time, the threat never materialized, and the idea was dropped.[111]

The head attorney in the case representing the petitioners, and the most prominent legal figure aside from the justices, Scott J. Bullock continued to fight the case in different ways after the decision was handed down. Working through the Institute for Justice, Bullock began taking measures the moment the public was aware of the decision. He called media outlets, organized protests in New London and elsewhere, and assisted Susette Kelo through the rigors of speaking before a Senate Committee and host of news reporters.[112] He is still currently a practicing attorney, and an active and contributing member of the Institute. He has organized and spoken at several conferences, and continues to author articles on eminent domain and the *Kelo* case.

The NLDC came under heavy fire immediately. The corporation had been portrayed negatively throughout the eight-year process, and because of this they sought to quickly evict Kelo and her neighbors from the neighborhood, but were met with waves of protests in front of their offices, the city hall, and around the nation. Governor Jodi Rell began to see the political nature of the problem. Although the previous governor had funded and worked with the NLDC's plans for New London, the post-*Kelo* decision made Rell fearful of the backlash. She issued a press release where she extolled the virtues of property ownership and denounced the Supreme Court decision. Rell withdrew support for the NLDC from the Office of the Governor.[113]

After hearing of the governor's defection, the NLDC began to act quickly. The President of the NLDC, Admiral Dave Goebel (ret.), sent out investigators to dig up scandal on Susette Kelo personally. Once this happened, Kelo and her neighbors staged a protest in front of Goebel's personal residence on a Sunday afternoon where he was entertaining guests. Thanks to her connections and popularity, the crowd swelled to an immense size. At one point another of her neighbors drove up in a Humvee dressed like General George S. Patton, egging the crowd on. Goebel could legally do nothing to stop the rally. After the crowd had gone away, the NLDC began sending out eviction notices immediately. Eviction notices were rescinded and issued again over the next several months.

The governor finally got involved, not wanting to see the investment ($70 million) go to waste. A mediator was called to help work out the problem. Perhaps the most significant blow came in September 2005 when the City of New London, with a persistent crowd of protestors outside city hall, voted 6–0 to cut ties with the NLDC. The NLDC forced Goebel to resign in exchange for the city's reinstatement of the NLDC.[114] Over the next year, the NLDC continued its negotiations with the neighbors and the protestors, and finally received the backing of Governor Rell again. She had had enough of the political drama, and in order to speed the up the process, she offered much more than fair-market value to the holdout neighbors in return for their cooperation. Eventually, one by one, they all left. In the end, the NLDC was able to remove each of the residents, including Susette Kelo, but its reputation was forever tarnished. In November 2009, several years after the neighborhood was cleared, the crown jewel of the project, the Pfizer Corporation, announced it would not build its new headquarters in New London.[115] The site was abandoned, and now stands an empty field where locals dump their trash and feral cats occupy the once promising lots.[116]

As of 2012, the mayor of New London, Daryl Finizio, announced that the NLDC would be changing its name to the Renaissance City Development Association. The *New London Patch* reported that the mayor also said, "the change will also include updates, revisions, and expansions of the organization's strategic plan and mission statement," but that it "will remain a community-based not-for-profit organization."[117] The mayor also mentioned the resignation of Michael Joplin, the NLDC's president after Goebel, and a restructuring that would only allow for the city, not any other agency or corporation, to exercise the power of eminent domain.[118]

The City of New London continues to suffer under its own problems. Recent statistics are grim. People living below the poverty line are at 17.9%, which is higher than the national average by nearly 3%. The median income was $45,509 in 2011, which was lower than the national average by $7,000, and lower than Connecticut's average by $23,000.[119] As is expected with such numbers, the crime rate is also rising in New London. In 2011, both murders and assaults were the highest they had been in over a decade, and thefts, burglaries, and rapes were all higher than the national average.[120] In short, for all of the case's deference to city planners, sympathetic legislatures, and advanced economic forecasters, the city remains in worse shape than it was a decade ago. Perhaps some of this can be blamed on the popular reaction (especially in the case of Pfizer leaving), but this has always been a tension in popular government: experts and administrators against the public. For New London the tension continues to breed poverty and crime.

As for Susette Kelo, the main player in the whole affair, her life was forever changed. From the moment the decision was handed down, she was actively involved in protesting and fighting the decision using any legal means (which failed with the decision) or political means (through protests, testimony, and public speaking) she could. When she testified before the Senate, and later the House of Representatives, she began in the same way, "I am the Kelo in *Kelo v. City of New London*."[121] One of the justices from the Connecticut Supreme Court, Richard Palmer, found Kelo at a private gathering and personally apologized to her for all of the trouble the decision had caused.[122] At one point, talks were being made to have a film made of the affair starring Brooke Shields as Susette Kelo.[123] As of 2013, no more word of the film has been mentioned.

Kelo found herself the spokesperson for private property owners throughout the nation. She and her neighbors ardently fought the city and NLDC after the decision, and Kelo personally made speeches on radio and television programs. After the decision was handed down, the city gave her a final date to leave her house before the bulldozers came in. The Fox News program Hannity & Colmes came out to her house, along with scores of other media, and set up in front of her house, waiting to see what would happen. Hannity asked Kelo, "Did you ever dream that one day you'd have a landmark Supreme Court decision with your name on it?" Kelo soberly replied, "It's more like a living nightmare than a dream."[124]

In the end, Kelo was left with one neighbor, Michael Cristofaro, in her holdout against the NLDC. Once she realized her neighborhood would never be full of the same people who had fought the battle with her, she decided to reach a compromise with the city. The compromise reached was one of the strangest in American legal history. After a lengthy discussion in June 2006 with mediators, Kelo had the idea of the city paying for her home to go with her. Slat-by-slat, and brick-by-brick, the little pink house she had renovated and protected was moved to a lot across the Thames River to the City of Groton. Overlooking the same waterfront, Kelo found a lot for sale by an owner who recognized her as "the lady from right over there."[125] Along with a sizeable monetary settlement, Kelo relocated, and as promised, the house was rebuilt in June 2008.[126] The house still stands, and Kelo still lives in it, with one minor change: a large sign on the front which reads in prominent lettering: The Kelo House.[127]

CONCLUSION

The Court's decision in *Kelo* set off a storm that consumed the nation for a very brief time.[128] The media was launched into a frenzy, making the plight of Kelo and her neighbors national news. Polls and protests showed that much of the nation was behind Kelo. However, as with many democratic furies, it quickly cooled, and in the end the decision was abandoned and forgotten. The political backlash largely mirrored the public's temperament. The Founders understood that ultimately personal ambition would animate public officials to follow the crowds, and state and federal legislators acted in largely the same way their constituents did. They cooled as their constituents cooled. With exception of a few legislators who still fight against economic redevelopment takings and *Kelo*, the matter has recently been met with tepidity in legislatures.

The Supreme Court set a precedent for redevelopment takings in *Kelo* that has been consistently followed until the present day. Both the courts at the national and state levels continue to use it, some to a higher degree than others. The decision did not spark a furious increase in takings, but it has shown society the sometimes-dichotomous limits of private ownership and community. The case served to reinforce the broad understanding of public use from both *Berman* and *Midkiff.* Whether the decision will be overturned is yet to be seen, but at the present time it continues to define public use, police powers, and the legal interpretation of the Fifth Amendment.

The academic backlash has been large, with both sides being covered from every angle. Much, but not all, of the academic literature has criticized the ruling as well as offered new solutions to the problem of economic takings. Partisans, think tanks, bloggers, as well as law professors and political scientists have weighed in on the decision. Academic scholarship tends to hold on to matters long after they cease to be popular, and it will be fascinating to see where it leads many years from now.

It would be difficult to say that Susette Kelo won the battle against eminent domain. Then again, she kept her house, received a very generous compensatory sum, and brought New London, the NLDC, and state public officials to the bargaining table. To this day, her neighborhood in Fort Trumbull stands empty as a tribute to the battle once waged there. Whether that is justice for the citizens in the still-depressed city of New London is another matter, but one that must be taken seriously. After almost a decade after the *Kelo* affair, the City of New London still remains in bad shape. As far as winners and losers go, *Kelo* is in the eye of the beholder.

NOTES

1. See chapter 4.
2. Main, *Bulldozed,* 175. This ironically fulfilled Stevens' hopes for the states to satiate the public outcry at the decision. At the end of the majority opinion he wrote, "We emphasize that nothing in our opinion precludes any State from placing further restrictions on its exercise of the takings power." (*Kelo v. New London,* 545 U.S. 469 (2005)).
3. Howard Troxler, "High Court Takes Fifth, Proceeds to Ruin It," *St. Petersburg Times,* June 28, 2005, B1.
4. Those who have left the bench since the *Kelo* decision were: Rehnquist (2005), O'Connor (2006), Souter (2009), and Stevens (2010).
5. Main, *Bulldozed,* 175.
6. "Stealing Home: Letting Government Take Property for Development Risks Abuse," *Houston Chronicle*, July 25, 2005, accessed May 3, 2013, http://www.chron.com/opinion/editorials/article/Stealing-home-Letting-government-take-property-1953507.php.
7. Todd Jackson, "Private—keep off: aftershocks of Kelo v. city of New London," *The Roanoke Times*, July 18, 2005, accessed May 20, 2013, http://ww2.roanoke.com//news/roanoke%5c27712.html.
8. Jeff Jacoby, "Eminent Injustice in New London," *The Boston Globe*, June 26, 2005, accessed May 3, 2013, http://www.boston.com/news/globe/editorial_opinion/oped/articles/2005/06/26/eminent_injustice_in_new_london/.

9. Avi Salzman and Laura Manseurs, "For Homeowners, Frustration and Anger at Court Ruling," *The New York Times*, June 24, 2005, accessed September 12, 2012, http://www.nytimes.com/2005/06/24/national/24newlondon.html?_r=0.

10. Main, *Bulldozed*, 175.

11. Les Christie, "Taking your home away," *CNN/Money*, August 3, 2005, accessed May 3, 2013, http://money.cnn.com/2005/07/25/real_estate/investment_prop/eminent_domain_v_development/.

12. Kyle Scott, *The Price of Politics: Lessons from Kelo v. New London,* (New York: Rowman & Littlefield, 2009), 125.

13. Benedict, *Little Pink House*, 262.

14. Scott, *The Price of Politics*, 128.

15. Ibid., 128.

16. Ibid., 122–30 (esp. 127–28).

17. Cf. chapter 6.

18. Main, *Bulldozed*, 174.

19. Christie, "Taking your home away."

20. "Poll: Readers favor eminent domain restrictions," *Jacksonville Business Journal*, April 25, 2006, accessed May 3, 2013, http://www.bizjournals.com/jacksonville/stories/2006/04/24/daily10.html.

21. Somin, "The Limits of Backlash," 104.

22. Janice Nadler, Shari Seidman Diamond and Matthew M. Patton, "Government Takings of Private Property: Kelo and the Perfect Storm in Public Opinion and Constitutional Controversy," in *Public Opinion and Constitutional Controversy*, eds. Nathaniel Persily, Jack Citrin, and Patrick Egan (New York: Oxford University Press Inc., 2008), Kindle Edition.

23. John Paul Stevens, "Judicial Predilections," *Nevada Law Journal* 6, (2005): 4.

24. Publius, *Federalist No. 57, The Avalon Project*, February 19, 1788, accessed May 31, 2013, http://avalon.law.yale.edu/18th_century/fed57.asp.

25. Benedict, *Little Pink House*, 346.

26. "Testimony of Susette Kelo," United States Senate Committee of the Judiciary, September 20, 2005, accessed October 15, 2012, http://www.judiciary.senate.gov/hearings/testimony.cfm?id=e655f9e2809e5476862f735da10a78d5&wit_id=e655f9e2809e5476862f735da10a78d5-2-1.

27. Jess Bravin, "Justice Stevens on His 'Most Unpopular Opinion'," *Wall Street Journal*, November 11, 2011, accessed May 31, 2013, http://online.wsj.com/article/SB10001424052970204358004577032071046475782.html.

28. Ibid.

29. See also Nadler, Diamond, and Patton, "Government Takings of Private Property," 287–310.

30. "Statement of The Honorable Patrick Leahy," United States Senate Committee of the Judiciary, September 20, 2005, accessed October 15, 2012, http://www.judiciary.senate.gov/hearings/testimony.cfm?id=e655f9e2809e5476862f735da10a78d5&wit_id=e655f9e2809e5476862f735da10a78d5-0-2.

31. "Statement of The Honorable John Coryn," United States Senate Committee of the Judiciary, September 20, 2005, accessed October 15, 2012, http://www.judiciary.senate.gov/hearings/testimony.cfm?id=e655f9e2809e5476862f735da10a78d5&wit_id=e655f9e2809e5476862f735da10a78d5-0-0.

32. Benedict, *Little Pink House*, 347.

33. Ibid., 347.

34. S. 1895—*109th Congress: Private Property Rights Protection Act.* (2005), accessed June 2, 2013, from http://www.govtrack.us/congress/bills/109/s1895.

35. Somin, 121.

36. S. 48—*110th Congress: Private Property Rights Protection Act.* (2007), accessed May 31, 2013, from http://www.govtrack.us/congress/bills/110/s48.

37. S. 3873—*109th Congress: Private Property Rights Protection Act of 2006.* (2006). accessed May 21, 2013, http://www.govtrack.us/congress/bills/109/s387.

38. H.R. 3135—*109th Congress: Private Property Rights Protection Act of 2005*. (2005). accessed May 21, 2013, from http://www.govtrack.us/congress/bills/109/hr3135.

39. S. 3873—*109th Congress: Private Property Rights Protection Act of 2006*. (2006). accessed May 21, 2013, http://www.govtrack.us/congress/bills/109/s387; S. 48—*110th Congress: Private Property Rights Protection Act*. (2007), accessed May 31, 2013, from http://www.govtrack.us/congress/bills/110/s48; S. 3873—*109th Congress: Private Property Rights Protection Act of 2006*. (2006). accessed May 21, 2013, http://www.govtrack.us/congress/bills/109/s387; and H.R. 3135—*109th Congress: Private Property Rights Protection Act of 2005*. (2005). accessed May 21, 2013, from http://www.govtrack.us/congress/bills/109/hr3135.

40. Somin, "The Limits of Backlash," 124.

41. Ibid., 124.

42. "Testimony of Susette Kelo," United States House Committee on the Judiciary, Subcommittee on the Constitution and Civil Justice, April 18, 2013, accessed May 31, 2013, http://judiciary.house.gov/hearings/113th/04182013/Kelo.pdf.

43. H.R. 1944—*113th Congress: Private Property Rights Protection Act of 2013* (2013), accessed June 2, 2013, from http://www.govtrack.us/congress/bills/113/hr194.

44. Somin, "The Limits of Backlash," 110.

45. Ibid., 110.

46. Ibid., 110–11.

47. Harvey M. Jacobs and Ellen M. Bassett, "All Sound, No Fury? The Impacts of State-Based *Kelo* Laws," *Planning and Environmental Law* 63, (2011): 7.

48. Ibid., 7.

49. Scott, *The Price of Politics*, 132–45.

50. Bullock, "The Inadequacy of the Planning Process," 92–94.

51. Stephen Greenhut. "Redevelopment Resurrection?" May 23, 2014, *City Journal*, accessed May 23, 2014, http://www.city-journal.org/2014/cjc0523sg.html.

52. Adam Summers. "Master of Your Domain: The Impact of the *Kelo* Decision," June 26, 2006, *Reason Foundation*, accessed May 30, 2013, http://reason.org/news/show/122529.html.

53. See also Steven J. Eagle. "Assembling Land for Urban Redevelopment: The Case for Owner Participation," *Property Rights: Eminent Domain and Regulatory Takings Re-Examined*, Bruce L. Benson ed., (New York: Palgrave Macmillan, 2010), 7–26.

54. Ibid., 132.

55. Bravin, "Justice Stevens," November 11, 2011.

56. Some of these cases include: *Fideicomiso de la Tierra del Cano Martin Pena v. Fortuno* (2010), *Caribbean Airport Facilities, Inc. v. Vazquez* (2013), *Priolo v. Town of Kingston* (2012), *Garcia-Rubiera v. Fortuño* (2010), *Goldstein v. Pataki* (2007, 2008), *Buffalo Teachers Fed'n v. Tobe* (2005), *Didden v. Vill. of Port Chester* (2006), *Faith Temple Church v. Town of Brighton Whittaker v. County of Lawrence*, 674 F. Supp. 2d 668 (Dist. Court, WD Pennsylvania 2009), among many, many others.

57. *Haywood v. Curtis* 555 U.S. 729 (2009) (Thomas, J., dissenting).

58. Ibid.

59. *Vartelas v. Holder*, 566 U.S. ___ (2012) (Scalia, J., dissenting).

60. Ibid.

61. Debra Cassens Weiss, "Scalia Lumps Kelo Decision with Dred Scott and Roe v. Wade" *ABA Journal*, October 19, 2011, accessed May 30, 2013.

62. *Whittaker v. County of Lawrence*, 674 F.Supp.2d 668 (Dist. Court, WD Pennsylvania 2009).

63. Ibid.

64. Ibid., quoting *Kelo v. New London* (2005).

65. *Goldstein v. Pataki*, 516 F.3d 50 (2d Cir. 2008).

66. Ibid.

67. *Kelo v. New London*, 545 U.S. 469 (2005) (O'Connor, J., dissenting).

68. *Kelo v. New London*, 545 U.S. 469 (2005) (Kennedy, J., dissenting).

69. *Goldstein v. Pataki*, 516 F.3d 50 (2d Cir. 2008).

70. Michael McCarthy, "First Look: Inside Brooklyn Nets new $1 billion Arena," *USA Today*, May 22, 2012, accessed May 30, 2013, http://content.usatoday.com/communities/game-

on/post/2012/05/first-look-inside-the-brooklyn-nets-new-arena-barclays-center-nba-bruce-ratner-jay-z/1#.U4tjasamBg0.

71. *Fideicomiso de la Tierra del Cano Martin Pena v. Fortuno* 604 F.3d 7 (1st Cir. 2010).

72. Ibid.

73. Ibid., quotations citing *Midkiff.*

74. Ibid.

75. Ibid. (Torruella, J., concurring).

76. Scott, *The Price of Politics*, 119–32.

77. Bravin, "Justice Stevens," November 11, 2011.

78. Brief of Amica Curiae for Jane Jacobs, *Kelo v. New London*. No 04-108. FindLaw.com, Accessed October 2, 2012. supreme.lp.findlaw.com/supreme_court/docket/2004/February.html#04-108.

79. Ilya Somin, "Controlling the Grasping Hand: Economic Development Takings after Kelo," *Supreme Court Economic Review* 15 (2007):183–271.

80. Somin, "*The Limits of Backlash*," 121.

81. Ilya Somin, "University of Michigan Law School Talk on Property Rights Since *Kelo*," *The Volokh Conspiracy*, March 7, 2013, accessed May 30, 2013, http://www.volokh.com/2013/03/07/university-of-michigan-law-school-talk-on-property-rights-since-kelo/.

82. Epstein, *Takings*.

83. Brief of Amicus Curiae for The CATO Institute, *Kelo v. New London*, No 04-108 (found at FindLaw.com, supreme.lp.findlaw.com/supreme_court/docket/2004/February.html#04-108).

84. Robert C. Ellickson, "Federalism and *Kelo*: A Question for Richard Epstein," *Tulsa Law Review* 44 (2009): 763.

85. Richard A. Epstein, "Public Use in a Post-*Kelo* World," *Supreme Court Economic Review* 17 (2009): 151–71.

86. Richard Epstein, *The Classical Liberal Constitution: The Uncertain Quest for Limited Government.* (Cambridge: Harvard University Press, 2014), 358.

87. Cf. Richard Sincere, "Richard Epstein notes how Kelo sparked more scrutiny of eminent domain," Examiner.com, January 7, 2012, accessed October 12, 2013, http://www.examiner.com/article/richard-epstein-notes-how-kelo-sparked-more-scrutiny-of-eminent-domain; and Richard A. Epstein, "Supreme Folly," *Wall Street Journal*, June 27, 2005, accessed May 30, 2013, http://online.wsj.com/article/0,,SB111982975240969952,00.html?mod=opinion&ojcontent=otep.

88. James W. Ely, Jr., "Post-*Kelo* Reform: Is the Glass Half Full of Half Empty?" *Supreme Court Economic Review* 17 (2009): 127–50.

89. Stevens, "Judicial Predilections," 4.

90. Julia D. Mahoney, "Kelo's Legacy: Eminent Domain and the Future of Property Rights," *The Supreme Court Review* 2005 (2005): 126.

91. Cf. the discussion of amici briefs for West Harlem Business Group, Develop Don't Destroy (Brooklyn) Inc., and The Becket Fund for Religious Liberty in chapter 3.

92. Ibid., 132–33.

93. Andrew P. Morriss, "Symbol or Substance? An Empirical Assessment of State Reponses to Kelo," *Supreme Court Economic Review* 17 (2009), 237–78, 241.

94. Bruce L. Benson and Matthew Brown, "Eminent Domain for Private Use: Is it Justified by Market Failure or an Example of Government Failure?" in *Property Rights: Eminent Domain and Regulatory Takings Re-Examined*, ed. Bruce L. Benson (New York: Palgrave Macmillan, 2010), 149–72.

95. Eagle, "Assembling Land for Urban Redevelopment," 7–26.

96. Bullock, "The Inadequacy of the Planning Process," 89–100.

97. Joseph Blocher, "Private Business as Public Good: Hotel Development and *Kelo*," *Yale Law & Policy Review* 24 (2006): 363–97.

98. Peter J. Boettke, Christopher J. Coyne, and Peter T. Leeson, "Land Grab: Takings, the Market Process, and Regime Uncertainty," in *Property Rights: Eminent Domain and Regulatory Takings Re-Examined*, ed. Bruce L. Benson's (New York: Palgrave Macmillan, 2010), 173–86.

99. Amnon Lehavi and Amir N. Licht, "Eminent Domain, Inc.," *Columbia Law Review* 107 (2007), 1704–48.

100. "Five Years After *Kelo*: The Sweeping Backlash Against One of the Supreme Court's Most-Despised Decisions," *Institute for Justice*, 2010, accessed May 1, 2013, http://www.ij.org/five-years-after-kelo-the-sweeping-backlash-against-one-of-the-supreme-courts-most-despised-decisions.

101. Janet Levy, "The Aftermath of the *Kelo* Ruling," *American Thinker*, June 28, 2006, accessed May 1, 2013, http://www.americanthinker.com/2006/06/the_aftermath_of_the_kelo_ruli.html.

102. Ronald D. Utt, "States Vote to Strengthen Property Rights," *Heritage Foundation*. February 1, 2007, accessed May 31, 2013, http://www.heritage.org/research/reports/2007/02/states-vote-to-strengthen-property-rights.

103. Erik Kain, "Liberals should be Upset by the Kelo Case," September 15, 2011, *Forbes*, accessed May 13, 2013, http://www.forbes.com/sites/erikkain/2011/09/15/liberals-should-be-anti-kelo/.

104. Abraham Bell and Gideon Parchomovsky, "The Uselessness of Public Use," *Columbia Law Review* 106 (2006): 1416.

105. John R. Nolon, "The Mighty Myths of *Kelo*," *Government, Law, and Policy Journal* 9 (2009): 10–15.

106. Ellickson, "Federalism and *Kelo*," 751, 762–63.

107. Heather K. Gerken, "Federalism as the New Nationalism: An Overview," *Yale Law Journal* 123 (2014): 1889.

108. Bravin, "Justice Stevens."

109. Lexington, "The Worst Decision of Justice Stevens."

110. Stevens, "Judicial Predilections," *Nevada Law Journal* 6 (2005): 4.

111. David de Sola, "Souter's Home an Activist Target," *CNN*, January 22, 2006, accessed May 13, 2013, http://www.cnn.com/2006/LAW/01/21/eminent.domain/.

112. Benedict, *Little Pink House*, 322–247.

113. Ibid., 331–32.

114. Ibid., 323–82.

115. Patrick McGeehan, "Pfizer to Leave City that Won the Land Use Case," *The New York Times*, November 12, 2009, accessed May 30, 2013, http://www.nytimes.com/2009/11/13/nyregion/13pfizer.html?_r=0.

116. Kerry Picket, "PICKET: '05 Kelo Decision a Failure; CT site remains a dump," *The Washington Times*, accessed May 30, 2013, http://www.washingtontimes.com/blog/watercooler/2011/sep/3/picket-05-kelo-decision-failure-ct-site-remains-du/.

117. Dirk Langeveld, "Mayor Announces Reorganization of NLDC," *New London Patch*, April 26, 2012, accessed October 9, 2012, http://newlondon.patch.com/groups/politics-and-elections/p/mayor-announces-reorganization-of-nldc.

118. Ibid.

119. 2010 U.S. Census, accessed May 1, 2014 (http://ci.new-london.ct.us).

120. "Crime Rates in New London by Year," *City-Data.com*, accessed May 31, 2013, http://www.city-data.com/crime/crime-New-London-Connecticut.html.

121. "Testimony of Susette Kelo," *United States House Committee of the Judiciary*, September 20, 2005, accessed May 1, 2014, http://judiciary.house.gov/_files/hearings/113th/04182013/Kelo.pdf.

122. Debra Cassens Weiss, "Connecticut Justice Apologized to Kelo Plaintiff at a Private Gathering," September 14, 2011, *ABAJournal*, accessed May 31, 2013, http://www.abajournal.com/news/article/connecticut_justice_apologized_to_kelo_plaintiff_at_a_private_gathering/.

123. Debra Cassens Weiss. "Brooke Shields to Star in TV Movie Chronicling Kelo Eminent Domain Case." September 20, 2011, *ABAJournal*, accessed May 31, 2013, http://www.abajournal.com/news/article/brooke_shields_to_star_in_tv_movie_chronicling_kelo_eminent_domain_case/.

124. Benedict, *Little Pink House*, 362.

125. Ibid., 375.

126. Scott Bullock, “Not For Sale,” June 23, 2008, *Reason.com*, accessed May 31, 2013, http://reason.com/archives/2008/06/23/not-for-sale.
127. Benedict, *Little Pink House*, 374.
128. Nadler, Diamond, and Patton, “Government Takings of Private Property.”

Chapter Nine

Conclusion

In the 1964 film *Goldfinger*, Ian Fleming's James Bond discovers a secret plan to destroy the nation's gold in Fort Knox using an atomic bomb. Prisoner of the criminal mastermind, Auric Goldfinger, Bond desperately racks his brain for a way to stop the device. Tensely yet leisurely conversing over mint juleps at Goldfinger's sprawling Kentucky estate, Bond asks for the specific details about the plan:

BOND

Brilliant. But the atomic device, as you call it, is already, obviously in this country.

GOLDFINGER

Obviously.

BOND

But bringing it to Fort Knox, uh, undetected could be risky—very risky.

GOLDFINGER

Oh the contrary, Mister Bond. The risk is all on your side. If the authorities should attempt to locate it, who knows where it might be exploded, eh? Perhaps the Polaris submarine pens at New London . . .[1]

Despite the fictional Goldfinger's threat, no atomic bomb was ever detonated in New London. Previously, New London had always been on the forefront of the national consciousness because of its nuclear submarine base. Ironically, it was only after the base closed that the Supreme Court dropped a political bomb that would explode in popular furor and drastically alter the landscape of property rights all across the nation. *Kelo v. New London* engulfed both the city and the entire nation for almost a year and had a lasting effect on Americans' minds the likes of which only a Bond-like supervillain could imagine. The case heightened the intense suspicion of citizens against the power of their own government, and although the protests and rallies have died out, there is still an undercurrent of suspicion that seems to sit just beneath the surface waiting to explode once more.

The decision in *Kelo* was not completely unexpected or shocking, nor did it overturn any Supreme Court precedent over the past one hundred years. However, the decision did bring the takings issue back into focus for many Americans. *Kelo* reminded them that they were not insulated from government taking their land for public use—whatever that phrase's interpretation might be. Most Americans did not like the interpretation of the Public Use Clause to include economic takings because many saw it as a tyrannical attack on private property. As has been shown, the new interpretation was not wholly novel but had its roots in precedent. Whether those roots were rotten is something still debated, but it is difficult to deny that the case came from a historically broad interpretation of the Fifth Amendment that has continued for decades.

In a very real sense, the public was not in an uproar over the new interpretation but instead what had been going on over the past century. Hotly criticized and loudly debated, the furor quickly dissipated, and the decision faded back into the shadows. The eminent domain landscape has hardly changed in most states and has not changed at all at the federal level. Bloggers and interest groups (such as the Institute for Justice) still rally citizens to change the laws, but the effects have varied across the nation.

The larger questions raised by the case are numerous: Did *Kelo* cement and embolden a more central-planning-friendly government? Did it highlight a doctrinal rift between ruler and ruled? Is defining the meaning of public use under the Fifth Amendment a police power? Should an interpretation of the Takings Clause be left to the states? Is economic redevelopment a valid public use? The majority issued its own answers to these questions, but as shown, the citizens have largely rejected the ruling.

PUBLIC USE AND THE FIFTH AMENDMENT

Without question, the largest contribution of the ruling was to the modern understanding of public use. The Court's ever-broadening interpretation of the Public Use Clause was further defined in *Kelo*. Despite what Justice O'Connor wrote, the precedent seems to have been pointing towards the decision for some time, beginning in the late nineteenth century. As the justices noted in their respective opinions, the new interpretation of public use began with *Fallbrook* in 1896 with the clause being reinterpreted as "public purpose." Following *Fallbrook* were *Clark* and *Strickley*, which further solidified and even broadened the *Fallbrook* interpretation of public purpose. In *Clark*, Justice Peckham noted that the definition of public use could change with time and place, saying that "what is a public use may frequently and largely depend upon the facts surrounding the subject."[2] The following year, Justice Holmes wrote in *Strickley*, "In discussing what constitutes a public use, it [Supreme Court] recognized the inadequacy of *use by the general public* as a universal test."[3] By 1906 (the year *Strickley* was decided), the Public Use Clause had become synonymous with public purpose, which meant something far broader than "use by the general public."

In 1954, the Court ruled on *Berman* and again interpreted the clause broadly. Justice Douglas gave the power to states to determine the proper interpretation of public use that built on *Clark*'s deference to "the facts surrounding the object." Public use became subject to time and place, and because he believed that local legislatures understood time and place for their citizens better than any Federal constitutional protections, the role of the judiciary became limited. Douglas wrote, "The role of the judiciary in determining whether that power is being exercised for a public purpose is an extremely narrow one."[4] Thirty years later, the Court ruled in *Midkiff* (1984) that public use included a power of "regulating oligopoly and the evils associated with it."[5] This drew the boundary of public use to include regulating the property market and "the evils associated with it." It also reinforced the *Berman* decision that the judiciary's role in determining public use "is an extremely narrow one."[6]

By the time the Supreme Court heard *Kelo*, it had already firmly established that the Public Use Clause was broad, subject to time and place, and was to be defined by legislatures. *Kelo*'s contribution was to ask if a state could also include economic redevelopment as part of the public use definition. The slim majority agreed that redevelopment was a valid public use based on the logic of precedent, and they further left the determinations of public use up to the states. For the four dissenting justices, this had gone too far and tipped the balance towards the states at the expense of the natural rights found in the Constitution. Justice Thomas went so far as to write that the whole line of cases had been wrong since *Fallbrook*, and that the original meaning of the Fifth Amendment had long since vanished form the Court's rulings.

Justice Thomas advocated returning to the original and strict understanding of the Public Use Clause, and there is a strong case to be made for his proposal. There are two reasons his proposal should be taken seriously. First, the public seems to understand the Public Use Clause in a pre-*Fallbrook* interpretation. Polls and statistics are not available on the reactions to both *Berman* and *Midkiff*, but general polls surrounding these decades show a remarkable propensity for Americans to see private property as "sacred."[6] As noted with *Kelo*, however, the polls showed a resounding dislike of the decision, even across party lines. Perhaps the rise of new forms of media, along with a more judicial-savvy public, has created more coverage and polling, but it seems the general public is still wedded to the idea that private property is a sacred natural right that should never be infringed upon unless for a necessary general use by the public. Following Thomas's interpretation would most likely comport with the majority of citizens' beliefs on the matter.

The second reason Thomas' dissent should be taken seriously is that subjecting the definition of a constitutional term to fifty different legislatorial opinions will lead to a confusing and frustrating mess for property owners and potential property owners. The Court's current deference makes it difficult to understand the meaning of the Public Use Clause because it varies from state to state. Although Robert C. Ellickson and others have described the usefulness of federalism in crafting state public policy through experimentation, variations in takings leaves people's fundamental rights exposed to abuse. When the very notion of private property is challenged to different degrees in different states, two problems become apparent. First, the Constitution, which should be universal within the borders of the United States, becomes a matter of interpretation based on political acumen. It has already been shown that state legislatures are often unduly influenced by more politically powerful actors, and this could easily include those with money to be made from a redevelopment plan or stadium. It would not take much to show (but not prove) how a plan could potentially make money and benefit the public. The possibility for corruption is far too high in a system dealing with private-to-private takings. Citizens would find themselves in the dangerous position of losing a natural right by virtue of where they live. To use the same logic, it would be as if states were able to interpret the Eighth Amendment's "no cruel or unusual punishment" provision state by state. Hardly anyone would feel secure in a state that suddenly passed a law that the medieval rack or public flogging was not cruel or unusual. Richard Epstein spoke directly to this point in his most recent book *The Classical Liberal Constitution: The Uncertain Quest for Limited Government* (2014): "It is examples like these [*Poletown*, *Midkiff*, and *Kelo*] then that make it imperative to keep a tight rein on public uses lest government power be used to move resources from A to B in ways that heighten the level of political intrigue, as particular groups vie to have the state exercise its condemnation power in their own direction."[7]

This leads to the second problem, that citizens often do not always have the mobility or capital to leave the state if they do not like a policy. The evidence has shown (especially in *Poletown*), it is often minorities and the lower class that suffer the most under redevelopment takings, and it is hardly conceivable to believe they could simply move somewhere else when eminent domain laws are changed. Cost of living between states, job security, and especially family concerns are all major obstacles for citizens to overcome if they wish to move to a different state.

It is not difficult to see how state interpretations might lead to different and creative definitions of public use in the wake of *Kelo*. Without a uniform guide, future experiments on the law are problematic and citizens will bear the brunt of fickle legislatures. Using the uniformity of what Thomas suggests (and seemingly most Americans agree with) would reinforce the solid bedrock principle of the "sacred" nature of private property.

POLICE POWERS

Kelo also more fully established the Court's interpretation of police powers. The power of the states to police their own citizens was originally laid forth by the novel idea of federalism during the framing of the Constitution. This doctrine was necessarily vague, as the fledgling republic was still wrestling with questions of sovereignty on many issues. While the majority in *Kelo* tried to reinforce what it believed was a state power, it sent a mixed signal to both the states and the national government. That the power to define public use falls under the blanket of the police power is subject to scrutiny at least as much as the Fourth Amendment's search and seizure prohibition. States are heavily scrutinized by the courts for search and seizure violations and are continually held to a narrow interpretation of the Fourth Amendment, and yet, they have now been given much more leeway in the broad interpretation of when to take a citizen's house or land away.

The governing power was always supposed to be shared by both the state and national governments as Publius wrote in *Federalist No. 39*:

> The proposed Constitution, therefore, is, in strictness, neither a national nor a federal Constitution, but a composition of both. In its foundation it is federal, not national; in the sources from which the ordinary powers of the government are drawn, it is partly federal and partly national; in the operation of these powers, it is national, not federal; in the extent of them, again, it is federal, not national; and, finally, in the authoritative mode of introducing amendments, it is neither wholly federal nor wholly national.[8]

States should always retain their own power to decide important local issues such as police, fire, morals, agricultural concerns, health, etc., which have always been part of the traditional police powers. Another traditional state police power has always been building infrastructure and planning cities, which sometimes requires the use of eminent domain. However, eminent domain should always be limited to a strict public use as the original understanding of the Takings Clause laid out in the Fifth Amendment. In order to keep the system of limited government functioning properly, property rights, some of the most important in the American regime, must be recognized and respected to a uniform degree.

Since *Kelo*, judges have been given a more difficult task to accomplish. Justice O'Connor pointed out that judges are now given the responsibility of "divining" the intent of those who carried out a redevelopment plan.[9] Trying to distinguish between a good faith economic redevelopment plan and simply "enriching the private individual who proposed it" can become incredibly difficult, especially since laws and circumstances vary in each state.[10] Enumerated rights in the Constitution should be clearly defined and adhered to, but the decision in *Kelo* has opened up the takings doctrine to fifty different interpretations.

Continuing reliance on unpopular precedent, as the decision in *Kelo* did, will lead to more intricate and endlessly labyrinthine property laws which citizens will continue to be repulsed by—or not understand at all. Patrick Henry knew that such a government would be the most dangerous to the "middling and lower" classes who could not understand the plain words of the law. In his original opposition to the Constitution, he feared that the Constitution would prove too unworkable and impossible to understand. At the Virginia Ratifying Convention in 1788 he said, "There will be no checks, no real balances, in this Government: What can avail your specious imaginary balances, your rope-dancing, chain-rattling, ridiculous ideal checks and contrivances?"[11] Going back to a traditionally held view of property, or moving closer towards it, would produce the most uniform and well-understood eminent domain laws, which would ultimately be safest and the most fair for the republic. If changes needed to be made to the language and understanding of the Constitution, they should be made by the Article V amending process, which the people themselves would agree with and be able to understand.

CONCLUSION

The Court's decision continued a trend of precedent that saw an ever-broadening interpretation of public use, and it is not difficult to see the abuse state and local legislatures can exercise. The Takings Clause, as Justice Kennedy mentioned, "has become a term of art."[12] Justice O'Connor would probably note that it is a term of art that "anyone but the 'stupid staff[er]'" would be able to manipulate.[13] Since the decision, redevelopment and economic takings have seen resurgence. As noted in chapter 8, there have been many redevelopment takings cases that have been heard and validated by *Kelo* in federal courts, including *Goldstein v. Pataki* (2008), *Fideicomiso de la Tierra del Cano Martin Pena v. Fortuno* (2010), and *Whittaker v. County of Lawrence* (2011). In 2014, the city of Orlando, Florida, filed suit in court to seize a church's land for one of the parcels desired for a Major League Soccer stadium.[14] In Atlantic City, New Jersey, a state redevelopment agency is attempting to use eminent domain against a private homeowner in order to clear his house for a casino development project.[15] In April 2014, the popular Netflix series *House of Cards'* production company was almost taken by the Maryland legislature because it was considering moving production out of state. The bill seizing the production company was passed by the lower chamber (House of Delegates), but failed in a General Assembly of Maryland conference committee.[16]

As scholars and lawyers continue to examine the *Kelo* decision, it remains to be seen how large the legacy and impact of the case will ultimately be. Legally, the decision marked a new line of interpretation of the Fifth Amendment. Socially, it highlighted the tension between the governors and the governed for a brief moment and brought out the inherent tensions of property rights in the regime. Where the Court and the regime will go from here is not entirely clear, but *Kelo* reminded the United States that property still does play a vital role in human affairs.

NOTES

1. Ian Fleming, Richard Maibaum, and Paul Dehn, *Goldfinger*, Directed by: Guy Hamilton. London: United Artists, 1964.
2. *Clark v. Nash*, 198 U.S. 361 (1905).
3. *Strickley v. Highland Boy Gold Mining Co.*, 200 U.S. 527 (1906), italics added.
4. *Berman v. Parker*, 348 U.S. 26 (1954).
5. *Hawaii Housing Authority v. Midkiff* 467 U.S. 229 (1984).
6. Nadler, Diamond, and Patton, "Government Takings of Private Property."
7. Richard Epstein, *The Classical Liberal Constitution: The Uncertain Quest for Limited Government.* (Cambridge: Harvard University Press, 2014), 358.
8. Publius, *Federalist No. 39*, *The Avalon Project*, January 16, 1788, accessed May 28, 2013, http://avalon.law.yale.edu/18th_century/fed39.asp.
9. *Kelo v. New London*, 545 U.S. 469 (2005) (O'Connor, J., dissenting).
10. *Goldstein v. Pataki*, 516 F.3d 50 (2d Cir. 2008)
11. Patrick Henry, Speech at the Virginia Ratifying Convention, June 5, 1788, in eds. Philip B. Kurland and Ralph Lerner, *The Founders' Constitution* (Chicago: University of Chicago Press, 1987), accessed May 10, 2013, http://press-pubs.uchicago.edu/founders/.
12. *Eastern Enterprises v. Apfel*, 524 U.S. 498 (1998) (Kennedy, J. concurring).
13. Ibid.
14. Mark Schlueb, "Orlando Files Suit to Take Church Land for Soccer Stadium," *Orlando Sentinel*, May 20, 2014, accessed May 20, 2014, http://articles.orlandosentinel.com/2014-05-20/news/os-church-soccer-stadium-court-20140520_1_orlando-city-soccer-club-faith-deliverance-temple-church-land.

15. Damon Root, "Atlantic City Wants to Bulldoze a Home to Benefit a Casino," *Reason.com*, May 20, 2014, accessed May 20, 2014, http://reason.com/archives/2014/05/20/atlantic-city-wants-to-bulldoze-a-home-t.

16. Alex Jackson, "General Assembly conference committee kills 'House of Cards' eminent domain provision," *CapitalGazette.com*, April 3, 2014, accessed April 10, 2014, http://www.capitalgazette.com/news/general_assembly/general-assembly-conference-committee-kills-house-of-cards-eminent-domain/article_04064c33-7693-5b32-9b4f-237d929d6ec7.html.

Bibliography

Amar, Akhil Reed. *The Bill of Rights: Creation and Reconstruction*. New Haven: Yale University Press, 2000.

Barros, Benjamin. "Nothing 'Errant' About it: The *Berman* and *Midkiff* Conference Notes and How the Supreme Court Got to Kelo With its Eyes Wide Open." Widener Law School Legal Studies Research Paper No. 08–30, 2007. Accessed May 23, 2014. http://ssrn.com/abstract=902926 or http://dx.doi.org/10.2139/ssrn.902926, 1–21.

Baude, William. "Rethinking the Federal Eminent Domain Power," *The Yale Law Journal* 122 (2013): 1738–1825.

Bell, Abraham and Gideon Parchomovsky. "Takings Reassessed." *Virginia Law Review* 87 (2001): 276–318.

———. "The Uselessness of Public Use," *Columbia Law Review* 106 (2006): 1419–21.

Benedict, Jeff. *Little Pink House: A True Story of Defiance and Courage*. New York: Grand Central Publishing, 2009.

Benson, Bruce L. and Matthew Brown. "Eminent Domain for Private Use: Is it Justified by Market Failure or an Example of Government Failure?" In *Property Rights: Eminent Domain and Regulatory Takings Re-Examined*, ed. Bruce L. Benson. New York: Palgrave Macmillan, 2010, 149–172.

Berliner, Dana. "Public Power, Private Gain." 2009. Institute for Justice Website. Accessed August 18, 2012. http://www.castlecoalition.org/index.php?option=com_content&task=view&id=312.

Blackstone, Sir William. *Commentaries on the Laws of England in Four Books. Notes selected from the editions of Archibold, Christian, Coleridge, Chitty, Stewart, Kerr, and others, Barron Field's Analysis, and Additional Notes, and a Life of the Author by George Sharswood, In Two Volumes*. Vol. I. Philadelphia: J.B. Lippincott Co., 1893. Accessed May 3, 2013. http://oll.libertyfund.org/index.php?option=com_staticxt&staticfile=show.php%3Ftitle=2140&layout=html#chapter_198690.

———. *Commentaries on the Laws of England* (A Facsimile of the First Edition of 1765–1769). Vol. II. Chicago: University of Chicago Press, 1979.

Blocher, Joseph. "Private Business as Public Good: Hotel Development and *Kelo*," *Yale Law & Policy Review* 24 (2006): 363–397

Boettke, Peter J., Christopher J. Coyne, and Peter T. Leeson, "Land Grab: Takings, the Market Process, and Regime Uncertainty," in *Property Rights: Eminent Domain and Regulatory Takings Re-Examined*, ed. Bruce L. Benson. New York: Palgrave Macmillan, 2010. 173–186.

Bravin, Jess. "Justice Stevens on His 'Most Unpopular Opinion'." *Wall Street Journal*, November 11, 2011. Accessed May 31, 2013. http://online.wsj.com/article/SB10001424052970204358004577032071046475782.html.

Brief of Amici Curiae for The American Farm Bureau Federation and the Farm Bureau Federations of the Following States: California, Connecticut, Florida, Indiana, Iowa, Kansas, Louisiana, Michigan, New Haven County, New Jersey, New York, North Carolina, Ohio, Oklahoma, Pennsylvania, Rhode Island, Texas, Utah, and Virginia. *Kelo v. New London*, No 04–108. FindLaw.com. Accessed October 2, 2012. supreme.lp.findlaw.com/supreme_court/docket/2004/February.html#04–108.

Brief of Amicus Curiae for the Becket Fund for Religious Liberty. *Kelo v. New London*. No 04–108. FindLaw.com. Accessed October 2, 2012. supreme.lp.findlaw.com/supreme_court/docket/2004/February.html#04–108.

Brief of Amici Curiae for Brooklyn United for Innovative Local Development (BUILD), Rev. Herbert Daughtry, and the New York City and Vicinity Carpenters Labor-Management Corporation in Support of the Respondents, *Kelo v. New London*. No 04–108. FindLaw.com. Accessed October 2, 2012. supreme.lp.findlaw.com/supreme_court/docket/2004/February.html#04–108.

Brief of Amici Curiae for the Cascade Policy Institute, American Association of Small Property Owners, Grassroots Institute of Hawaii, James Madison Institute, John Locke Foundation, Illinois Policy Institute, Indiana Policy Review Foundation, Oregonians in Action Legal Center, Pioneer Institute, Sutherland Institute, and Tennessee Center for Policy Research; and Brief for The New London Railroad Company, Inc., *Kelo v. New London*. No 04–108. FindLaw.com. Accessed October 2, 2012. supreme.lp.findlaw.com/supreme_court/docket/2004/February.html#04–108.

Brief of Amicus Curiae for The CATO Institute. *Kelo v. New London*. No 04–108. FindLaw.com. Accessed October 2, 2012. supreme.lp.findlaw.com/supreme_court/docket/2004/February.html#04–108.

Brief of Amicus Curiae for Claremont Institute. *Kelo v. New London*. No 04–108. FindLaw.com. Accessed October 2, 2012. supreme.lp.findlaw.com/supreme_court/docket/2004/February.html#04–108.

Brief of Amici Curiae for David L. Callies, James T. Ely, Paula A. Franzese, Nicole Stelle Garnett, James E. Krier, Daniel R. Mandelker, John Coepland Nagle, John Nolon, J.B. Ruhl, Shelley Ross Saxer, A. Dan Tarlock, Laura Underkuffler, and Edward F. Ziegler, *Kelo v. New London*. No 04–108. FindLaw.com. Accessed October 2, 2012. supreme.lp.findlaw.com/supreme_court/docket/2004/February.html#04–108.

Brief of Amici Curiae for Develop Don't Destroy (Brooklyn) Inc. and The West Harlem Business Group. *Kelo v. New London*. No 04–108. FindLaw.com. Accessed October 2, 2012. supreme.lp.findlaw.com/supreme_court/docket/2004/February.html#04–108.

Brief of Amica Curiae for Jane Jacobs, *Kelo v. New London*. No 04–108. FindLaw.com. Accessed October 2, 2012. supreme.lp.findlaw.com/supreme_court/docket/2004/February.html#04–108.

Brief of Amici Curiae for Law Professors Robert H. Freilich, Richard Briffault, Julie Cheslik, Janice C. Griffith, Tim Iglesias, Julian Conrad Jurgensmayer, Anita Miller, Thomas E. Roberts, Patricia E. Salkin, Edward J. Sullivan, Robert R.M. Verchick, Judith Welch Wegner, and Alan Weinstein in Support of the Respondents, *Kelo v. New London*. No 04–108. FindLaw.com. Accessed October 2, 2012. supreme.lp.findlaw.com/supreme_court/docket/2004/February.html#04–108.

Brief of Amici Curiae for The Connecticut Conference of Municipalities and the State Municipal Leagues of Alabama; Arkansas; California; Colorado; Florida; Georgia; Illinois; Indiana; Iowa; Kansas; Kentucky; Louisiana; Maryland; Massachusetts; Michigan; Minnesota; Missouri; New Hampshire; New Jersey; New Mexico; New York; North Carolina; Ohio; Oklahoma; Pennsylvania; Rhode Island; South Carolina; South Dakota; Texas; West Virginia and Wisconsin in Support of Respondents, *Kelo v. New London*. No 04–108. FindLaw.com. Accessed October 2, 2012. supreme.lp.findlaw.com/supreme_court/docket/2004/February.html#04–108.

Brief of Amici Curiae for The National Association for the Advancement of Colored People, AARP, Hispanic Alliance of Atlantic County, Inc., Citizens in Action, Cramer Hill Resident Association, Inc., and the Southern Christian Leadership Conference, *Kelo v. New London*. No 04–108. FindLaw.com. Accessed October 2, 2012. supreme.lp.findlaw.com/supreme_court/docket/2004/February.html#04–108.

Brief of Amici Curiae for The National Association of Home Builders and the National Association of Realtors. *Kelo v. New London*. No 04–108. FindLaw.com. Accessed October 2, 2012. supreme.lp.findlaw.com/supreme_court/docket/2004/February.html#04–108.

Brief of Amici Curiae for The National League of Cities, National Conference of State Legislatures, U.S. Conference of Mayors, Council of State Government, National Association of Counties, International Municipal Lawyers Association, and International City/County Management Association, *Kelo v. New London*. No 04–108. FindLaw.com. Accessed October 2, 2012. supreme.lp.findlaw.com/supreme_court/docket/2004/February.html#04–108.

Bukowczk, John J. "The Decline and Fall of a Detroit Neighborhood: Poletown vs. G.M. and the City of Detroit." *Washington and Lee Law Review* 41 (1984), 49–76.

Bullock, Scott. "Not For Sale." June 23, 2008, *Reason.com*. Accessed May 31, 2013. http://reason.com/archives/2008/06/23/not-for-sale.

Bullock, Scott G. "The Inadequacy of the Planning Process for Protecting Property Owners from the Abuse of Eminent Domain for Private Development." In *Property Rights: Eminent Domain and Regulatory Takings Re-Examined*, ed. Bruce L. Benson, 89–100. New York: Palgrave Macmillan, 2010.

Calabresi, Steven G. "Federalism and the Rehnquist Court: A Normative Defense," *Annals of the American Academy of Political and Social Science* 574 (2001): 24–46.

Christie, Les. "Taking your home away." *CNN/Money*, August 3, 2005. Accessed May 3, 2013. http://money.cnn.com/2005/07/25/real_estate/investment_prop/eminent_domain_v_deveopment/.

Connecticut General Statutes. 132 C. § 8. Accessed January 2, 2013. http://www.cga.ct.gov/2011/pub/chap132.htm.

Constitution of the State of Connecticut, Art. I, §11.

The Constitution of the United States of America: Analysis, and Interpretation. Ed. Congressional Research Service. Washington, D.C.: Government Printing Office, 1992. Accessed May 3, 2013. http://www.gpo.gov/fdsys/pkg/GPO-CONAN-1992/pdf/GPO-CONAN-1992.pdf.

"Crime Rates in New London by Year," *City-Data.com*, accessed May 31, 2013, http://www.city-data.com/crime/crime-New-London-Connecticut.html.

Dagan, Hanoch. "Takings and Distributive Justice." *Virginia Law Review* 85 (1999): 741–804.

Department of Energy and Environmental Protection. "The Battle of Groton Heights and The Burning of New London." Accessed May 12, 2013. http://www.ct.gov/deep/lib/deep/stateparks/general_info/the_battle_of_groton_heights_and_the_burning_of_new_london.pdf.

Eagle, Steven J. "Assembling Land for Urban Redevelopment: The Case for Owner Participation." In *Property Rights: Eminent Domain and Regulatory Takings Re-Examined*, ed. Bruce L. Benson, 7–26. New York: Palgrave Macmillan, 2010.

Ellickson, Robert C. "Federalism and *Kelo*: A Question for Richard Epstein." *Tulsa Law Review* 44 (2009): 751–764.

Ely, Jr., James W. "Post-*Kelo* Reform: Is the Glass Half Full of Half Empty?" *Supreme Court Economic Review* 17 (2009): 127–150.

Epstein, Richard A. *The Classical Liberal Constitution: The Uncertain Quest for Limited Government*. Cambridge: Harvard University Press, 2014.

———. "Public Use in a Post-*Kelo* World." *Supreme Court Economic Review* 17 (2009): 151–71.

———. "Supreme Folly." *Wall Street Journal*, June 27, 2005. Accessed May 30, 2013. http://online.wsj.com/article/0,,SB111982975240969952,00.html?mod=opinion&ojcontent=otep.

———. *Takings: Private Property and the Power of Eminent Domain*. Cambridge: Harvard University Press, 1985.

"Five Years After *Kelo*: The Sweeping Backlash Against One of the Supreme Court's Most-Despised Decisions." *Institute for Justice*, 2010. Accessed May 1, 2013. http://www.ij.org/

five-years-after-kelo-the-sweeping-backlash-against-one-of-the-supreme-courts-most-despised-decisions.

Fleming, Ian, Richard Maibaum, and Paul Dehn. *Goldfinger*. Directed by: Guy Hamilton. London: United Artists, 1964.

"From Pierre L'Enfant, Editorial Note, 21 September, 1791." *The Papers of George Washington Digital Edition*, ed. Theodore J. Crackel. Charlottesville: University of Virginia Press, Rotunda, 2008. Accessed May 12, 2014. http://founders.archives.gov/documents/Washington/05–09–02–0124.

Gerken, Heather K. "Federalism as the New Nationalism: An Overview," *Yale Law Journal* 123 (2014).

Google Maps. "New London, CT." Accessed May 31, 2013. https://www.google.com/maps/place/New+London,+CT/@41.3458062,-72.1057119,12z/data=!3m1!4b1!4m2!3m1!1s0x89e60e6eb612cdbd:0xd01603e69c2b939d).

Greenhut, Stephen G. "Redevelopment Resurrection?" *City Journal*, May 23, 2014. Accessed May 23, 2014. http://www.city-journal.org/2014/cjc0523sg.html.

Guadani, Claire. "New London Development Corporation Case Study." ClaireGuadani.com. Accessed March 21, 2013. http://www.clairegaudiani.com/default.aspx.

Henry, Patrick. "Speech at the Virginia Ratifying Convention," June 4, 1788, In *The Founders' Constitution*. Philip B. Kurland and Ralph Lerner, eds. Chicago: University of Chicago Press, 1987. Accessed February 28, 2010. http://press-pubs.uchicago.edu/founders/.

———. "Speech at the Virginia Ratifying Convention." June 5, 1788. In *The Founders' Constitution*. Philip B. Kurland and Ralph Lerner, eds. Chicago: University of Chicago Press, 1987. Accessed February 28, 2010. http://press-pubs.uchicago.edu/founders/.

Holmes, Oliver Wendell, "The Path of the Law" *Harvard Law Review* 457 (1897). Accessed July 11, 2009. http://constitution.org/lrev/owh/path_law.htm.

H.R. 1944–*113th Congress: Private Property Rights Protection Act of 2013*. 2013. Accessed June 2, 2013. http://www.govtrack.us/congress/bills/113/hr194.

H.R. 3135–*109th Congress: Private Property Rights Protection Act of 2005*. 2005. GovTrack Website. Accessed May 21, 2013. http://www.govtrack.us/congress/bills/109/hr3135.

Hughes, Charles Evans, *Addresses of Charles Evans Hughes: 1906–1916*. New York: G.P. Putnam's Sons, 1916.

Jackson, Alex. "General Assembly conference committee kills 'House of Cards' eminent domain provision." *CapitalGazette.com*, April 3, 2014. Accessed April 10, 2014. http://www.capitalgazette.com/news/general_assembly/general-assembly-conference-committee-kills-house-of-cards-eminent-domain/article_04064c33–7693–5b32–9b4f-237d929d6ec7.html.

Jackson, Todd. "Private—keep off: aftershocks of Kelo v. city of New London." *The Roanoke Times*, July 18, 2005. Accessed May 20, 2013. http://ww2.roanoke.com//news/roanoke%5c27712.html.

Jacobs, Harvey M. and Ellen M. Bassett. "All Sound, No Fury? The Impacts of State-Based *Kelo* Laws." *Planning and Environmental Law* 63, (2011): 3–8.

Jacoby, Jeff. "Eminent Injustice in New London." *The Boston Globe*, June 26, 2005. Accessed May 3, 2013. http://www.boston.com/news/globe/editorial_opinion/oped/articles/2005/06/26/eminent_injustice_in_new_london/.

Jaffa, Harry V. *Crisis of the House Divided: An Interpretation of the Issues in the Lincoln-Douglas Debates*. Chicago: University of Chicago Press, 1959.

Jefferson, Thomas. *Notes on the State of Virginia*. The Avalon Project Website. Accessed May 24, 2013. http://avalon.law.yale.edu/18th_century/jeffvir.asp.

———. "Observations on L'Enfant's Letter." In *The Papers of Thomas Jefferson Digital Edition*, eds. Barbara B. Oberg and J. Jefferson Looney. Charlottesville: University of Virginia Press, Rotunda, 2008. Accessed May 12, 2014. http://founders.archives.gov/documents/Washington/05–09–02–0124.

Kain, Erik. "Liberals should be Upset by the Kelo Case." *Forbes*, September 15, 2011. Accessed May 13, 2013. http://www.forbes.com/sites/erikkain/2011/09/15/liberals-should-be-anti-kelo/.

Langeveld, Dirk. "Mayor Announces Reorganization of NLDC." *New London Patch*, April 26, 2012. Accessed October 9, 2012. http://newlondon.patch.com/groups/politics-and-elections/p/mayor-announces-reorganization-of-nldc.

L'Enfant, Pierre. "From Pierre L'Enfant, George town [Md.], December 7th 1791." In *The Papers of George Washington Digital Edition*, ed. Theodore J. Crackel. Charlottesville: University of Virginia Press, Rotunda, 2008. Accessed May 12, 2014, http://founders.archives.gov/documents/Washington/05–09–02–0124.

Lehavi, Amnon, and Amir N. Licht, "Eminent Domain, Inc.," *Columbia Law Review* 107, (2007): 1704–48.

Levy, Janet. "The Aftermath of the *Kelo* Ruling." *American Thinker*, June 28, 2006. Accessed May 1, 2013. http://www.americanthinker.com/2006/06/the_aftermath_of_the_kelo_ruli.html.

Levy, Leonard W., Charles Fairman, and Stanley Morrison. *Fourteenth Amendment and the Bill of Rights: The Incorporation Theory*. New York: De Capo Press, 1970.

Levy, Robert A., and William Mellor, *The Dirty Dozen: How Twelve Supreme Court Cases Radically Expanded Government and Eroded Freedom*. New York: Sentinel, 2008.

Lexington. "The Worst Decision of Justice Stevens." *The Economist*, April 14, 2010. Accessed October 10, 2013. http://www.economist.com/blogs/lexington/2010/04/kelo_john_paul_stevenss_worst_decision.

Locke, John. *Two Treatises of Government*, ed. Thomas Hollis. London: A. Millar et al., 1764. Accessed May 23, 2014. http://oll.libertyfund.org/titles/222.

Madison, James. "Notes (July 5, 1787)." In *The Records of the Federal Convention of 1787*. Vol. I, ed. Max Farrand. New Haven: Yale University Press, 1911.

Magna Carta. The Constitution Society. Accessed May 3, 2013. http://www.constitution.org/eng/magnacar.htm.

Mahoney, Julia D. "Kelo's Legacy: Eminent Domain and the Future of Property Rights." *The Supreme Court Review* 2005 (2005).

Main, Carla T. *Bulldozed: "Kelo," Eminent Domain, and the American Lust for Land*. New York: Encounter Books, 2007.

McCarthy, Michael. "First Look: Inside Brooklyn Nets new $1 billion Arena." *USA Today*, May 22, 2012. Accessed May 30, 2013. http://content.usatoday.com/communities/gameon/post/2012/05/first-look-inside-the-brooklyn-nets-new-arena-barclays-center-nba-bruce-ratner-jay-z/1#.U4tjasamBg0.

McCloskey, Robert G. "Economic Due Process and the Supreme Court: An Exhumation and Reburial," *The Supreme Court Review* 1962 (1962).

McGeehan, Patrick. "Pfizer to Leave City that Won the Land Use Case." *The New York Times*, November 12, 2009. Accessed May 30, 2013. http://www.nytimes.com/2009/11/13/nyregion/13pfizer.html?_r=0.

Moreno, Paul. "Poletown Neighborhood Council v. Detroit: Private Property and Public Use." *Michigan Bar Journal* 88, (2009): 18–23.

Morriss, Andrew P. "Symbol or Substance? An Empirical Assessment of State Reponses to Kelo," *Supreme Court Economic Review* 17 (2009), 237–78.

Nadler, Janice, Shari Seidman Diamond, and Matthew M. Patton. "Government Takings of Private Property: Kelo and the Perfect Storm in Public Opinion and Constitutional Controversy." In *Public Opinion and Constitutional Controversy*. Nathaniel Persily, Jack Citrin, and Patrick Egan eds. New York: Oxford University Press Inc., 2008, Kindle Edition.

National Park Service. "The L'Enfant and McMillan Plans." Accessed March 3, 2013. http://www.nps.gov/nr/travel/wash/lenfant.htm.

New London Historic Waterfront. "Upcoming Fun Events." Accessed October 10, 2012. http://www.newlondonmainstreet.org/pub/gen/eventspage.

Nichols, Philip. *The Law of Eminent Domain: A Treatise on the Principles Which Affect the Taking of Property for the Public Use*. Albany: Matthew Bender & Company Incorporated, 1917.

Nolon, John R. "The Mighty Myths of *Kelo*," *Government, Law, and Policy Journal* 9 (2009): 10–15.

Picket, Kerry. "PICKET: '05 Kelo Decision a Failure; CT site remains a dump." *The Washington Times*, Accessed May 30, 2013. http://www.washingtontimes.com/blog/watercooler/2011/sep/3/picket-05–kelo-decision-failure-ct-site-remains-du/.

"Poll: Readers favor eminent domain restrictions." *Jacksonville Business Journal*, April 25, 2006. Accessed May 3, 2013. http://www.bizjournals.com/jacksonville/stories/2006/04/24/daily10.html.

Pollock, Sir Frederick, and Frederic William Maitland. *The History of English Law before the Time of Edward I.* Vol. 2. Indianapolis: Liberty Fund, 2010. Accessed online May 2, 2013. http://oll.libertyfund.org/index.php?option=com_staticxt&staticfile=show.php%3Ftitle=2314&layout=html#chapter_219571.

Publius. "Federalist No. 8." November 20, 1787. *The Constitution Society*. Accessed May 28, 2013. http://www.constitution.org/fed/federa08.htm.

———. "Federalist No. 39." January 16, 1788. *The Avalon Project*. Accessed May 28, 2013. http://avalon.law.yale.edu/18th_century/fed39.asp.

———. "Federalist No. 45." January 26, 1788. *The Constitution Society*. Accessed May 28, 2013. http://www.constitution.org/fed/federa45.htm.

———. "Federalist No. 57." February 19, 1788. *The Avalon Project*, February 19, 1788. Accessed May 31, 2013. http://avalon.law.yale.edu/18th_century/fed57.asp.

"Putting the New back in New London." *The Economist*, June 13, 1998. Accessed February 11, 2013. http://www.economist.com/node/134291.

Risen, James. "Poletown Becomes Just a Memory: GM Plant Opens, Replacing Old Detroit Neighborhood." *Los Angeles Times*, September 18, 1985. Accessed May 13, 2013. http://articles.latimes.com/1985–09–18/business/fi-6228_1_gm-plant.

Robertson, William. *The History of the Reign of Emperor Charles V With A View of the Progress of Society in Europe from the Subversion of the Roman Empire to the Beginning of the Sixteenth Century*. (New York: J&J Harper, 1829), 71.

Root, Damon. "Atlantic City Wants to Bulldoze a Home to Benefit a Casino." *Reason.com*, May 20, 2014. Accessed May 20, 2014. http://reason.com/archives/2014/05/20/atlantic-city-wants-to-bulldoze-a-home-t.

Rossum, Ralph and G. Alan Tarr. *American Constitutional Law*. Vol. I. Boulder: Westview Press, 2010.

S. 1895–*109th Congress: Private Property Rights Protection Act*. 2005. GovTrack Website. Accessed June 2, 2013. http://www.govtrack.us/congress/bills/109/s1895.

S. 3873–*109th Congress: Private Property Rights Protection Act of 2006*. 2006. GovTrack Website. Accessed May 21, 2013. http://www.govtrack.us/congress/bills/109/s387.

S. 48–*110th Congress: Private Property Rights Protection Act*. 2007. GovTrack Website. Accessed May 31, 2013. http://www.govtrack.us/congress/bills/110/s48.

Salkin, Patricia E., Lora A. Lucero, and Allyson Phillips. "Friends of the Court: The Role of Amicus Curiae in *Kelo v. City of New London*." In *Eminent Domain Use and Abuse: Kelo in Context*, eds. Dwight H. Merriam and Mary Massaron Ross, Chicago: American Bar Association, 2006.

Salzman, Avi and Laura Manseurs, "For Homeowners, Frustration and Anger at Court Ruling." *The New York Times*, June 24, 2005. Accessed September 12, 2012. http://www.nytimes.com/2005/06/24/national/24newlondon.html?_r=0.

Sargent, J.F. and Ricardo R. Read. "The 5 Most Terrifying Supreme Court Decisions." Cracked.com, September 6, 2012. Accessed October 31st, 2013. http://www.cracked.com/article_19991_the-5–most-terrifying-supreme-court-decisions.html.

Schlueb, Mark. "Orlando Files Suit to Take Church Land for Soccer Stadium." *Orlando Sentinel*, May 20, 2014. Accessed May 20, 2014. http://articles.orlandosentinel.com/2014–05–20/news/os-church-soccer-stadium-court-20140520_1_orlando-city-soccer-club-faith-deliverance-temple-church-land.

Scott, Kyle. *The Price of Politics: Lessons from Kelo v. New London*. New York: Rowman & Littlefield, 2009.

Sincere, Richard. "Richard Epstein notes how Kelo sparked more scrutiny of eminent domain." *Examiner*, January 7, 2012. Accessed October 12, 2013. http://www.examiner.com/article/richard-epstein-notes-how-kelo-sparked-more-scrutiny-of-eminent-domain.

Sola, David de. "Souter's Home an Activist Target." *CNN*, January 22, 2006. Accessed May 13, 2013. http://www.cnn.com/2006/LAW/01/21/eminent.domain/.

Somin, Ilya. "Controlling the Grasping Hand: Economic Development Takings after Kelo." *Supreme Court Economic Review* 15 (2007): 183–271.

———. "The Limits of Backlash: Assessing the Political Response to *Kelo*." In *Property Rights: Eminent Domain and Regulatory Takings Re-Examined*, ed. Bruce L. Benson, 101–48. New York: Palgrave Macmillan, 2010.

———. "University of Michigan Law School Talk on Property Rights Since *Kelo*." *The Volokh Conspiracy*, March 7, 2013. Accessed May 30, 2013. http://www.volokh.com/2013/03/07/university-of-michigan-law-school-talk-on-property-rights-since-kelo/.

"Statement of The Honorable John Coryn." *United States Senate Committee of the Judiciary*. September 20, 2005. Accessed October 15, 2012. http://www.judiciary.senate.gov/hearings/testimony.cfm?id=e655f9e2809e5476862f735da10a78d5& wit_id=e655f9e2809e5476862f735da10a78d5–0–0.

"Statement of The Honorable Patrick Leahy." *United States Senate Committee of the Judiciary*. September 20, 2005. Accessed October 15, 2012. http://www.judiciary.senate.gov/hearings/testimony.cfm?id=e655f9e2809e5476862f735da10a78d5& wit_id=e655f9e2809e5476862f735da10a78d5–0–2.

"Stealing Home: Letting Government Take Property for Development Risks Abuse." *Houston Chronicle*, July 25, 2005. Accessed May 3, 2013. http://www.chron.com/opinion/editorials/article/Stealing-home-Letting-government-take-property-1953507.php.

Stevens, John Paul. "Judicial Predilections." *Nevada Law Journal* 6, (2005): 1–6.

Stoebuck, William B. "A General Theory of Eminent Domain," *Washington Law Review* 47, (1972).

Summers, Adam. "Master of Your Domain: The Impact of the *Kelo* Decision." *Reason Foundation*, June 26, 2006. Accessed May 30, 2013. http://reason.org/news/show/122529.html.

"Susette Kelo, et al., Petitioners v. City of New London, Connecticut, et al." Supreme Court of the United States Website. Accessed May 23rd, 2014. http://www.supremecourt.gov/Search.aspx?FileName=/docketfiles/04–108.htm.

Susette Kelo et al. v. City of New London, et al., Supreme Court Case 04–108, Oral Argument Transcript. Alderson Reporting Company (2005). Supreme Court of the United States Website. Accessed March 20, 2012. http://www.supremecourt.gov/oral_arguments/argument_transcripts/04–108.pdf.

"Testimony of Susette Kelo." *United States House Committee on the Judiciary, Subcommittee on the Constitution and Civil Justice*, April 18, 2013. Accessed May 31, 2013. http://judiciary.house.gov/hearings/113th/04182013/Kelo.pdf.

"Testimony of Susette Kelo." *United States Senate Committee of the Judiciary*. September 20, 2005. Accessed October 15, 2012. http://www.judiciary.senate.gov/hearings/testimony.cfm?id=e655f9e2809e5476862f735da10a78d5& wit_id=e655f9e2809e5476862f735da10a78d5–2–1.

The New London Gazette. "Surprises, Features, and Facts of New London, Connecticut, USA." Accessed May 13, 2013. http://newlondongazette.com/surprise.html.

———. "The Richest Gem of the Sound." Accessed May 13, 2013, http://newlondongazette.com/fisherisland.html.

"The Rise and Fall of Economic Substantive Due Process: Overview," Justia.com. Accessed June 1, 2013. http://law.justia.com/constitution/us/amendment-14/07–economic-substantive-due-process.html.

Tocqueville, Alexis de. *Democracy in America*, Translated by Harvey C. Mansfield and Delba Winthrop. Chicago: University of Chicago Press, 2000.

Treanor, William Michael. "The Original Understanding of the Takings Clause and the Political Process," *Columbia Law Review* 95 (1995): 782–887.

Troxler, Howard. "High Court Takes Fifth, Proceeds to Ruin It." *St. Petersburg Times*, June 28, 2005, B1.

Tucker, St. George. "*Blackstone's Commentaries: With Notes of Reference to the Constitution and Laws of the Federal Government of the United States and of the Commonwealth of Virginia*." 5 vols. Philadelphia, 1803. Reprint. South Hackensack, N.J.: Rothman Reprints,

1969. In *The Founders' Constitution*. Philip B. Kurland and Ralph Lerner, eds. Chicago: University of Chicago Press, 1987. Accessed February 28, 2010. http://press-pubs.uchicago.edu/founders/.

"Tuesday February 22, 2005." FindLaw.com. Accessed May 12, 2012. http://supreme.lp.findlaw.com/supreme_court/docket/2004/february.html.

Utt, Ronald D. "States Vote to Strengthen Property Rights." *Heritage Foundation*, February 1, 2007. Accessed May 31, 2013. http://www.heritage.org/research/reports/2007/02/states-vote-to-strengthen-property-rights.

U.S. Census Bureau. "New London (city) Connecticut." Accessed May 31, 2013. http://quickfacts.census.gov/qfd/states/09/0952280.html.

Wardle, Lynn D. "The Judicial Imposition of Same-Sex Marriage: The Boundaries of Judicial Legitimacy and Legitimate Redefinition of Marriage." *Washburn Law Journal* 50 (2010): 79–107.

Washington, George. "To Thomas Jefferson, Philadelphia, January 18th, 1792." In *The Papers of George Washington Digital Edition*, ed. Theodore J. Crackel. Charlottesville: University of Virginia Press, Rotunda, 2008. Accessed May 12, 2014. http://founders.archives.gov/documents/Washington/05–09–02–0124.

Watson, Bradley C.S. *Living Constitution, Dying Faith: Progressivism and the New Science of Jurisprudence*. Wilmington: ISI Books, 2009.

Weiss, Debra Cassens. "Brooke Shields to Star in TV Movie Chronicling Kelo Eminent Domain Case." September 20, 2011, *ABAJournal*. Accessed May 31, 2013. http://www.abajournal.com/news/article/brooke_shields_to_star_in_tv_movie_chronicling_kelo_eminent_domain_case/.

———. "Connecticut Justice Apologized to Kelo Plaintiff at a Private Gathering." September 14, 2011, *ABAJournal*. Accessed May 31, 2013. http://www.abajournal.com/news/article/connecticut_justice_apologized_to_kelo_plaintiff_at_a_private_gathering/.

———. "Scalia Lumps Kelo Decision with Dred Scott and Roe v. Wade." *ABA Journal*, October 19, 2011. Accessed May 12, 2013. http://www.abajournal.com/news/article/scalia_lumps_kelo_decision_with_dred_scott_and_roe_v._wade/.

West, Thomas G. *Vindicating the Founders: Race, Sex, Class, and Justice in the Origins of America*. New York: Rowman & Littlefield Publishers Inc., 1997.

Whittington, Keith. *Constitutional Interpretation: Textual Meaning, Original Intent, and Judicial Review*. Lawrence: University Press of Kansas, 1999.

Wolfe, Christopher. *The Rise of Modern Judicial Review: From Constitutional Interpretation to Judge-Made Law*. New York: Rowman and Littlefield Publishers, 1994.

Cases Cited

99 Cents Only Stores v. Lancaster Redevelopment Authority, 237 F. Supp. 2d 1123 (CD Cal. 2001).

Armstrong v. United States, 364 U. S. 40 (1960).

Barron v. City of Baltimore, 32 U.S. 243 (1833).

Berman v. Parker, 348 U.S. 26 (1954).

Brown v. Legal Foundation of Wash., 538 U.S. 216 (2003).

Buffalo Teachers Federation v. Tobe, 446 F.Supp.2d 134 , 137 (W.D.N.Y.2005).

Bugryn v. Bristol, 63 Conn. App. 98, 774 A. 2d 1042 (2001).

Calder v. Bull, 3 Dall. 386 (1798).

Caribbean Airport Facilities, Inc. v. Vazquez, (2013).

Cincinnati v. Vester, 281 U.S. 439 (1930).

City of Boerne v. Flores, 521 U.S. 507 (1997).

City of Duluth v. State, 390 N.W.2d 757, 763 (Minn. 1986).

City of Jamestown v. Leevers Supermarkets, Inc., 552 N.W.2d 365, 369 (N.D. 1996).

Clark v. Nash, 198 U.S. 361 (1905).

County of Wayne v. Hathcock, 684 N.W. 2d 455 (Mich. 2004).

Didden v. Village of Port Chester, 173 Fed. Appx. 931 (2d Cir. 2006).

Eastern Enterprises v. Apfel, 524 U.S. 498 (1998).

Faith Temple Church v. Town of Brighton, 348 F. Supp. 2d 18 (W.D.N.Y. 2004).

Fallbrook Irrigation District v. Bradley (1896)

FCC v. Beach Communications, Inc., 508 U.S. 307 (1993).

Fideicomiso De La Tierra v . Fortuno , 604 F.3d 7 (1st Cir. 2010).

Garcia-Rubiera v. Fortuño, 752 F.Supp.2d 180 (D.P.R.2010).

Gohld Realty Co. v. Hartford, 141 Conn. 135, A. 2d 365 (1954).

Goldstein v. Pataki, 488 F.Supp.2d 254 (E.D.N.Y.2007).

Goldstein v. Pataki, 516 F.3d 50 (2d Cir. 2008).

Graham v. Houlihan, 147 Conn. 321, 160 A.2d 745 (1960).

Gregory Marina, Inc. v. Detroit, 378 Mich. 364, 396, 144 N.W.2d 503 (1966).

Hairston v. Danville & Western R. Co. 208 U.S. 598 (1908).

Hawaii Housing Authority v. Midkiff, 467 US 229 (1984).

Haywood v. Curtis 556 U.S. 729 (2009).

Head v. Amoskeag Mfg. Co., 113 U.S. 9 (1885).

Hogue v. Port of Seattle, 54 Wash. 2d 799, 341 P.2d 171, 187 (Wash. 1959)

In the Matter of Northeast Parent & Child Society, Inc. v. Schenectady, 114 A.D.2d 741, 494 N.Y.S.2d 503 (N.Y. 1985).

Lingle v. Chevron USA Inc. 544 U.S. 528 (2005).

Madisonville Traction Co. v. St. Bernard Mining Co., 196 U.S. 239 (1905).
Marbury v. Madison, 5 U.S. 137 (1803).
Missouri Pacific Railroad Corporation v. State of Nebraska, 164 U.S. 403 (1896).
Missouri Pacific Railway Co. v. Humes, 115 U.S. 512 (1885).
Mistretta v. United States, 488 U.S. 361 (1989).
Monongahela Nav. Co. v. United States, 148 U. S. 312 (1893).
Mt. Vernon-Woodberry Cotton Duck Co. v. Alabama Interstate Power Co., 240 U. S. 30 (1916).
Munn v. Illinois, 94 U.S. 113 (1877).
National Railroad Passenger Corporation v. Boston & Maine Corp., 503 U.S. 407, (1992)
New York v. United States, 505 U.S. 144 (1992).
Oliver Brown, et al. v. Board of Education of Topeka, et al., 347 U.S. 483 (1954).
Old Dominion Land Co. v. United States, 269 U. S. 55 (1925).
Palazzolo v. Rhode Island, 533 U.S. 606 (2001).
Pequonnock Yacht Club, Inc. v. Bridgeport, 259 Conn. 601 (2002).
Poletown Neighborhood Council v. Detroit, 410 Mich. 616, 304 N. W. 2d 455 (1981).
Printz v. U.S, 521 U.S. 98 (1997).
Priolo v. Town of Kingston, Mass., 839 F.Supp.2d 454 (2012).
Rindge Co. v. County of Los Angeles, 262 U. S. 700 (1923).
Ruckelshaus v. Monsanto, Co. (1984).
Strickley v. Highland Boy Gold Mining Co., 200 U.S. 527 (1906).
Susette Kelo et al. v. City of New London et al., 2002 Conn. Super. LEXIS 789 (2002).
Susette Kelo et al. v. City of New London et al., 2004 Conn. LEXIS 54 (2004).
Susette Kelo et al. v. City of New London, et al., 545 U.S. 469 (2005).
Sweetwater Valley Civic Assoc., Inc. v. City of National City, 18 Cal. 3d 270, 555 P.2d 1099, 133 Cal. Rptr. 859, 863 (Cal. 1976).
Tahoe-Sierra Preservation Council, Inc. v. Tahoe Regional Planning Agency, 535 U.S. 302 (2002).
Thompson v. Consolidated Gas Corp., 300 U.S. 55, 80 (1937).
United States v. Alvarez 567 U.S. ___ (2012)
United States v. Carolene Products Company, 304 U.S. 144 (1938).
United States v. Gettysburg Electric R. Co. 160 U.S. 668 (1896).
United States v. Lopez, 514 U.S. 549 (1995).
United States v. Morrison, 120 S. Ct. 1740 (2000).
Van Horne's Lessee v. Dorrance, 2 U.S. 304 (1795).
Vartelas v. Holder, 566 U.S. ___ (2012).
Village of Willowbrook v. Olech, 528 U.S. 562 (2000).
Whittaker v. County of Lawrence, 674 F. Supp. 2d 668 (Dist. Court, WD Pennsylvania 2009).
Wilkinson v. Leland, 2 Pet. 627 (1829).
Williamson v. Lee Optical, Inc., 348 U.S. 483 (1955).
Williamington Parking Auth. v. Land with Improvements, 521 A.2d 227 (Del. 1987).
Wright v. United States, 302 U. S. 583 (1938).

Index

About the Author

Guy F. Burnett is assistant professor of government and foreign affairs at Hampden-Sydney College in Virginia and the director of the Center for the Study of the Constitution. He earned his B.S. from Utah State University, his M.A. from the University of Utah, and his Ph.D. from Claremont Graduate University. He has taught and lectured on American Politics, Constitutional Law, and Political Philosophy at Hampden-Sydney College, the University of Alaska Anchorage, Central Texas College (Camp Pendleton), and aboard the USS George Washington (CVN-73). In 2013, he founded the William H. Seward Lecture Series at the University of Alaska Anchorage. He has given lectures on various topics including law, the Constitution, the Supreme Court, the First Amendment, and property rights, and has published articles in *The Claremont Review of Books*, *City Journal*, *Political Behavior*, and *Society*.